Advanced
Adobe PageMaker

CLASSROOM IN A BOOK™

Library of Congress Catalog No.: 95-81204 (Macintosh)   95-81205 (Windows)

ISBN: 1-56830-261-4 (Macintosh)   1-56830-262-2 (Windows)

10 9 8 7 6 5 4 3 2   First Printing: January 1996

The content of this book is furnished for informational use only, is subject to change without notice, and should not be construed as a commitment by Adobe Systems Incorporated. Adobe Systems Incorporated assumes no responsibility for any errors or inaccuracies that may appear in this book. The software and typefaces mentioned in this book are furnished under license and may be used or copied only in accordance with the terms of such license.

PANTONE ® Computer video simulations displayed may not match PANTONE-identified solid color standards. Use current PANTONE Color Reference Manuals for accurate color. All trademarks noted herein are either the property of Pantone, Inc. or their respective companies. PANTONE Open Color Environment™ (POCE™) © Pantone, Inc. 1994.

Pantone, Inc. is the copyright owner of PANTONE Open Color Environment™ (POCE™) and Software, which are licensed to Adobe to distribute for use only in combination with Adobe PageMaker. PANTONE Open Color Environment™ (POCE™) and Software may not be copied onto another diskette or into memory unless as part of the execution of Adobe PageMaker.

PostScript® is a trademark of Adobe Systems Incorporated ("Adobe"), registered in the United States and elsewhere. PostScript can refer both to the PostScript language as specified by Adobe and to Adobe's implementation of its PostScript language interpreter.

Any references to "PostScript printers," "PostScript files," or "PostScript drivers" refer, respectively, to printers, files, and driver programs written in or supporting the PostScript language. References in this book to the "PostScript language" are intended to emphasize Adobe's standard definition of that language.

Adobe, the Adobe Press logo, Acrobat, Acrobat Exchange, Adobe Dimensions, Adobe Illustrator, PageMaker, Adobe Photoshop, Adobe Teach, Adobe Type Manager, Adobe Garamond, Birch, Madrone, Minion, Myriad, Poplar, Trajan, Classroom in a Book, Classroom in a Box, and PostScript are trademarks of Adobe Systems Incorporated. Macintosh is a registered trademark of Apple Computer, Inc., and Windows is a registered trademark of Microsoft Corporation. Kodak Photo CD is a trademark of Eastman Kodak Company. PANTONE is a registered trademark and Hexachrome is a trademark of Pantone, Inc. All other trademarks are the property of their respective owners.

Printed in the United States of America by Shepard Poorman Communications, Indianapolis, Indiana using 100% computer-to-plate technology (filmless process).

Published simultaneously in Canada.

Adobe Press books are published and distributed by Macmillan Computer Publishing USA. For individual orders, or for educational, corporate, or retail sales accounts, call 800-428-5331, or 317-581-3500. For information, address Macmillan Computer Publishing, 201 W. 103rd Street, Indianapolis, IN 46290.

Part Number: 0197 3857 (Macintosh)   0297 2191 (Windows)

CONTENTS

This introduction includes a description of the book, its intended audience, recommended prerequisites, cross-platform compatibility issues, and a brief overview of each project.

In addition to outlining required and recommended hardware and software needed to execute the projects in this book and to play Adobe Teach™ movies, this section describes the files and fonts found on the CD-ROM disc that is included with the book.

You get a virtuoso review of PageMaker basics: importing text, working with styles and text blocks, applying color and tints, and working with graphic objects. In addition, you learn some new tricks: colorizing bitmaps, using the new multiple master pages, creating starbursts with the new polygon tool, and using advanced techniques with the new rotation and cropping tools.

You watch this beautifully designed guidebook come to life as you add text and graphics to the template that's provided. In the course of creating this piece, you learn a lot of new tricks with styles and acquire expertise with text blocks. You add some fancy bullets with the Bullets and Numbering plug-in and use the new Build Booklet plug-in to create two-up pages.

Assembling this complex catalog gives you a chance to master a whole collection of professional layout techniques. You learn to use the pasteboard effectively, import Kodak Photo CD™ images, create text runarounds, explore graphics linking issues, create designer rules, and use the Find/Change command to format text.

To create this beautiful six-panel brochure, you create a diecut, define a color for a varnished finish, apply a Gallery Effect® filter to a photograph, and use the Mask command to create a circular image. You use the Build Booklet plug-in to create spreads and you use the Create Adobe PDF command —available from within PageMaker—to generate a high-quality proof.

You use Adobe Table 2.5 to build a table as an OLE2 object that can be edited from within PageMaker. To convert the background image to PANTONE® Hexachrome™ colors, you first learn the basics of color management and then apply a source profile to the image and create a preseparation file for it. Finally, you make it available online by creating a PDF file for viewing with Acrobat® Reader or Acrobat Exchange.™

Use PageMaker to create a page for the World Wide Web! This project discusses the design issues that confront Web authors and then takes you through the process of adding links and anchors to your publication and of converting your PageMaker publication to an HTML file by using the HTML Author plug-in.

This project focuses on design, layout, and typographic issues. You learn to construct an invisible layout grid and use it to create complex pages with the unified appearance that is the hallmark of professional design. You play with some advanced image control features and work with kerning, tracking, and controlling hyphenation, as well as the Guide Manager and the spelling checker.

It's easier than you think to combine publications into a book and generate a table of contents and index. This project takes you through all the steps: you learn to create and use a Book List and to use PageMaker's many resources for adding index markers, generating and formatting the index, and creating a table of contents that's both easy and beautiful.

WHY AN ADVANCED BOOK?

Graphic designers, desktop publishers, publication professionals, and the whole range of people involved with print preparation use Adobe PageMaker software to create a variety of professional-quality publications. PageMaker

WHY AN ADVANCED BOOK?

6 includes over 50 new tools and resources to provide increased ease and flexibility in document composition tasks.

The *Advanced Adobe PageMaker* volume of the *Classroom in a Book* series introduces the latest approach to color management, OLE2 (Object Linking and Embedding) objects, output options, graphics handling features such as Kodak Photo CD and PANTONE Hexachrome™ colors, multiple master pages, and several new tools. This book covers advanced tips and techniques for using the new tools and features such as the Create Adobe PDF command, which lets you convert your PageMaker publication to a PDF document. In one of the projects, you use the HTML Author plug-in to convert your PageMaker publication to an HTML document for viewing on the World Wide Web.

Use Advanced Adobe PageMaker to discover a more convenient way of working with Adobe PageMaker, and to gain stronger creative control and improved production capabilities.

ADVANCED PREREQUISITES

Advanced Adobe PageMaker is designed for users who are familiar with Adobe PageMaker and for users of other page layout software who want to explore PageMaker. Since this book shows you advanced techniques for using Adobe PageMaker, the instructional material assumes that you know the application, or at least basic page layout functions. You must also know your computer and some general graphic arts terminology.

If you are new to page layout, begin with *Class-*

room in a Book: Adobe PageMaker, then proceed to this book, *Advanced Adobe PageMaker*. Visit your local bookstore to find either of these books, as well as *Classroom in a Book* volumes on Adobe Photoshop, Adobe Illustrator, Adobe Premier, and Adobe AfterEffects. You can order these books directly from the publisher by calling 800-428-5331.

SELF-PACED LEARNING FOR BUSY USERS

Developed and tested at Adobe Systems, each book in the *Classroom in a Book* series features a collection of design projects. Each project consists of step-by-step instructions for creating publications. Not only do you set the pace, it's up to you when and where you choose to do the work.

CROSS-PLATFORM COMPATIBILITY

Adobe PageMaker features the same functional interface across both Macintosh® and Windows platforms. This book has been developed especially for use on Macintosh and Windows 95. It has not been tested with any earlier versions of Windows. Once you learn Adobe PageMaker on one platform, you'll find it easy to use on other platforms. The following dialog boxes illustrate just how similar Adobe PageMaker is across platforms.

Rather than illustrate this book with dialog boxes from a specific platform, or alternate among the three platforms, we altered the appearance of Macintosh dialog boxes to simulate dialog boxes for all platforms. The dialog box shown below illustrates the cross-platform version of the dialog boxes in the previous illustration.

Filenames are all provided in a DOS-compliant form.

A SEMINAR IN A BOOK

This book includes eight advanced PageMaker projects. Each one contains step-by-step instructions for creating a publication, along with lots of explanations, tips, and techniques.

With international sports and recreation as the central theme for the book, you will assemble publications for a variety of fictitious companies such as designers, publishers, and advertising agencies. Within this context, you'll work on a sporting event ticket design, a guidebook to the Tour de France, a brochure for a Swiss mountaineering school, a Web page featuring sports around the world, and more.

The first project provides a quick review and can also serve as an introduction to Adobe PageMaker for people who have been using other page layout programs. It also gives an overview of some of the newest page design features, including new tools, grouping and locking commands, and masking.

In Project 2, you explore a variety of advanced style options and work with imported style sheets. You also use the Build Booklet plug-in to create an eight-page booklet with 2-up saddlestitched imposition.

Project 3 is a highly designed catalog of recreational equipment. You work with text wraps, clipping paths, Kodak Photo CDs, managing links, and a variety of issues relating to imported text and graphics.

The emphasis in Project 4, a six-color brochure for a Swiss mountaineering school, is color publishing, using the new automatic trapping feature, prepress issues, and printing separations. You create a die cut and convert the finished file to Adobe PDF format for viewing with Acrobat Reader or Acrobat Exchange.

In Project 5, an oversize soccer poster, you create a table using Adobe Table 2.5 as an OLE server and you work with PANTONE Hexachrome colors. You are introduced to Kodak's color management system and learn to assign a source profile to an image and to preseparate it. After completing the poster, you convert the poster to Adobe Acrobat PDF format using PageMaker's Create Adobe PDF command.

Project 6 is the Web page project. You create a page for a Web site and then use the HTML Author tool to convert it to HTML format for use with a Web browser.

You develop sophisticated layout and typographic skills in Project 7, a designer newsletter that uses a layout grid, Expert Kerning, and other advanced PageMaker design resources. You also augment your expertise with the Story Editor and learn to check spelling.

Project 8 is a complete book. You manage pagination, create a Book List, insert index markers, and generate a table of contents and an index.

Adobe® PageMaker® 6 offers tools for everybody in the publishing cycle: graphic artists, designers, writers, editors, production artists, and prepress professionals. With Adobe PageMaker it is possible to integrate text and graphics from many

WHAT YOU NEED TO KNOW

sources into virtually any kind of publication, from newsletters and brochures to color catalogs and magazines, with maximum precision and control.

PREREQUISITES

Before beginning to use *Classroom in a Book: Advanced Adobe PageMaker*™, you should have a working knowledge of the platform on which you'll be working. You should know how to use the mouse and should be familiar with the standard menus and commands of your Macintosh or Windows interface. You should also know how to open, save, and close files. If you need to review these techniques, refer to the documentation that comes with your system.

ABOUT CLASSROOM IN A BOOK

Classroom in a Book teaches you the techniques that you need to get the most out of Adobe PageMaker. The projects in this book center on a theme of an international sports. The publications you'll assemble include a ticket, a booklet, a catalog, a brochure, a poster, a Web page, a designer newsletter, and a complete book. You use the new Create Adobe PDF feature to convert two of the projects to PDF (Portable Document Format) files for proofing and online distribution.

Unlike a real work environment, *Classroom in a Book* is designed to let you move at your own pace, and even make mistakes! Although each project provides step-by-step instructions for creating a specific publication, there is room for exploration and experimentation. You may follow the book from start to finish or pick whichever lesson interests you the most.

Classroom in a Book is not meant to replace documentation that comes with Adobe PageMaker. Only the commands and options used in the lessons are explained in this book. For comprehensive information about all of the program's features, refer to the *Adobe PageMaker User Guide.*

HOW TO GET STARTED

Before you begin using the *Advanced Adobe PageMaker*, you need to make sure that your system is set up correctly, and that you have installed the required software and hardware. The following list summarizes what you need to do:

• Check the system requirements.

• Install Adobe PageMaker 6. For Project 5, you also need to install Adobe Table 2.5 and the QuarkXPress® Converter. Projects 4 and 5 both require that Adobe Acrobat Distiller and Adobe Acrobat Reader be installed.

• Install the fonts included on the *Advanced Adobe PageMaker* CD-ROM.

• Copy the project files from the *Advanced Adobe PageMaker* CD-ROM to your hard drive. Files for Macintosh platforms and for Windows platforms are stored in separate sections of the CD-ROM. Your system will "see" only its own files when you display the CD-ROM's directory. The required files for each project are stored in a folder named with the project number.

Important information

Be sure to take a look at the *PM CIB Readme* file (Macintosh) or the *CIBRead.txt* file (Windows) located in the root directory of the *Advanced Adobe PageMaker* CD-ROM. It contains additional information and last-minute updates that you will not find elsewhere.

Checking system requirements

To access the *Advanced Adobe PageMaker* CD-ROM, you need a double-speed or faster CD-ROM drive. To execute the lessons in this book, your system must include the hardware and software described below.

Macintosh:

- 8 MB of free RAM (16 MB preferable)
- Apple System 7.1 or later
- 20–40 MB free hard drive space
- 9" (Powerbook) or 12" monitor (640×780 pixels)
- Double-speed or faster CD-ROM player
- Adobe Acrobat Distiller and Adobe Acrobat Reader

Power Macintosh:

- 10 MB of free RAM (16 MB preferable)
- Apple System 7.1.2 or later
- 20–40 MB free hard drive space
- 9" (Powerbook) or 12" monitor (640×780 pixels)
- Double-speed or faster CD-ROM player
- Adobe Acrobat Distiller and Adobe Acrobat Reader

Windows 95:

- Computer with 486 or Pentium processor
- 10 MB of free RAM
- 20–40 MB free hard drive space
- Super VGA or XGA display card (at least 256 colors and at least 640×480 resolution)
- Double-speed or faster CD-ROM player
- Windows 95
- Adobe Acrobat Distiller and Adobe Acrobat Reader

Installing the Adobe PageMaker program

This book does not include the Adobe PageMaker software. You must purchase that software separately. Use the *Adobe PageMaker 6.0 Getting Started* booklet that comes with the Adobe PageMaker software to install the Adobe PageMaker application.

Installing Adobe Acrobat Distiller

Adobe Acrobat Distiller PE (Personal Edition) is part of the Adobe PageMaker 6 distribution. You must install it separately, however. It is not part of the basic PageMaker installation. The Personal

Edition of Distiller converts PageMaker files to PDF format. You can purchase the full version, which converts files from any application that can write PostScript output.

Macintosh:

1 On the PageMaker 6 CD-ROM (not the CIB CD-ROM), open the *Acrobat Distiller Install* folder and then open the *disk 1* folder.

2 Double-click *Installer* and follow the prompts.

Windows:

1 On the PageMaker 6 CD-ROM (not the CIB CD-ROM), open the *acrodist* folder and then open the *disk1* folder.

2 Double-click *Installer* and follow the prompts.

Installing Acrobat Reader 2.1

You can use the Adobe Acrobat Reader application that is distributed on the *Advanced Adobe PageMaker* CD-ROM to view any file that is in PDF format. You will need it to view your PDF files if you choose to create Adobe PDF files in Projects 4 or 5. It is not part of the basic PageMaker installation. You must install it as a separate application.

Macintosh:

1 On the *Classroom in a Book: Advanced Adobe PageMaker* CD-ROM, open the *Acrobat Reader Install* folder.

2 Double-click the *ReadMe-Reader2.1* file for information about the application and how to install it.

Windows:

1 On the *Classroom in a Book: Advanced Adobe PageMaker* CD-ROM, open the *acroread* folder and then open the *disk1* folder.

2 Double-click the *readme-r.txt* file for information about the application and how to install it.

Installing the fonts

In addition to some commonly used fonts, all lessons included in this book feature Adobe Originals® fonts. These fonts are found on the Classroom in a Book CD-ROM in the Fonts folder. For information on how to install these fonts, refer to the *PM CIB Readme* file (Macintosh) or *the CIBRead.txt* file (Windows) on the Classroom in a Book CD-ROM.

The specific fonts needed for each project are listed at the beginning of the project. Collectively, the following fonts are required for the projects in this book:

Font	Projects
AGaramond™	7, 8
Birch™	5
Corvinus Skyline™	7, 8
Minion™	2, 3
MyriadMM™	1, 2, 3, 4, 5, 6, 8
Zapf Dingbats	2

Copying the Classroom in a Book files

The *Advanced Adobe PageMaker* CD-ROM includes all necessary files for all the projects. You may copy whichever files you need to your system.

Note: Since the files on the Advanced Adobe PageMaker CD-ROM are not locked, it is possible to make and save changes to them after they have been copied to your system. If you make unwanted changes to a PageMaker publication file on your system, choose Revert from the File menu to restore it. If you inadvertently save any changes to a file, you can recopy the file from the Classroom in a Book CD-ROM to view the original file.

IMAGE FILES

The image files on the *Advanced Adobe PageMaker* CD-ROM are all under copyright and may not be copied or distributed. They are all provided in relatively low-resolution format, usually 100 dpi, since they are intended for use only on screen.

SAVING YOUR WORK FILES

Create a folder or directory called *Projects*. The instructions for each project include directions for creating a work file and saving it in this location. This keeps your work files separate from the project elements so that it's easier to keep track of your files.

THROWING AWAY PREFERENCES

As you begin each project, you'll see an instruction telling you to delete your PageMaker preferences or configuration file. That's because the steps in the projects assume that the settings in each dialog box are the default settings, unless you have been instructed to make a change. Deleting the preferences or configuration file ensures this default environment. On a Macintosh, you will find the preferences file in the Preferences folder within the System folder. It is named *Adobe PageMaker 6.x Prefs*. On a Power Mac its name is *Adobe PageMaker 6.xP Prefs*. On Windows platforms, you should throw \pm6\rsrc\ usenglish\pm6.cnf into the recycle bin. You must empty the trash or recycle bin after dragging the preferences file into it. You can make this process faster and easier by creating an alias (Macintosh) or a shortcut (Windows).

FILENAMES

Although Macintosh and Windows 95 both support long file names, the files provided on the *Advanced Adobe PageMaker* CD-ROM all have the older, DOS-compliant names. In Windows 95, you can choose whether the portion of the name following the period (the extension) is visible by changing the setting in View > Options.

PLACING GUIDELINES

The Projects frequently include an instruction to place a ruler guide to assist you in placing an object on the document page. When you see a phrase such as "drag a guide to approximately 1.88," drag the guide from the ruler and look at the Y value in the Control palette for horizontal guides or at the X value for vertical guides. The word "approximately" is present because the monitor and zoom factor both affect which values appear in the Control palette as you drag. You may never see 1.88, for example, so just drag the guide to as close a value as you can manage. Zooming in or out a little will probably permit you to place the guide at the exact value.

USING INTERIM FILES

An *interim file* is a file that contains the project publication at a certain stage of completion. There is at least one for each project. There is a note in each chapter at the point where an interim file was created. You can skip the initial part of a project and pick it up at the point where the interim file is noted. Open the designated interim template and save it to your *Projects* folder or directory as a work file, just as you do at the beginning of a project. You can then continue the project from that point.

The following interim files are included in the project folders or directories:

01Inter1.pt6	*05Inter2.pt6*
02Inter1.pt6	*06Inter1.pt6*
03Inter1.pt6	*07Inter1.pt6*
04Inter1.pt6	*08Inter1.pt6*
05Inter1.pt6	

ABOUT PICAS

Picas are a unit that is in common use in the publishing and graphic arts fields. Type size and leading are always specified in picas, and graphics professionals there tend to use picas for all document measurements. Several of the projects in this book specify picas as the unit for measurements and for the rulers. There are 6 picas to the inch and 12 points to a pica.

WATCHING ADOBE TEACH™ MOVIES

Adobe Teach movies are QuickTime movies included on the *Classroom in a Book* CD-ROM. You can watch a movie to see a preview of what's to come in a lesson, or you can go back

and review the movie after you've tried a new technique. You can even watch a movie right now. The Adobe Teach movie icon appears in the text whenever it's time to watch a movie.

Additional system requirements

To watch Adobe Teach™ movies, your system must meet or exceed the following additional requirements:

Macintosh or Power Macintosh:
• QuickTime™ 2.1 installed on your system
• Sound Manager 3.1 installed on your system
• Adobe Acrobat Reader 2.1

Note: To install QuickTime, place the QuickTime extension from the QuickTime folder into your System folder.

To play Adobe Teach movies, you must set your monitor to 256 colors.

Windows:
• Multimedia-capable computer
• QuickTime™ 2.0 for Windows installed on your system
• Adobe Acrobat Reader 2.1

Each Adobe Teach movie can be played by clicking an icon in a PDF file provided on the Classroom in a Book CD-ROM. To see a movie, follow these instructions:

Playing the movies

The following instructions assume that you are playing the movies from the Classroom in a Book CD-ROM. If you wish, you can copy the movie folder to your hard drive.

Macintosh:

1 Quit the Adobe PageMaker application.

2 Open the Adobe PageMaker™ CIB folder on the *Classroom in a Book* CD-ROM, and then open the Adobe Teach™ movies folder.

3 Double-click the Adobe Teach™ movie menu icon to launch Adobe Acrobat Reader and open the movie menu window.

The Movie menu is a PDF file.

5 In the Movie menu window, click a camera icon above the desired movie title to open a movie.

6 To play the movie, click the arrow button in the lower left corner of the display window. To adjust the volume, choose the volume level from the speaker pop-up menu in the lower left corner of the movie window. You can replay a movie or a portion of a movie by dragging the progress indicator to the left.

7 To close a movie, click the close box in the upper left corner of the movie window to return to the Movie menu screen.

8 To exit the Movie menu screen, hold down the Command key and press the period key. You can then exit Adobe Acrobat Reader by holding down the Command key and pressing **Q**.

Windows:

1 Open the Double-click on the \APMCIB\ Movies\ ATMOVWIN file. This launches Acrobat Reader and displays the Adobe Teach Start screen.

The Movie Menu screen is a PDF (Portable Document Format) file.

3 Position the grabber pointer over the movie icon above the title you wish to view. When the grabber turns to a hand pointer, click the icon. The movie Start screen appears in MoviePlayer.

4 Click the forward arrow to start the movie.

5 When the movie is over, choose Exit from the File menu to exit Movie Play and return to the Adobe Teach Start screen.

6 Watch another movie by repeating the previous steps, or choose Exit from the File menu to exit Adobe Acrobat.

READ THE MANUAL

For comprehensive information about all of the application features, refer to the *Adobe PageMaker User Guide*. You will find the Quick Reference Card, packaged with PageMaker, a useful companion as you work through the projects in this book.

Ticket 1

THE IRON CITY ARENA

2100 WHITE PINE ROAD, ISHPHEMING, MI

HOOPLAS VS. DRIBBLERS

DOORS @ 7PM

THU SEPT 3 1998 1:00 PM

SEC	ROW	SEAT	PRICE
FLOOR	**GEN**	**ADM**	**22.50**

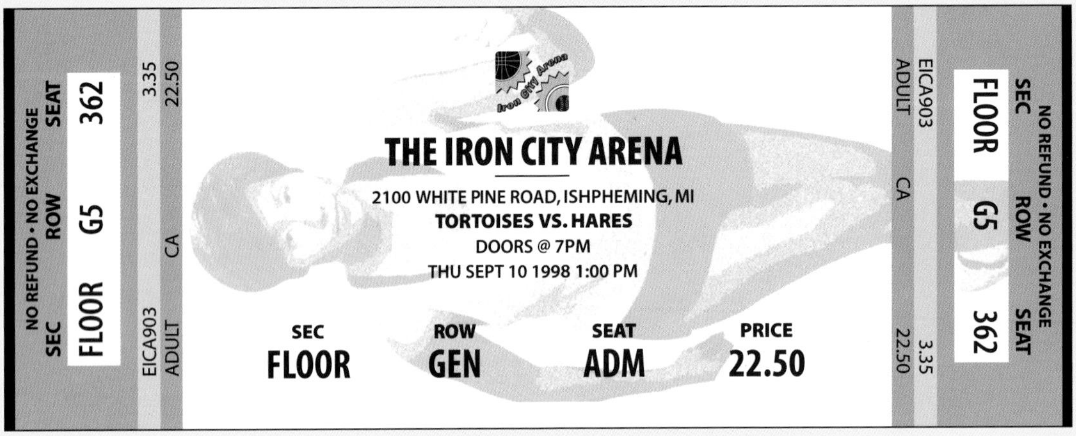

NO REFUND · NO EXCHANGE
SEC FLOOR ROW G5 SEAT 362
EICA903 3.35
ADULT CA 22.50

NO REFUND · NO EXCHANGE
SEC FLOOR ROW G5 SEAT 362
EICA903 3.35
ADULT CA 22.50

Ticket 2

THE IRON CITY ARENA

2100 WHITE PINE ROAD, ISHPHEMING, MI

TORTOISES VS. HARES

DOORS @ 7PM

THU SEPT 10 1998 1:00 PM

SEC	ROW	SEAT	PRICE
FLOOR	**GEN**	**ADM**	**22.50**

NO REFUND · NO EXCHANGE
SEC FLOOR ROW G5 SEAT 362
EICA903 3.35
ADULT CA 22.50

NO REFUND · NO EXCHANGE
SEC FLOOR ROW G5 SEAT 362
EICA903 3.35
ADULT CA 22.50

· UNITED STATES ·

1

This project introduces a number of Adobe PageMaker's newest page layout features. It also provides a review of basic procedures for those who are familiar with page layout

SPORTING EVENT TICKETS

programs and want to start exploring the advanced features available in Adobe PageMaker. ■ The end product in this project is a pair of sample tickets, one for a basketball game and one for a track event. They are exactly the same in layout and style. Only the event information, color, and background image differ. A strategic use of master pages eliminates all duplication of effort. Nothing that is the same on both tickets has to be created twice. Creating the logo on the ticket is also part of this project. In a separate publication, you employ several new tools and features to draw starbursts, arrange and group the components, and finally export the whole graphic as an EPS file that you then place in the ticket file.

In this project, you design and create a ticket layout that will be a component of a sales presentation to a sporting event ticketing agency. Each ticket has the same layout, but the different events are distinguished by different colors and

SPORTING-EVENT TICKETS

different background images. When you have completed the project, you have a color composite for each event. In the real world, you would print these on a color printer and present them to the agency.

For this project, you set up an Adobe PageMaker publication and place the text and graphic elements on a master page. You then use the new multiple master page feature to duplicate the original master page. The duplicates are the starting point for two additional master pages that are specific to the two events. In a separate file, you create a logo, export it as an EPS (Encapsulated PostScript) file, and then place it in your ticket publication. You import and manipulate several graphic images, and then use these master pages to create a basketball ticket and a track-meet ticket. The master pages make it possible for you to create tickets that have many elements in common without having to repeat any work.

This project covers:

- Multiple master pages

- Polygon, crop, and rotate tools

- Mask command

- Group and Lock Position commands

- Scripts

- Print dialog box

You also review basic PageMaker features, including placing and formatting text, placing and manipulating graphics, using drawing tools, creating text styles, and working with color.

It should take you about 2 hours to complete this project .

BEFORE YOU BEGIN

1 Return all settings to their defaults by deleting the *Adobe PageMaker 6.x Prefs* file from the *Preferences* folder (Macintosh) or by removing \pm6\rsrc\usenglish\pm6.cnf from the drive containing PageMaker (Windows).

2 Make sure the Myriad Multiple Master family of fonts is installed on your system.

3 Launch the Adobe PageMaker application, then open the *01Final.pm6* file in *01Project* to see what you're creating in Project 1.

4 After examining the ticket on page 1, click the page 2 icon in the lower left corner of the Publication window to examine the second ticket. Notice the similarities and differences in the two tickets.

Leave the final file open so you can use it as a reference during the lesson.

SETTING UP THE DOCUMENT

You begin by creating a new document. All measurements in this project are in inches except the point size, leading, and rule thicknesses, which are always in points.

1 Choose New from the File menu. In the Document Setup dialog box, set the Dimensions to 5.25 by 2 inches and set the Orientation to Wide. Turn the Double-sided option off, then set the Left and Right margins to 0.2 and the Top and Bottom margins to 0.25. Click OK.

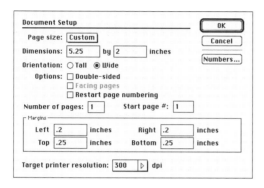

2 Save your new file in *Projects* as *01Work.pm6*.

REVIEWING THE PUBLICATION WINDOW

After creating a new document, you see the page centered vertically in the window. The page is surrounded by the pasteboard, which can be used to store graphics and text. The pasteboard is accessible from each page of the document. The vertical and horizontal rulers allow you to position objects on the page. You can also drag ruler guides from the rulers, and you can reset the zero point using the icon at the intersection of the rulers in the top left corner of the Publication window. In the lower left corner are the page icons and master page icons that you use for navigating between pages.

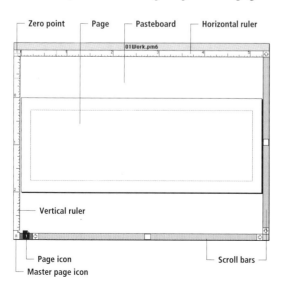

Palettes

The Toolbox palette contains drawing and viewing tools, the Colors palette contains the colors used in the open publication, and the Styles palette includes all the text styles for the publication. The Control palette provides a variety of functions including text formatting and object positioning. Other available palettes include Master Pages, Scripts, and the Library. You can access any of these palettes from the Window menu.

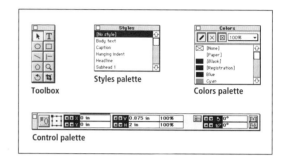

SETTING UP MASTER PAGES

You'll begin by setting up several master pages. A master page contains elements that appear on any document page that has that master page applied to it. You can apply any master page to any document page, and you also have the option of applying no master page at all to a document page, or of hiding the master page elements on a selected document page. In PageMaker 6, you can create as many master pages as you need, which gives you great flexibility in designing sophisticated publications that use different layouts for different pages. In this project, you use a series of master pages to create two backgrounds for the two sporting events. You start setting up the master page by importing and formatting text on the Document Master master page.

1 Click the master page icon at the bottom of the Publication window.

Clicking the master page icon displays the master page that is used by the current document page. You can press and hold (Macintosh) or right-click (Windows) on the icon to display a menu of defined master pages and select the one you want

TIP: USING THE

TEXT TOOL, DOUBLE-

CLICK TEXT TO SELECT

A WORD. TRIPLE-

CLICK TEXT TO SELECT

A PARAGRAPH.

to display. You get to do that later in this project. For now, the only master page is Document Master, which is the default that is created with every new document.

2 Choose Place from the File menu (or use the keyboard shortcut) to display the Place Document dialog box. Navigate to *01Project*, select *01Addr.doc* and click OK (Macintosh) or Open (Windows).

Whenever you place a file into PageMaker, the loaded icon shows the type of file you are importing. In this case, the loaded text icon appears.

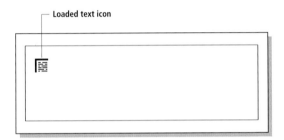

Loaded text icon

3 Click the loaded text icon anywhere within the margins of the ticket.

The text flows in and fills the space between the side margins. Windowshade handles appear at the top and bottom of the text block. You use the pointer tool to resize or move text blocks. Use the text tool to apply type specifications.

FORMATTING TEXT

You next format the address on the master page by changing the font, size and alignment, and by defining a rule that is part of the paragraph style.

1 Click the text tool in the Toolbox, then triple-click the first line of text to select it.

2 Choose Type Specs from the Type menu, then choose MyriadMM 830 Black 300 Cond from the Font submenu. Set the Size to 14 points and leave the other settings as they are. Click OK.

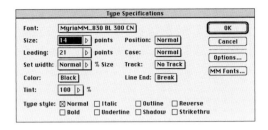

PageMaker offers you a number of ways to specify type settings. You can use the Font, Size, Style, and other submenus that are at the available on the Type menu. You can display the Type Specifications dialog box as you did here, or you can use the Control palette. It's just a matter of convenience and personal work style. You will get to explore all three techniques in this project.

3 Choose Paragraph from the Type menu, then choose Center from the Alignment menu. Don't click OK yet.

Now you create a rule as part of the paragraph definition.

4 Still in the Paragraph Specifications dialog box, click the Rules button. In the Rules dialog box, enable Rule Below Paragraph. In the Rule Below part of the dialog box, choose .5 from the Line Style menu and set Line Width to Width of Text. Finally, set the left and right indents to 0.55. Don't click OK yet.

Be sure to make your settings in the bottom part of the dialog box, not the upper half, which is for Rule Above settings.

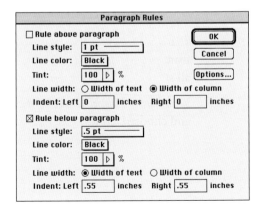

TIP: ANOTHER WAY
TO CREATE A STYLE
FROM SELECTED TEXT
IS TO COMMAND-
CLICK (MACINTOSH)
OR CONTROL-CLICK
(WINDOWS) ON
[NO STYLE] AT THE TOP
OF THE LIST IN THE
STYLES PALETTE.

5 Click the Options button, then enter .05 in the Bottom box for Inches Below Baseline.

6 Press the Option key (Macintosh) or Shift key (Windows) and click OK to get out of the nested dialog boxes.

The formatted text now has a rule attached 0.05 inches below the baseline.

> **THE IRON CITY ARENA**
> 2100 WHITE PINE ROAD, ISHPHEMING, MI
> NAME OF THE EVENT
> DOORS @ 7PM
> THU SEPT 3 1998 1:00 PM

CREATING A PARAGRAPH STYLE

A paragraph style is a whole set of character and paragraph attributes that are identified with a name. Choosing the attributes and assigning a name is known as *defining a paragraph style.* Once a style has been defined, you can select any paragraph and apply that style to it. This is called *applying the style to the paragraph.* In just that one step, the paragraph acquires all the formatting defined for the style.

There are two methods you can use to create a style in PageMaker; you can format the text first and then create a style based on that paragraph, or you can define a style by using the Define Styles dialog boxes to specify the attributes. In the following steps, you create a style based on the text you just formatted.

1 To display the Styles palette, choose Styles from the Window menu. The Styles palette lists all styles currently defined in the publication.

2 Make sure the first line of text is still selected and choose Define Styles from the Type menu.

3 Make sure that the word **Selection** is highlighted, and then click the New button. Name the new style **Stadium**, press Option (Macintosh) or Shift (Windows), and click OK to accept the definition and exit the nested dialog boxes.

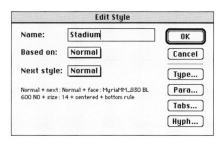

The new paragraph style appears in the Styles palette. You may need to resize the palette to see it.

4 Click Stadium in the Styles palette to apply the new style to the selected text.

Defining a style from selected text does not automatically apply that style to the text.

CREATING ANOTHER STYLE

This time, you create a style before formatting the text.

1 Use the text tool to select the next four lines of text, and then choose Define Styles from the Type menu.

2 Click the New button, and name the new style **Event Info**. Then click the Type button, set the font to Myriad 565 Semibold 600 Norm, the size to 6.5 points, the leading to 8.5 points, and click OK.

Note: The words Event *and* Info *must be capitalized. Later, you import styles from 01Final.pm6 and it's important for the names to match exactly so you don't get two versions in your Styles list.*

3 Click the Para button, choose Center from the Alignment menu, and exit the nested dialog boxes.

4 Click Event Info in the Styles palette to apply the style to the four lines of text.

5 With the pointer tool, drag the end handles of the text block in so that the text block is not much wider than the text. Don't worry about the position. You take care of that later.

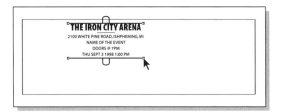

The bottom handle of the text block should be empty and no lines should break.

6 Save the file at frequent intervals as you work.

POSITIONING TEXT

Next, you drag some horizontal and vertical ruler guides to help you position the text on the master page.

1 Make sure that the Control palette is displayed and then drag a ruler guide from the horizontal ruler. Watch the Y value in the Control palette to position the guide at or near 0.75.

Note: Watching the X and Y values in the Control palette is an easy way to position vertical and horizontal guides precisely. When you are dragging a guide, there is also a hairline in the ruler that you can use to help you position the guide. It's a matter of convenience and personal work style.

2 Drag a ruler guide from the vertical ruler until the X value in the Control palette is approximately 1.883.

3 Using the pointer tool, drag the text block so that the first baseline rests on the horizontal guide and the left edge of the first line ("The Iron City Arena") rests against the vertical guide.

USING SCRIPTS

PageMaker provides some default paragraph styles whenever you create a new document. You may want to delete these styles so that they don't take up room in the Styles palette. You can delete these styles manually, but you can also use one of the new PageMaker scripts. Scripts are used to automate repetitive tasks. You can use the preprogrammed scripts available in the Scripts palette, and you can also create your own scripts.

Removing the default styles

1 Choose Scripts from the Window menu.

The Scripts palette appears.

Scripts palette

PageMaker 6 comes with a useful collection of prepared scripts. Spend a little time looking through the different categories to see what script tools are available to you.

2 In the Scripts palette, click the triangle (Macintosh) or plus sign (Windows) next to Text and then the Styles triangle or plus sign. Double-click Remove Default Styles (Macintosh) RMStyles (Windows).

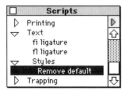

The script removes the default styles from the Styles palette, leaving just the two styles you created, plus the Normal style that was imported with the text that you placed.

3 Close the Scripts palette.

USING INDENTS AND TABS

Next you place the "Section, Row..." text and set indents and tabs to align it.

1 Take a look at *01Final.pm6* to see how the text across the bottom of the ticket looks.

2 Display the Place Document dialog box, click *01SecRow.doc*, and make sure that As New Story is enabled. Click OK (Macintosh) or Open (Windows).

3 To flow the text onto the page, click with the loaded text icon between the margins and below the text you just finished formatting.

This time you use the Control palette to format the text.

4 Select the new text with the text tool, be sure the character view of the Control palette is displayed, and choose Myriad 830 Bold 600 Norm from the font pop-up menu. Enter 7 points in the Size box. To apply the settings, click the Apply button, or press Return (Macintosh) or Enter (Windows).

5 Choose Indents/Tabs from the Type menu.

The Indents/Tabs ruler appears. The left indent marker is a split triangle. The lower half controls the left indent and the upper half controls the first line indent of the selected paragraphs. The right triangle matches the right margin. The smaller triangles represent default tabs.

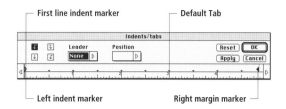

6 Drag the left indent marker (make sure to grab the bottom half of the triangle) to the 1.219 inch mark on the Indents/tabs ruler. Click the Apply button to see the effect of the setting.

The text moves in from the left margin by the specified amount. Notice that when you drag the bottom (left-indent) triangle, the top triangle moves with it, in order to retain the indent of the first line relative to the rest of the paragraph.

Note: You can click the Apply button to preview the effects of any of your settings. This is optional, however, because your settings are applied when you click OK to exit the Indents/tabs dialog box.

7 In the Indents/tabs ruler, click the Center tab button, and then type **2.031** into the Position box. Click the triangle at the right of the Position box (Macintosh) or click the Position button (Windows) to display the pop-up menu, and choose Add Tab.

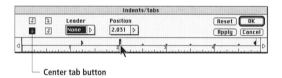

This sets a center-aligned tab at 2.031 inches. When you set a tab, PageMaker removes all the preset tabs that are to the left of the new tab.

Another way to set a tab is to click the ruler of the Indents/tabs dialog box at the approximate place it should be and then drag the tab until the number in the Position box tells you it's exactly where you want it.

8 To set a tab at 2.812 inches, click a tab in that general area of the Indents/Tabs ruler and then drag the tab until the Position reads 2.812. Set a third tab at the 3.562-inch mark.

Notice that the two new tabs are also centered since you have not clicked a different tab alignment button.

9 Click OK to close the Indents/tabs dialog box.

10 Drag a horizontal ruler guide so that the Y value in the Control palette is 1.57. Select the text block with the pointer, and drag it so that the baseline rests on the guide.

11 This is a good time to save your work. Remember to save often. You don't have to wait until you've finished a major part.

USING THE ZOOM AND DRAWING TOOLS

The Toolbox contains a zoom tool for changing the magnification of the document; it also contains several drawing tools for creating graphic elements. In the next steps, you zoom in on the right side of the ticket and draw a rectangle.

1 Click the zoom tool in the Toolbox, drag a marquee around the right quarter of the ticket and a bit of the pasteboard to the right of it.

Notice that the view pans if you move against the side of the window as you are dragging the marquee. Now you have magnified the area so that you can perform detailed steps in it.

2 Click the rectangle tool and draw a rectangle of any convenient size anywhere on the pasteboard just to the right of the ticket.

USING THE CONTROL PALETTE

Use the Control palette to size and position selected objects. When an object is selected, the Control palette displays a proxy with reference points that match the selection handles of the selected object. Before using the Control palette

to set the size or position of an object, first click one of the reference points on the proxy. Then settings that you make in the Control palette will be relative to the corresponding point on the selected object.

Note: If you click a reference point twice, it changes to a double-headed arrow. Then settings that you make in the Control palette will affect only the part of the object corresponding to the reference point. Click the point again to toggle it back to a square reference point.

1 With the rectangle selected, click the upper right reference point on the proxy. Enter **5.25** for the X coordinate and **0** for the Y coordinate.

Upper right reference point

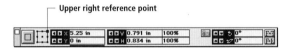

2 Still in the Control palette, set the size of the rectangle by entering **0.875** for the width and 2 for the height. Click the Apply button, or press Return (Macintosh) or Enter (Windows) to apply the settings.

The top right corner of the rectangle is now positioned at the top right corner of the ticket.

Next, you give the rectangle a heavy line thickness to achieve the look of a rectangle with a transparent rectangle in the middle.

3 With the rectangle selected, choose Line from the Element menu and Custom from the submenu. Enter **22** for Line Weight, and click OK.

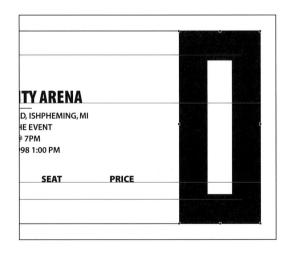

Notice that the thick line weight has not changed the outer dimensions of the rectangle. PageMaker draws rules by starting at the outside and "growing" them toward the inside. Horizontal rules start from the top and grow downward as the line thickness increases.

DEFINING COLORS AND TINTS

Next, you define the colors that you will need in the publication. As you define each color, it appears in the Colors palette. In addition to these defined colors, every PageMaker document has a set of default colors: None, Paper, Black, Registration, Blue, Cyan, Green, Magenta, Red, and Yellow. You can add colors by importing them along with an EPS file, or you can create them by using the Define Colors command.

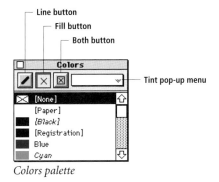

Colors palette

You can remove unused colors by running a script or by clicking the Remove Unused button in the Define Colors dialog box. In the following steps, you use the script in order to become familiar with the Scripts palette.

Removing unused colors

1 Display the Colors palette by choosing Colors from the Window menu.

This step isn't essential, but it lets you see what's happening. You're going to need the Colors palette soon, anyway.

2 In the Scripts palette, click the triangle (Macintosh) or plus sign (Windows) next to Color, then double-click Remove Unused (Macintosh) or RMunused (Windows).

All unused colors are removed from the Colors palette. The colors surrounded by brackets, such as [Black] cannot be removed.

3 Close the Scripts palette.

Defining a new color

1 Choose Define Colors from the Element menu and click the New button.

2 Choose Spot from the Type pop-up menu, and choose PANTONE Coated from the Libraries pop-up menu. Enter **442** in the PANTONE box at the top to select PANTONE 442 CVC, and click OK.

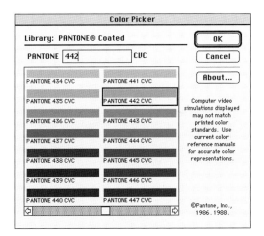

3 Click OK again to add the color to the Colors palette.

4 To define a second color, click the New button once more, and click the Libraries button to choose PANTONE Coated again. Type **5295** to select the color and click OK.

5 Press the Option key (Macintosh) or Shift key (Windows) and click OK to add the color to the Colors palette and exit the nested dialog boxes.

Note that the two PANTONE colors have been added to the Colors palette.

TIP: YOU CAN ALSO COPY AND PASTE USING THE KEYBOARD. ON A MACINTOSH, COMMAND-C COPIES AND COMMAND-V PASTES. IN WINDOWS, THE COMMANDS ARE CONTROL-C AND CONTROL-V, RESPECTIVELY.

6 To apply color to the rectangle, select it with the pointer tool, click the Line button in the Colors palette, and click PANTONE 442.

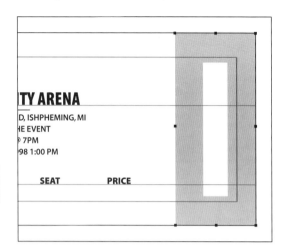

Note: There are three buttons at the top of the Colors palette. The first one is the Line button, the second one is the Fill button, and the rightmost one is the Both (line and fill) button.

Applying a tint

Next, you draw two more rectangles and apply a tint to one of them.

1 With the rectangle tool selected, draw a rectangle of any size anywhere on the ticket.

2 Click the upper left reference point of the proxy in the Control palette. Enter **4.485** for X, **0** for Y, **0.111** for the width and **2.0** for the height, and apply the settings.

3 With the new rectangle selected, click the Both button in the Colors palette, click PANTONE 442, and select 30% from the Tint pop-up menu.

The line and fill of the rectangle is now a 30% tint of PANTONE 442.

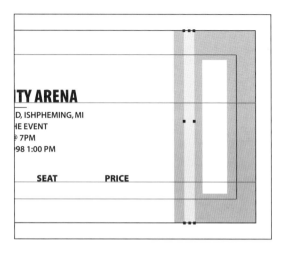

Now you create another rectangle by copying and pasting the one you just finished.

1 Select the narrow rectangle, and choose Copy from the Edit menu.

2 To paste the copy exactly on top of the original rectangle, you use a technique called *Power Paste*. Press the Option key (Macintosh) or Shift key (Windows) and choose Paste from the Edit menu. The keyboard shortcut is Option-Shift-V (Macintosh) or Control-Shift-P (Windows).

Note: When you use "normal" paste, PageMaker offsets the copy slightly so that it's easier to see. For some purposes, it's desirable to have the copy exactly on top of the original. That's what Power Paste does. If you Power Paste something onto a new page, its position on the new page is exactly the same as the position of the thing you copied.

3 With the copy selected, click the Both button in the Colors palette, select Black in the Colors palette, and set the tint to 100%. This sets the line and fill of the new rectangle to solid black.

4 To position the rectangle, press the Shift key to constrain movement to 90-degree increments and press and hold on the rectangle with the pointer tool until you can see the four-arrowhead pointer. Then continue to hold down the Shift key as you drag the rectangle to the right until it aligns with the right edge of the ticket.

TIP: TO COPY A FEW STYLES FROM ANOTHER FILE, RATHER THAN ALL OF THEM, SELECT TEXT TAGGED WITH THE STYLES THAT YOU WANT AND COPY IT INTO THE NEW DOCUMENT. THE STYLES ARE ADDED TO THE STYLES PALETTE.

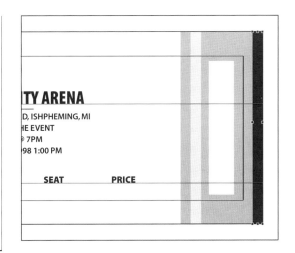

3 Click the left nudge arrow next to Width to decrease the width of the rectangle by ¹⁄₁₀-inch increments until the width is 0.051 inch.

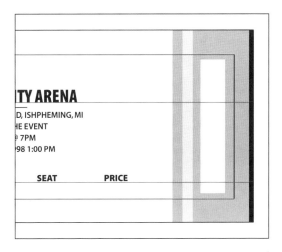

RESIZING USING THE CONTROL PALETTE

You can use the Control palette to resize a selected object.

1 With the black rectangle still selected, double-click the middle left reference point of the Control palette proxy.

Left-center reference point

A double-headed arrow appears. Settings that you make in the Control palette will now apply only to the side corresponding to the selected reference point. The effect is like dragging the selected handle with the mouse.

2 Save your work. Then experiment by changing the width of the selected object when the reference point is a double arrow. Look at what happens, and then Undo the change. Reselect the proxy reference point so that it toggles back to being a square, and then make the same width setting again, and notice the difference in behavior. Undo the second change. If necessary, choose Revert from the File menu to get back to where you were before your experiment.

ADDING TEXT IN PAGEMAKER

Now you finish adding elements to the right side of the ticket master page. This time, instead of importing text, you use the text tool to enter type directly onto the page. Adobe PageMaker offers you two environments in which you can add type. You can always type directly into Layout view—the view you've been working in. However, if you have a large amount of text and want to work in a word-processing environment, without the complexities of the layout, PageMaker includes Story Editor view, which functions as an easy-to-use word processor. It includes features such as spell checking and find/replace.

1 Display the ticket at actual size.

2 Select the text tool, then click on the pasteboard above the ticket.

3 Type **SEC**, press the Tab key, type **ROW**, press the Tab key again, and type **SEAT**.

4 With the pointer tool, click on the text that you just typed, and notice that the text block is the same width as the space between the right and left page margins.

TIP: ON A MACINTOSH, PRESS COMMAND OPTION AND THEN CLICK ANYWHERE ON THE PAGE TO TOGGLE BETWEEN FIT IN WINDOW AND ACTUAL SIZE VIEWS. IN WINDOWS, RIGHT-CLICK TO TOGGLE BETWEEN THEM.

By default, placed text flows from margin to margin. You can control the width of a text block in advance by drawing a bounding box before you type. You use this technique to create your next line of text.

5 With the text tool selected, drag the text cursor on the pasteboard to create an invisible bounding box about 3 inches wide.

When you drag a bounding box, text that you type stays within the area you define, rather than expanding out to the width of the page margins as your last text block did.

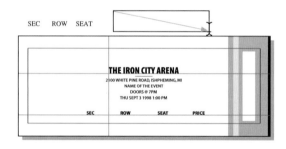

This bounding box prevents the text handles from going all the way across the page.

6 Type **NO REFUNDS • NO EXCHANGES.** To type the bullet in the middle, press Option-8 (Macintosh) or Control-Shift-8 (Windows).

Notice that the width of the text block is the width of the bounding box that you drew before you typed.

COPYING STYLES FROM ANOTHER PUBLICATION

In previous steps, you learned how to create paragraph styles. Now you learn how to copy styles from another PageMaker publication into your current publication. This technique is a powerful tool, because it means that you can use the same styles for many publications, without having to recreate them. It's an easy way to maintain a consistent look.

1 Choose Define Styles from the Type menu. Click the Copy button, then navigate to *01Project* and highlight *01Final.pm6.*

2 Click OK (Macintosh) or Open (Windows) to copy the styles from *01Final.pm6* into the current publication. Confirm that you want to copy them over the current styles, and then click OK once more to exit the Define Styles dialog box.

If a copied style has the same name as a style in the current file, the new style definition replaces the former definition of the style.

3 Use the text tool to click an insertion point in the "SEC ROW SEAT" text, and click the Vert.Row.1 style in the Styles palette to apply the newly copied style to the selected text.

This style has indents and tabs defined, so the text aligns with the tabs.

4 With the pointer tool, drag the handles on the right side of the text block in until the text block is the width of the text.

Reducing the size of the text block helps ensure that it doesn't get selected accidentally and tidies up your workspace.

5 Select the "NO REFUNDS" paragraph with the text tool and apply the No Refunds style from the Styles palette.

5 Drag the the two text text blocks that you just formatted over to the right-hand part of the ticket.

You'll position them more precisely a little later.

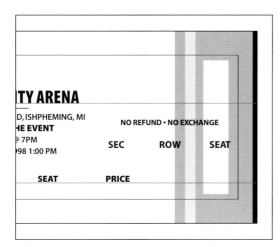

ROTATING OBJECTS

You can rotate objects by using the rotate tool from the Toolbox or by using the Rotate box in the Control palette. The rotate tool allows you to visually select the angle of rotation; the Control palette allows you to type in a specific position.

You begin by changing the view to Fit in Window so that the whole ticket is visible.

1 Choose View from the Layout menu and Fit in Window from the submenu.

2 With the pointer tool, select the "SEC ROW SEAT" text that you just dragged to the right end of the ticket, then click the rotate tool in the Toolbox. Position the Rotate cursor on the text block near the right end, then hold down the Shift key and drag clockwise until the text rotates 90 degrees, and the word "SEC" is toward the top of the ticket. Release the mouse button before releasing the Shift key.

Holding down the Shift key constrains the rotation to 45° increments or *jumps*.

3 Use the pointer tool and arrow keys to position the text block so that the top of the text block is against the right margin guide. Then select either middle side reference point in the Control palette proxy, and set the Y value equal to 1.

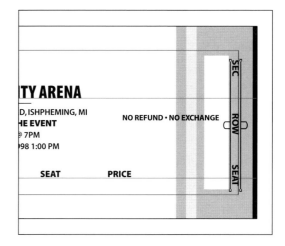

Next you use the Control palette to rotate the "no refunds" text.

4 Click the "NO REFUNDS" text with the pointer tool and resize the text block so that it's about the same width as the line of text. Select the center reference point on the proxy in the Control palette. Enter −90° in the Rotation box, and apply the setting.

Note: The number of degrees of rotation that you enter in the Control palette are absolute, not relative to the current position of the object. The diagram below shows where the top of the object is for each Rotation entry.

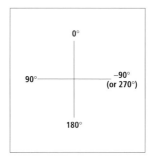

Using the Control palette to set rotation

5 Drag a ruler guide from the left ruler to 5.149. Use the pointer tool and arrow keys to position the text block so that the tops of the letters rest on the guide and the right side of the letter U in REFUNDS rests against the horizontal guide that you placed earlier at 0.75.

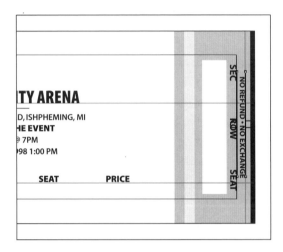

GROUPING ELEMENTS

Whenever you have several different elements that need to be treated as a single unit, you can use PageMaker 6's Group command to "glue" the objects together. A grouped object can be moved, reshaped, and resized without danger of the elements becoming separated. In the next steps, you group the objects on the right, then copy and paste them to the left half of the ticket.

1 With the pointer tool selected, press and drag all the way around the objects on the right quarter of the ticket to select them. To be sure of including all the elements at the end of the ticket, begin and end dragging on the pasteboard.

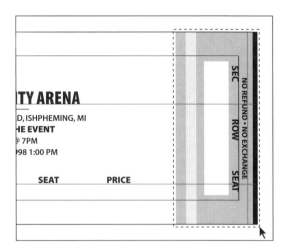

Notice that as you drag with the pointer tool, a dotted selection marquee shows you the selected area. This technique of marquee-dragging selects only objects that are *completely* enclosed by the marquee.

2 Choose Group from the Arrange menu.

All the selected elements are grouped into one object.

3 With the grouped object selected, copy it and Power Paste it to place it exactly on top of the original.

Now you rotate the copy and position it at the other end of the ticket. The newly pasted copy is selected, so you don't have to reselect it.

4 To rotate the copy, click the center reference point on the proxy in the Control palette, then enter **180** for rotation, and apply the setting.

5 Click the upper left reference point on the proxy, enter **0** for X and **0** for Y, and apply the settings.

A copy of the object that you created at the right end of the ticket now appears at the left end of the ticket, rotated 180 degrees.

6 Save *01Work.pm6*.

Note: An interim file is provided with the steps completed up to this point. If you want to complete the rest of this project without having to do the earlier steps, go to 01Project, *open* 01Inter1.pt6, *and save it in* Projects.

USING THE POLYGON TOOL

Now you open a new document and assemble a logo for the ticket. You import graphics and use drawing tools to create the logo and save it as an EPS file, which you then import into the ticket layout.

You start by examining the completed logo.

1 Choose *01Final.pm6* from the list of open documents in the Window menu, and use the zoom tool to magnify the logo.

The logo consists of three imported EPS files, plus several stars created with PageMaker 6's new polygon tool. A mask is used to hide portions of the logo.

2 Choose New from the File menu, then set the Dimensions to 5.25 by 4 inches. Choose the Wide option, deselect Double-sided, set all the margins to 0, and click OK.

3 Save the new file as *01Work2.pm6* in *Projects*.

Note: If you wish to skip the steps for creating the logo, you can go directly to the "Placing the Logo" section later in this project and place the file 01Final2.eps (Macintosh) or 01Final3.tif (Windows). Both files are in 01Project.

4 Double-click the polygon tool in the Toolbox. In the Polygon dialog box, enter **18** for Number of Sides and **15** for Star Inset, and click OK.

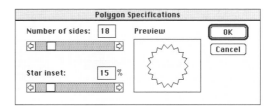

These settings will apply to all objects that you draw with the polygon tool. You can use the polygon tool for drawing multisided objects such as stars, triangles, pentagons, and any other polygons.

5 Draw a star shape of any size anywhere on the page.

6 In the Control palette, make sure the top left reference point on the proxy is selected. Set X to 0.408, Y to 0.15, width to 2.156, and height to 2.226, and apply the settings.

7 Select the star with the pointer tool, make sure the Both button on the Colors palette is selected, click Black, and choose 30% from the Tint pop-up menu.

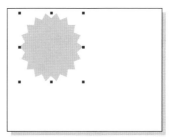

8 To create a drop shadow for the star shape, copy the shape and then paste. Don't use Power Paste.

9 With the copy still selected, set the tint to 100%, then choose Send Backward from the Arrange menu.

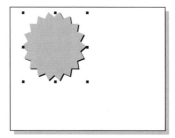

In PageMaker 6 you can choose to move an item forward or back one layer at a time (Bring Forward and Send Backward), as well as send it all the way to the front or to the back (Bring to Front and Send to Back).

10 Press the Shift key and click the light gray star, so that both objects are selected, and then copy the selection.

11 Paste the selection, make sure the top left reference point of the proxy is selected in the Control palette, and set X to 2.66 and Y to 1.668. Apply the settings.

12 Hold down the Shift key and click the gray star copy to deselect it. Enter 2.638 for X and 1.628 for Y to position the drop shadow to the left of the star.

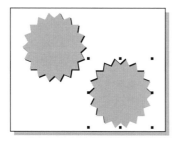

Take a look at the logo in *01Final.pm6* to make sure your design matches.

IMPORTING GRAPHICS

Next, you draw several circular elements and then import some graphics that were created in Adobe Illustrator.

1 Select the oval tool from the Toolbox, and draw an oval or circle of any size. In the Control palette, be sure that Proportional mode is not enabled (the button to the right of the width scale option), and set both the width and height to 1.396.

2 With the circle still selected, click the Fill button in the Colors palette, and set the fill to Paper.

3 Choose Line from the Element menu and Custom from the submenu. Set the line weight to 1.5 points and click OK.

Now you position the circle inside the lower right-hand star shape.

4 To position the circle precisely within the lower star, select the center point of the Control palette proxy, and then click the star with the pointer tool to select it. Write down the X and Y values (the coordinates) that appear in the Control palette. Next, select the circle, keep the center point of the proxy selected, enter the same coordinates, and apply them to the circle.

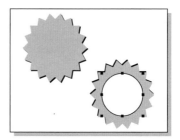

Note: There is an Align Objects command available on the Arrange menu, but it moves both of the selected objects to align them. When you require that one object remain unmoved, you need to use the technique described in these steps.

5 Copy the circle, and paste it. Use the Control palette to set the width and height to 1.219. Click the Fill button in the Colors palette, then change the color to Black and the tint to 30%. Center the new circle in the original circle by entering the same coordinates in the Control palette that you wrote down in Step 4. Apply the settings.

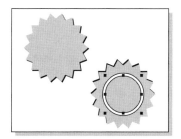

6 Display the Place Document dialog box. In *01Project*, select *01Ball1.eps* as an independent graphic. Click the loaded graphic icon to place the baseball image in the nested circles, and then make sure the center point of the proxy is still selected, and center the image in the lower star by entering the coordinates in the Control palette again.

Now you center a ball image in the upper left star shape. Make sure the center reference point of the proxy remains selected for the next two steps.

7 Select the left gray star shape and write down the X and Y coordinates.

8 Display the Place Document dialog box, and select *01Ball2.eps*. Click the loaded graphic icon to place the basketball image, then center the image in the left star by entering the coordinates from step 7 in the Control palette.

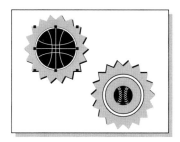

9 Display the Place Document dialog box, and select *01Logo.eps*. Click the loaded graphic icon to place the text image on the page. To position the image between the two stars, set X to 2.59 and Y to 2.001 in the Control palette.

Note: On Windows platforms, the background of 01Logo.eps displays as black. It will print correctly on PostScript printers.

10 Make sure the newly placed graphic is selected, and then choose Send to Back from the Arrange menu.

11 If you haven't saved your work recently, this is a good time to save the *01Work2.pm6* file.

CREATING A MASK

Now you are ready to create a mask for the logo. The new Mask command in PageMaker 6 allows you to use polygons, ovals, or rectangles to hide portions of an image. In the following steps, you create a rectangle with rounded corners, position it over the design you've been creating, and then select everything and create a mask that hides everything outside the rectangle.

1 Double-click the rectangle tool.

2 In the Rounded Corners dialog box, choose the upper right icon and click OK.

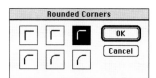

3 Draw a round-corner rectangle of any size on the pasteboard next to the page.

4 In the Control palette, make sure that the top left reference point of the proxy is selected and that the Proportional button is not selected. Set X to 1.283, Y to 0.953, width to 2.592, and height to 2.064. Apply the settings.

5 With the rounded rectangle still selected, click the Both button in the Colors palette, and click None.

You are not required to set the line and fill to None when creating a mask. This is just the nature of this particular design.

6 Choose Select All from the Edit menu.

In the next step, you create the mask and group the object in a single step. You can create a mask without grouping it by not holding down the Option or Shift key.

7 Hold down Option (Macintosh) or Shift (Windows) and choose Mask and Group from the Element menu.

Only the portion of the design that lies under the rectangle is visible, and the whole image is grouped into a single object.

8 Save *01Work2.pm6*.

SAVING AN EPS FILE

Now you save the logo as an EPS (Encapsulated PostScript) file so that you can import it and scale it in the ticket publication.

1 Display the Print Document dialog box.

2 Click the Options button and enable Write PostScript to File. Click the EPS radio button.

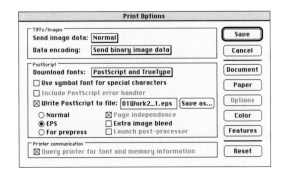

3 Click the Save As button (Macintosh) or the Browse button (Windows). Navigate to the *Projects* folder, and leave the name that is pre-selected for you.

4 Click OK (Macintosh) or Save (Windows), and then click Save. PageMaker saves the image to an EPS file with the designated name.

Choosing EPS causes PageMaker to create a graphic file that can be imported into other files or publications. If you choose to write to a PostScript file without enabling the EPS option, you create a PostScript file that can be output on any PostScript printer, but it can't be imported as a graphic.

Note: On Windows platforms, EPS files with WMS or TIFF preview images do not support transparent backgrounds or clipping paths, so you will see the background of this image onscreen when you place it in PageMaker. It will print correctly on a PostScript printer, however.

5 Save and close *01Work2.pm6*.

PLACING THE LOGO

1 Return to the master page of *01Work.pm6* and display the Place Document dialog box.

2 Navigate to *Projects* and select *01Work2_1.eps* (the EPS file you just created) as an independent graphic. If you are working on a Windows platform, you may prefer to place *01Final3.tif*, which will display correctly and will print correctly to non-PostScript printers. The EPS version will display as a gray box in Windows. Click with the loaded graphic icon on the pasteboard above the ticket to place the logo on the pasteboard.

Note: If you chose not to create the logo yourself, place 01Final2.eps *(Macintosh) or* 01Final3.tif *(Windows) from* 01Project. *(The EPS version will display as a gray box on Windows platforms but will print correctly to PostScript printers.)*

In the next steps, you reduce the size of the logo by using the percentage scale setting in the Control palette. You then use guides to place the logo on the ticket.

3 Select the newly imported logo, click the center reference point of the Control palette proxy, and make sure that Proportional mode (the button to the right of the Width scale box) is selected. Enter 14% for the width scale, and apply the setting.

4 Drag a vertical ruler guide to 2.43 and a horizontal guide to 0.5.

5 Align the lower left corner of the logo image with the intersection of the two ruler guides.

6 Save *01Work.pm6*.

CREATING NEW MASTER PAGES

You have now finished creating the Document Master master page. Since you are creating tickets for two different events, you next create two new master pages. Each one starts out as a duplicate of the Document Master that you have been working on. You then add unique elements to each new master page.

1 Choose Master Pages from the Window menu to display the Master Pages palette. With Document Master selected in the Master Pages palette, click the right-pointing triangle at the top of the palette and choose Duplicate from the Palette menu.

2 Type **Basketball** for the name of the new master page and click Duplicate.

PageMaker creates and displays a new master page named Basketball. It is a copy of the Document Master master page. By default, PageMaker creates a new master page by copying the master page that is highlighted in the palette at the time you choose Duplicate from the Palette menu. You can use a different master page as the starting point by choosing it from the Duplicate pop-up menu of existing master pages.

Now you are ready to add a new graphic to the Basketball master page.

USING A LIBRARY OF IMAGES

The Library palette is useful for storing and organizing graphics and text.

1 To be sure you are now working on the Basketball master page, look at the bottom of the window and notice that the master page icon is selected. Then look at the Master Pages palette and notice that Basketball is highlighted.

Note: If a master page is displayed, you can see its name by pressing and holding (Macintosh) or right-clicking (Windows) on the master page icon at the bottom of the window to pop up a list of existing master pages. There is a check mark next to the one that is displayed. You can display a different master page by selecting from this list. Similarly, if you have a document page displayed and want to know what master page it uses, you can tell either by seeing what page is highlighted in the Master Pages palette or by displaying the list from the master page icon at the bottom of the window and looking for the check mark.

2 If the Library palette is not already displayed, choose Library from the Window menu, then select 01Lib.pml from the Library dialog box.

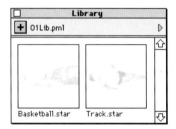

Note: If you have selected this library in this publication before, you don't see the Library dialog box. The library displays immediately.

3 Click the Basketball.star image, drag it from the library onto the ticket publication, and release the mouse button to flow the graphic onto the page. Click the graphic with the pointer tool to select it. Click the upper left reference point on the proxy, and then position the Basketball Star image by setting X to 0 and Y to −0.008.

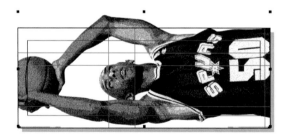

4 Click the cropping tool in the Toolbox.

The cropping tool is used to hide portions of a graphic.

5 Position the center of the cropping tool over the top center selection handle of the graphic, and then drag downward until the graphic is cropped to the top edge of the ticket.

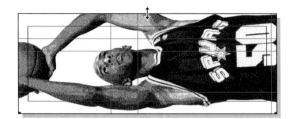

COLORIZING A BITMAP

PageMaker lets you apply colors to imported monochrome and grayscale bitmap images. The image that you just placed is a grayscale TIFF image and therefore falls into this category.

1 To colorize the basketball player image, make sure the image is selected and click the Fill button on the Colors palette.

2 Make sure that the Tint is set to 100% and click PANTONE 442 in the Colors palette to apply the color to the image.

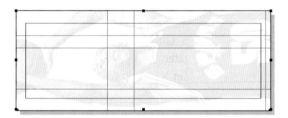

FINISHING THE MASTER PAGE

The Lock Position command ensures that you can't accidentally move an object.

1 With the image still selected, choose Send to Back from the Arrange menu.

2 Choose Lock Position from the Arrange menu.

3 Change the text that says "name of the event" to "Hooplas vs. Dribblers." Then select the text and click the All Caps button in the Control palette (the capital C button below the font name) to capitalize the text.

4 Save *01Work.pm6.*

You have completed the master page for the basketball ticket.

CREATING ANOTHER MASTER PAGE

Now you create a second master page for the track-event ticket, once again using the material on the Document Master master page as the starting point.

1 Choose Duplicate from the Master Pages palette menu.

2 Choose Document Master from the Duplicate pop-up menu.

3 Enter **Track** for the name of the new master page, then click Duplicate.

You are now working on the new Track master page.

4 Drag the Track.star image from the Sports library anywhere onto the Track master page.

5 Click the image to select it, click the top left reference point on the Control palette proxy, and set X to **0.798** and Y to **0.008** to position the graphic on the ticket.

6 With the image still selected, make sure that Tint is set to 100% in the Colors palette and that the Fill button is selected. Click PANTONE 5295 in the Colors palette to colorize the black-and-white TIFF image of the track star. Choose Send to Back from the Arrange menu.

UNGROUPING OBJECTS

The next step is to change the color of the grouped objects at the ends of the ticket to match the color of the Track.star image.

1 With the pointer tool, select the grouped object at the right end of the Track master page, and choose Ungroup from the Arrange menu.

2 Click outside the page to deselect the collection of objects. Select the large rectangle, click the Line button on the Colors palette, and click PANTONE 5295.

3 Select the thin rectangle at the left of the same group, click the Both button on the Colors palette, and again apply PANTONE 5295.

Notice that the 30% tint value is retained when you change the color.

4 Select all the objects at the right end of the ticket, and choose Group from the Arrange menu.

Now you repeat the procedure for the left end of the Track master page, but you use a different technique for dealing with the grouped object.

5 To select only the large rectangle in the grouped object at the left end of the ticket, Command-click (Macintosh) or Control-click (Windows) the rectangle.

6 Click the Line button on the Colors palette and apply PANTONE 5295.

7 Now use the same technique to select the thin rectangle at the right of the grouped object, click the Both button on the Colors palette, and apply PANTONE 5295.

8 Select the "name of the event" text and change it to "TORTOISES VS. HARES." With the text selected, capitalize it by clicking the All Caps button in the Control palette.

9 Save *01Work.pm6.*

APPLYING MASTER PAGES

So far, you have been working only on the master pages of *01Work.pm6*. Now you apply the two different master pages to two document pages to create two tickets: one for basketball and one for track.

You begin by applying the Basketball master page to the document page.

1 Click the Page 1 icon to display the document page. Notice that the Document Master master page elements appear on the page. Then click the Basketball master page in the Master Pages palette to apply the Basketball master page to the document page.

The Basketball master elements appear on the document page.

Note: Clicking a master page name in the Master Pages palette has two entirely different effects, depending on whether you are displaying a master page or a document page at the time. If you have a master page displayed, you go to the master page that you clicked in the palette. That is how you move between master pages. If you have a document page displayed, however, clicking a master page name applies that master page to the document page that is displayed.

2 Display the Place Document dialog box and select *01Floor.doc* from *01Project*. Click on the pasteboard to place the text.

3 Highlight the first line with the text tool and cut it. Click just above the bottom margin anywhere between the side margins and paste.

4 Click an insertion point in the newly pasted text, and apply the Row.2 paragraph style.

5 With the pointer tool or the arrow keys, position the text block so that the baseline of the type rests on the bottom margin.

Because the style has the necessary indents and other formatting, the new line of text falls into its correct place under the line above. Go to a document page of *01Final.pm6* to see how your text should look.

6 Return to the text block on the pasteboard, select the next line, and apply the Vert.row.2 style.

7 Select the remaining two lines of text, and apply the Vert.row.3 style.

8 Use the pointer tool to resize the text block so that its width is not much more than the width of the text. Be sure that all of the text is displayed and that no lines break.

9 Select the text block with the pointer tool, click the center reference point on the Control palette proxy, and enter **−90°** into the rotation box in the Control palette. Apply the setting.

10 To position the text at the end of the ticket, select the top left reference point on the proxy, set the X value to **4.367** and the Y value to **0.25**.

11 Copy the text that you just positioned and Power Paste it. To rotate the copied text, enter **90°** in the Rotation box of the Control palette and apply the setting.

Note: Entering 90° in the Rotation box always places the top of the object on the left, regardless of the initial position of the object.

12 To position the rotated text at the left end of the ticket, click the bottom left reference point on the Control palette proxy, and set X to **0.34** and Y to **1.75**.

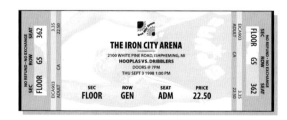

13 Save *01Work.pm6*.

CREATING THE SECOND TICKET

Now that you have completed the basketball ticket, you create the track event ticket by copying the text from the basketball document page and pasting it onto a new page that uses the Track master page.

1 On the document page, Select All and then Copy.

2 Add a new document page by choosing Insert Pages from the Layout menu. In the Insert Pages dialog box, set Insert to 1 and leave the position set to After the Current Page. To assign the Track master page to the new document page, choose Track from the Master Page pop-up menu. Click Insert.

PageMaker adds a new page that uses the Track master page and displays the new page.

3 Now Power Paste the text that you copied onto the new page.

Using Power Paste ensures that the text is placed on the new page exactly where it was on the old page.

These two simple steps have created a complete track event ticket.

PRODUCING THE PUBLICATION

The tickets will be enlarged and printed on a color printer, to use as comps in a presentation. If you have access to a color printer, select it and try printing. If you do not have access to a printer, you can still follow most of the steps.

PageMaker provides a multitude of printing features, including the ability to print in black and white, color composites, or color separations. You could also create an Acrobat PDF file for electronic distribution. See Projects 4 and 5 for instructions on how to use PageMaker's Create Adobe PDF feature.

The following instructions are for a color PostScript printer. Print this to a non-color printer by choosing a suitable PPD. You will have somewhat different options if you are printing to a non-PostScript printer.

1 Use Chooser to select your printer.

2 Display the Print Document dialog box. and select the Color General PPD.

3 Click the Paper button. In the Print Paper dialog box, you can see the new Print Fit view, which ensures that the selected page fits within the dimensions of the paper or film in your output devices. It accounts for paper and page orientation, negative or positive settings and printer's marks.

4 Enter **150%** in the Scale box and note how the Print Fit view changes.

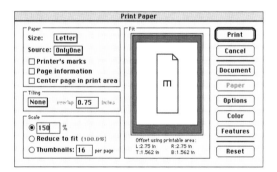

5 If you have a PostScript printer, click the Print button.

FINISHING UP

Close all open documents and quit PageMaker 6.

UNE COURSE CYCLISTE DE CLASSE MONDIALE: LE TOUR DE FRANCE

• FRANCE •

2

In this eight-page guidebook to the Tour de France, one of the world's great cycling events, you get a chance to go beyond the basics of using PageMaker's styles. As you construct

CYCLING GUIDEBOOK

this dramatic and playful piece, you learn sophisticated ways to put the power of paragraph styles to work for you. You import style sheets and become adept at manipulating text blocks. ■ When the piece is complete, you confront issues and opportunities in page imposition by using the Build Booklet plug-in to create a new publication in which the pages are arranged for two-up saddle stitching.

To create this guidebook, you begin by opening an Adobe PageMaker publication that has been partially completed. You then place two separate text files that have been formatted by using style sheets in a word-processing program. Next, you

CYCLING GUIDEBOOK

edit the styles and explore several style options. After completing the layout, you use the Build Booklet plug-in to build pages for printing two pages per sheet.

This project covers:

• Importing and using word-processing style sheets

• Editing styles

• Basing one style on an existing style

• Using the Bullets and Numbers plug-in

• Changing a word-processing style to a PageMaker style

• Replacing one style with another

• Separating and manipulating text blocks

• Creating a booklet by using the Build Booklet plug-in

At the end of this lesson, you'll have a eight-page, six-color booklet.

It should take you about 2 hours to complete this project .

BEFORE YOU BEGIN

1 Return all settings to their defaults by deleting the *Adobe PageMaker 6.x Prefs* file from the *Preferences* folder (Macintosh) or by removing *\pm6\rsrc\usenglish\pm6.cnf* from the drive containing PageMaker (Windows).

2 Make sure that Minion, Minion Italic, Zapf Dingbats, and the Myriad Multiple Master family of fonts are installed on your system.

For this lesson, you need to copy the French hyphenation and spelling dictionary to your Adobe PageMaker application directory.

3 To install the French dictionary, drag the *Français* folder from the *02Project* folder into the *Proximity* (Macintosh) or *PRX* (Windows 95) folder, located inside the *Linguist* folder. The *Linguist* folder is in the *RSRC* folder, which is in your *Adobe PageMaker* application folder.

4 Launch the Adobe PageMaker application, and then open the *02Final.pm6* file in *02Project*.

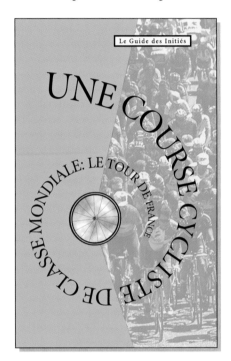

This publication is an eight-page booklet containing photographs, maps, and text. The text was entered and formatted in a popular word-processing application, then placed into the Adobe PageMaker document.

5 Leave this file open so you can use it as a visual reference during the lesson. Click the page icons in the lower left corner to examine each spread in the document. Zoom in where you wish to take a closer look.

TIP: TO OPEN THE STYLES PALETTE, PRESS COMMAND-Y (MACINTOSH) OR CONTROL-Y (WINDOWS).

SETTING UP THE DOCUMENT

Start by opening a document that has been partially completed for you.

1 Choose Open from the File menu, then select the *02Begin.pm6* file.

Since the focus of this project is working with imported text styles, a lot of the placing and positioning of graphic elements has been done for you. This booklet is an eight-page document, 6 inches by 9.5 inches in size. A number of photographs and illustrations have been placed, and several colorful graphic rectangles have been created and positioned. Several colors have already been defined in the Colors palette, including two Pantone fluorescent colors.

2 Choose Preferences from the File menu. Set the units for the Measurements and Vertical Ruler to Picas. In order to speed up screen redraw, click the Standard option in the Graphics display area. Click OK.

3 Choose Save As from the File menu, type **02Work.pm6** for the name, and save the publication into *Projects*.

Setting Column and Ruler Guides

The design of the publication is based on a three-column grid, with sidebars added for variety. In the next steps, you set up a three-column grid on the document master page. The three-column format will help you place the text on pages 3, 4, and 5.

1 Display the facing pages by choosing View from the Layout menu and Fit in Window from the submenu. The keyboard shortcut is Command-0 (Macintosh) or Control-0 (Windows). Another way to access Fit in Window view is to hold down Option (Macintosh) or Alt (Windows) and double-click the zoom tool in the Tools palette. Another way, that works on both platforms, is to Shift-click the page icon.

2 Choose Document Setup from the File menu, and set the Inside, Outside, and Top margins to 2p6, and the Bottom margin to 2p10, then click OK.

Note: The units for this publication are set to picas, the unit most commonly used in graphic design. "2p6" means 2 picas and 6 points. Type the entry exactly as shown in the instruction.

3 To display the underlying master page (Document Master), click the master page icon in the lower left corner of the window. Then choose Column Guides from the Layout menu, set the number of columns to 3 with a 1-pica gutter, and click OK.

4 Go to the page 2–3 spread.

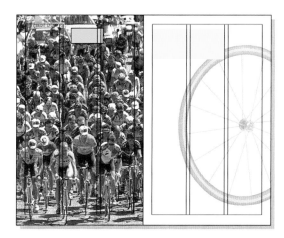

Because the Facing Pages option is enabled in the document setup, the pages display in pairs when the zoom factor is set to Fit in Window,

WORKING WITH IMPORTED STYLES

You'll import two text files into the guidebook. Both files were created in Microsoft Word and formatted by using Word's Style command.

A *style* is a set of character and paragraph formatting attributes that you apply to the text in your document. Once a style has been defined and named, you can select any paragraph and

TIP: TO TURN
THROUGH THE PAGES
OF YOUR PUBLICATION
AUTOMATICALLY, PRESS
SHIFT AND THEN CHOOSE
GO TO PAGE FROM
THE LAYOUT MENU.
CLICK THE MOUSE
BUTTON TO CANCEL.

apply that style. In just one step, all formatting defined for that style is applied to the paragraph. A *style sheet* is the set of styles that has been defined for a particular document.

Viewing styles

A list of styles that are in the current PageMaker publication is available in thee different places: in the Styles palette, in the Control palette, and on the Styles submenu of the Type menu. You can apply and edit styles by using the Styles palette or the Control palette. You can also apply them by using the Styles submenu of the Type menu, or you can edit them by choosing Define Styles from the Type menu.

PageMaker includes six default styles which you can edit to have any appearance you wish. If you prefer, you can create new styles or use the styles that are imported when you place a file from a word processor. When you create new styles or import styles, the style names appear in the Styles list.

Most word-processing programs have a Style command. When you import a word-processor file, the style sheets are imported along with the text (as long as the proper filters are included when you install PageMaker).

If you are not using styles, you aren't taking advantage of the power of PageMaker. Styles save you time when you apply and change formatting, and they give a consistent look to your publication.

Even in the case of this guidebook, which does not have a rigidly consistent style, you can take advantage of styles for basic formatting, and then apply special characteristics later.

While designing the guidebook, the graphic designer experimented with a variety of font and text styles. Now that all the design decisions have been made, you're ready to define the final text styles.

IMPORTING STYLES THAT MATCH PAGEMAKER STYLES

The translator who typed the French text in Word applied styles to the text. The style names used are identical to PageMaker's default style names, although the styles themselves are not defined at all the way they are in PageMaker. If you have Microsoft Word available on your system, you can open *02TextA.doc* and see that the text looks very plain, although the familiar PageMaker style names are used.

Because the style names are identical in the Word file and in PageMaker, the placed text will take on the style definitions set in PageMaker if you select Retain Format when you place the text. For this to work, the style name in the word processor must be *exactly* the same as those in PageMaker, including capitalization and word spacing. For example, a style named Body Text and one named Body text would be two different styles.

1 Go to page 3, and display the page at actual size view. On a Macintosh, you can toggle between Fit in Window view and Actual Size by holding down Command and Option keys and clicking anywhere on the page. In Windows, right-clicking toggles these views. Press Option (Macintosh) or Alt (Windows), and drag with the mouse to pan the page. Position it so that the top half of page 3 is in the center of your screen.

2 Display the Place Document dialog box, and click once on *02TextA.doc* to select it.

3 Be sure that As New Story and Retain Format are both selected and click OK (Macintosh) or Open (Windows).

When you select Retain Format, PageMaker uses the PageMaker style definition. (Remember that the styles have the same names in the Word file and in the PageMaker publication.) When the word processor style name has no counterpart in PageMaker, Retain Format retains the word processor style definition.

4 Press the Command (Macintosh) or Control (Windows) key to access automatic text flow. Then click the loaded text cursor inside the left column of page 3.

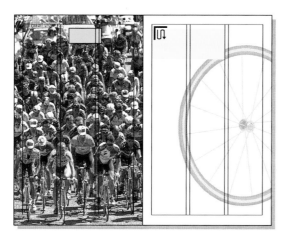

The text flows in through page 5 and takes on the formatting of the PageMaker styles.

EDITING STYLES

Next, you change the definition of the Body text paragraph style.

1 Go to page 3, and choose Define Styles from the Type menu.

2 Click the Body text style, then click the Edit button.

3 Click the Type button, then change the font to Minion Regular, the size to 9 points, and the leading to 13 points. Click OK.

4 Click the Para button, set the First indent to 0, select Justify from the Alignment pop-up menu, and choose Français from the Dictionary menu.

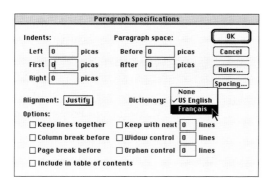

5 Press Option (Macintosh) or Shift (Windows) and click OK to accept your changes and get out of the nested dialog boxes.

Notice that the first few paragraphs of text have changed style. The rest of the body text has been formatted with the Normal style in the word processor and so is not affected by the change to the Body text style. You will fix that later in the lesson.

BASING STYLES ON OTHER STYLES

Styles in PageMaker can be based on other styles. For example, the Subhead 1 style is based on the Headline style. It contains all the characteristics of the Headline style, except the point size is smaller. Basing one style on another saves time when creating and editing styles. With PageMaker's default styles, the Headline style is the main format; Subhead 1 is based on the Headline style, and Subhead 2 is based on the Subhead 1 style. If you edit the font of the Headline style, all the styles that are based on the Headline style will change as well.

You next examine the current styles, then change the font of the Headline style and see how the Subhead 1 and Subhead 2 styles also change.

1 Select Define Styles from the Type menu.

2 Select the Subhead 1 style, then click Edit.

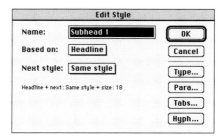

Notice that the Subhead 1 style is based on the Headline style. The Subhead 2 style is based on the Subhead 1 style. You can base a style on any other style in your publication.

3 Click Cancel, then double-click the Headline style. The Headline style is based on No Style because it is the top style in the hierarchy. Click Cancel.

Note: You can also specify what style text follows another style paragraph by using the Next Style pop-up menu. This feature works only on text that is typed directly into PageMaker.

4 To examine the three styles before you change them, display the Control palette by choosing it from the Window menu. Then click an insertion point in "1903" at the top of page 3. Notice that Headline is highlighted in the Styles palette because it is the style that is applied to the text. Look in the Character view of the Control palette, and notice that the font is Times. Now click in the next line ("La victoire…") and notice that it is Subhead 1 and that the font is still Times. Finally, click in "La stratégie" a little farther down the column. This paragraph is Subhead 2 and also has Times as the font.

5 To redefine the Headline style, Command-click (Macintosh) or Control-click (Windows) on the style name in the Styles palette and click the Type button. Change the font to MyriadMM 700 Bold 600 Norm, set the size to 42 points, choose Purple from the Color menu, and select Normal for the Type Style.

6 Press the Option (Macintosh) or Shift (Windows) key, then click the OK button to get out of the nested dialog boxes.

The font changes in all text tagged with the Headline, Subhead 1, or Subhead 2 style. This is an excellent way of ensuring that elements in a document remain consistent. Click the Subhead 1 and Subhead 2 text that you checked before, and notice that they have all changed to purple Myriad.

Now you fine-tune the Subhead 1 and Subhead 2 styles.

7 Choose Define Styles from the Type menu, then double-click the Subhead 1 style. Click the Type button, set the size to 26 points, and the leading to 32 points. Click OK twice to return to the Define Styles dialog box.

Notice that you edited the Headline style by accessing it from the Styles palette, and you edited this one by choosing it from the Define Styles dialog box. It doesn't matter which technique you use. The effect is the same.

8 Double-click the Subhead 2 style, then click the Type button and set the point size to 13 points and the leading to 13 points as well; exit from the nested dialog boxes.

9 Page through the document and notice that all text tagged with the Subhead 1 or Subhead 2 style has been changed to the new font and color.

10 Return to page 3, and save *02Work.pm6*.

Creating a Style based on another style

Now you'll create a second body text style that incorporates an indent. You'll base it on the regular Body text style.

1 Choose Define Styles from the Type menu, click the Body text style, then click the New button.

The Define Style dialog box appears with Body text selected in the Based On area.

2 Type **Body Text Indent** in the Name box.

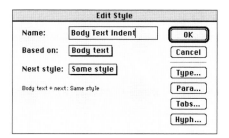

3 Click the Para button, then set the First line indent to .2i and exit the nested dialog boxes.

Typing an **i** after the number forces the unit to be inches, instead of the default unit (picas for this publication).

4 Scroll down and click an insertion point in the paragraph that starts "Quelques minutes…." Click the new Body Text Indent style in the Styles palette to apply it to the paragraph.

MANAGING TEXT THREADING

The text for this guidebook was typed into two different text files. When you place a text file into PageMaker, the text is a single story in a series of linked or *threaded* text blocks. For this particular design, some of the text needs to be broken into separate stories for ease in positioning on the page.

1 Change to Fit in Window view.

You want the text that starts with "1903" and ends just before "L'échappée" to be a story that is separate from the text that follows. To break the connection between text blocks, simply cut a portion of the text, then paste it back into position. Cutting and pasting creates a new story.

Before you cut the threading, you position the windowshades so that only the text that you want in the section is showing.

2 With the pointer tool, click the text block in the right column to select it. Drag the window-shade handle at the bottom up to the top margin so that the text block is completely rolled up.

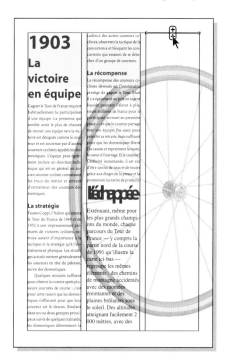

3 Select the middle text block, and drag the lower windowshade handle up to the middle of the phrase "L'échappée."

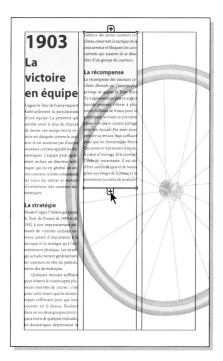

Since you can't display half a line of text, this procedure ensures that the last line of the section prior to the headline remains on the page.

4 Click the left text block with the pointer tool, and then Shift-click the remaining text block to add it to the selection.

5 Choose Cut from the Edit menu. The text disappears.

6 To paste the text so that it's in exactly the same position as before, use Power Paste: press the Option key (Macintosh) or the Alt key (Windows), and Paste.

The text reappears as a separate story, in precisely the same position as before. The empty window-shade handle at the bottom of the right text column indicates that the link with the rest of the text has been broken. The rest of the text now starts on page 4.

CHANGING MULTIPLE COLUMNS TO A SINGLE COLUMN

The design calls for the heading and first paragraph in the "La victoire en équipe" section to span two columns. In the following steps, you split the text without breaking the link between text blocks, then reposition the text and adjust the formatting.

1 To begin, you move the "1903" text to the yellow box on the left page. With the text tool selected, triple-click the "1903" paragraph to select the whole paragraph, including the line ending. Cut the paragraph, pan to the left to page 2, and zoom in on the yellow rectangle. Use the text tool to drag a bounding box inside the yellow rectangle and paste the text. Use the pointer tool to center the text block visually in the yellow rectangle.

2 Change to Fit in Window view and return to page 3.

3 To make room for the wider first paragraph, select the middle column with the pointer tool and drag the top windowshade handle down until it is below the bottom of the yellow box.

4 Select the left column text block, and drag the bottom windowshade handle up to bottom of the yellow rectangle. Then drag the right handle of the text block to the right margin of the middle column. The heading and first few lines span two columns.

TIP: IF YOU ACCI-
DENTALLY CLICK A
WINDOWSHADE
HANDLE AND GET
THE LOADED TEXT
CURSOR, YOU CAN
CANCEL THE CURSOR
BY CLICKING ANY TOOL
IN THE TOOLBOX.

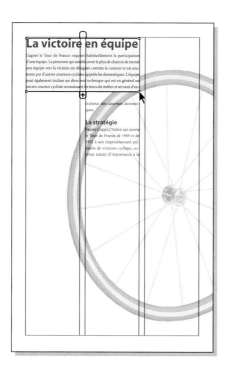

5 Use the text tool to select the first three lines of text in the first body text paragraph, then use the Control palette to set the font size to 16 points and the leading to 32 points.

6 Click the Paragraph button in the Control palette, and set the alignment to Force Justify by clicking the far-right alignment button.

7 To prevent any hyphenation in this paragraph, choose Hyphenation from the Type menu, click the Off button, and click OK.

8 Make sure that there are three lines of text visible in the wide text block below "La victoire en équipe." Lengthen the text block a little if necessary. Make sure that this text block spans the two columns.

9 Zoom in on the text that's in the middle column. To separate the first three lines from the preceding text, click at the beginning of the first narrow line, just in front of "le plus de chances," and press Return or Enter. Although it isn't readily apparent, the text is split into two paragraphs.

10 Notice that a plus sign appears next to the Body text style in the Styles palette. A plus sign indicates that additional formatting is overriding the original style. To reapply the Body text style to the second paragraph in the narrow column, click in the paragraph and then click Body text in the Styles palette.

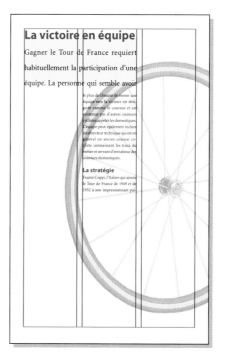

The text returns to the Body text style, and the plus sign disappears from the Body text style name in the Styles palette.

11 Drag a horizontal ruler guide to 5p7. Watch the Y value in the Control palette to position it. Then select the wide text block, and use the pointer tool, arrow keys, or nudge buttons to position it so that the baseline of the first line of body text ("Gagner le tour…") rests on the 5p7 guide.

12 With the pointer tool, click the plus sign in the bottom windowshade handle of the two-column text block. Click the loaded text cursor in the first column below the wide paragraph.

The text that was at the top of the narrow middle column is now in the left column.

Aligning the text

1 Drag a horizontal ruler guide down to 12p11, then position the narrow text block in the left column so that the baseline of the first line of text rests on the guide.

2 Drag a horizontal ruler guide down to 29p3, and then use the pointer tool to roll up the bottom windowshade handle of the left text block so the last line of text is resting on the guide. You'll have to position the bottom of the text block just a little below the guide to accomplish this.

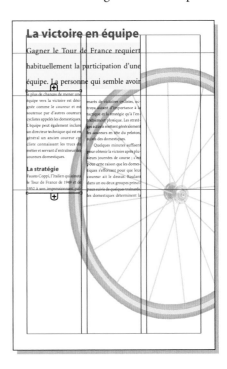

3 With the pointer tool, click the text block in the middle column to select it. Drag or nudge the text block so that the first baseline rests on the 12p11 guide. Drag down the bottom windowshade handle until the bottom line of text rests on the 29p3 guide.

4 Click the bottom handle of the middle text block to load the text icon, and click in the right column to flow in the remainder of the text. Position the top of the text block against the top margin, and drag the bottom windowshade handle down so that the last line of text rests on the 29p3 guide.

You've got the three narrow text blocks positioned. Now you return to the wide text block and use a baseline shift button in the Control palette to adjust the vertical position of a single line of type.

5 Select the entire subhead "La victoire en équipe" with the text tool, make sure the Character view of the Control palette is chosen, and click the baseline shift down arrow button until the bottom of the text rests on the top of the yellow rectangle (approximately –0p10).

Baseline shift ⎯

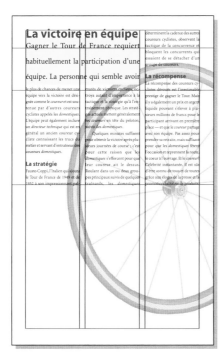

5 Save *02Work.pm6*. You should be saving your work at frequent intervals. We remind you only once in a while.

Finishing the first spread

To finish the first spread, you add two text sidebars that have already been formatted and stored in the library.

1 Choose Library from the Window menu. Highlight *02Lib.pml*, and click Open. The *02Lib.pml* library appears. Expand the library window so that you can see the two items.

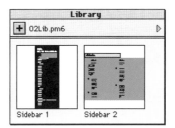

2 Drag the Sidebar 1 library item onto page 2. Position it so that the right edge of the rectangle aligns with the right edge of page 2, and the top edge of the rectangle aligns with the bottom edge of the "1903" rectangle.

The highlight effect for the first three lines of the sidebar text is created by three green rectangles that are positioned behind the text.

3 Go to page 3, and display the bottom half of it. Drag the Sidebar 2 library item onto page 3, and then position the green rectangle between the margins, with the bottom of the green rectangle on the bottom margin.

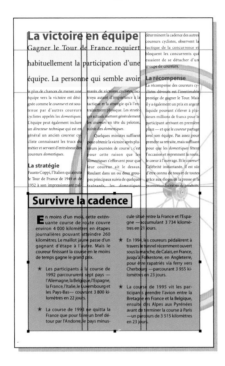

4 Save *02Work.pm6*.

Congratulations. You have completed the first spread of the guidebook.

Note: An interim file is provided with the steps completed up to this point. If you want to complete the rest of this project without having to do the earlier steps, go to 02Project, *open* 02Inter1.pt6, *and save it in* Projects.

REPLACING ONE STYLE WITH ANOTHER

There are a number of paragraphs that are still tagged with the Normal paragraph style that was applied to the text in Microsoft Word. You want all of the paragraphs to have the Body text style applied instead. The fastest and easiest way to do this is to use the Find/Change command to Find the Normal style and change it to Body text style. The asterisk next to the name Normal in the Styles palette indicates that it is an imported style.

1 Use the text tool to click several different body text paragraphs following the *L'échappée* headline. Notice that they are all tagged with the Normal paragraph style.

2 Use the text tool to click an insertion point anywhere in the text. Display the Story Editor by choosing Edit Story from the Edit menu.

3 Choose Change from the Utilities menu.

4 Click the Change dialog box, click the Para Attributes button to display the Change Paragraph Attributes dialog box.

5 Click the Find What: Para Style pop-up menu and choose Normal. Click the Change To: Para Style pop-up menu and choose Body text. Click OK.

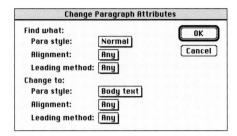

6 Notice that Find What and Change To are both underlined in the Change dialog box, indicating that one or more type or paragraph attributes are specified. These attribute specifications will remain selected until you remove them. The underlines are a reminder.

7 Leave the Find What and Change To boxes empty and click Change All.

PageMaker finds all occurrences of the Normal paragraph style and applies the Body text paragraph style to the text.

8 Now that you've completed the change, you want to remove the attribute specifications from Find What and Change To, so that they don't affect any other search. You could just click the Para Attributes button again and change the settings back to Any, but there's a shortcut: Hold down Option (Macintosh) or Alt (Windows) and click the Para Attributes button. This resets all the attributes to Any. Notice that the underlines disappear from the words *Find What* and *Change to* in the Change dialog box.

9 Click in the paragraphs that formerly had Normal applied and notice that they are now tagged with the Body text style.

REMOVING AN UNUSED STYLE

Your next step is to remove Normal from the Style list. This removes the clutter of unused styles from the list and ensures that it won't get applied by accident.

1 Choose Define Styles from the Type menu.

2 Highlight Normal in the style list and click the Remove button. Click OK.

3 Look in the Styles palette and notice that Normal is no longer in the list.

ALIGNING THE TEXT

Now you align the text blocks for the spread on pages 4 and 5. As you work, pan the page as necessary and use Zoom to see the area you are editing.

1 Select the headline text ("L'échappée") by triple-clicking with the text tool so that the line ending is included in the selection. Cut the selection and paste it onto the pasteboard above the page.

2 Drag horizontal ruler guides down to 7p7, 15p2, and 19p6.

3 Position the left and middle text blocks so that the baseline of the first line of text rests on the 7p7 guide. You can use any convenient combination of the techniques you have learned: use the pointer tool to roll down the top windowshade handles, Shift-drag the text blocks with the pointer, and use the arrow keys for the final exact positioning. Zoom in so that you can see the text clearly. Remember, it's the baseline of the type, not the top of the text block, that goes on the guide.

4 Scroll down, and drag the bottom windowshade handle of the left column so that the last baseline rests on the bottom margin. You need to pull the bottom of the windowshade just a little below the margin to do this.

5 Drag up on the windowshade handles for the middle column and the right column until the bottom baseline rests on the 19p6 guide.

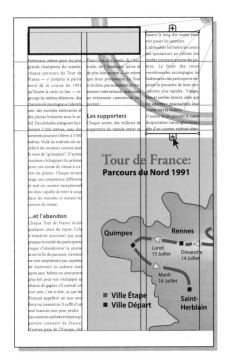

Any paragraph that doesn't directly follow a head needs to have Body Text Indent applied to it. In the next step, you apply this style to three paragraphs on page 4.

6 Apply the Body Text Indent style to the second paragraph after the "et l'abandon" head and to the second and third paragraphs after the "Les supporters" head.

You next finish page 4 by dragging the headline from the pasteboard where you placed it earlier into the bordered box that has been prepared for it.

7 Using the pointer tool, drag the headline ("L'échappée") into the yellow bordered box at the top left of the page. Use the arrow keys or the nudge buttons in the Control palette to position the text so that it is visually centered in the box.

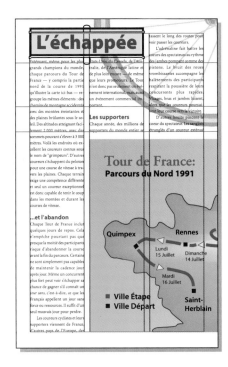

8 Load the text icon by clicking the bottom windowshade handle of the last text column on page 4. Click near the top of the first column on page 5 to flow the text onto the page.

9 Make sure that the top of the text block rests against the top margin of the page. Roll up the bottom of the text block so that the last baseline rests on the guide that's at 15p2. Load the text icon again, and flow text into the second column. Again, adjust the bottom of the text block so that the bottom baseline is on the 15p2 guide. Finally, load the text icon from this second text block, and flow the remaining text into the third column. Check *02Final.pm6* to confirm the positioning of the text.

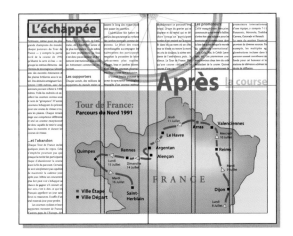

FINISHING PAGE 7

Now you place some text for the sidebar on page 7. As with the other text file that you placed in this project, the text was prepared in Microsoft Word and tagged with styles whose names are the same as style names in the PageMaker publication. You want to use the PageMaker definitions, so you enable Retain Format.

Note: When the styles applied in the word processor have names that are different from the PageMaker style names, enabling Retain Format retains the style definitions used in the word-processing application.

1 Go to page 7.

2 Choose Place from the File menu, select the *02TextB.doc* file, be sure the Retain Format option is selected, and click OK.

3 To place the text, choose the text tool and drag diagonally from the top left corner of the green rectangle to the lower right corner. See the following illustration for the exact ending position of the icon.

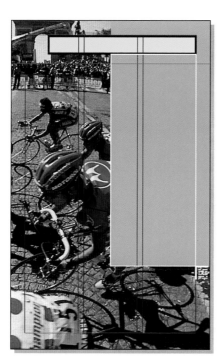

4 Select the heading ("Gagner... encore et toujours") by triple-clicking it with the text tool. Cut the selection, and then use the text tool to drag a bounding box in the yellow rectangle. Paste the cut headline into the yellow rectangle, and then use the arrow keys or the nudge buttons on the Control palette to center the headline in the yellow box.

The body text is on top of the headline, but you take care of that in a moment.

5 Drag a horizontal ruler guide down to 7p7, then move the body text block down so that the baseline of the first line rests on this guide. Make sure that the bottom handle of the text block is empty, indicating that all the text is displayed.

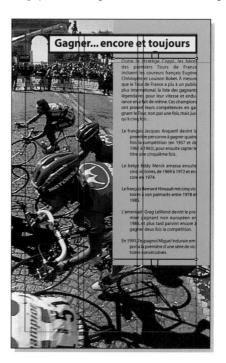

CONVERTING AN IMPORTED STYLE TO A PAGEMAKER STYLE

If you want to use an imported style in PageMaker, it's a good idea to convert the style to the PageMaker format. In the following steps, you convert the Sidebar Head and Sidebar Text styles to PageMaker styles.

1 Choose Define Styles from the Type menu, and click the Sidebar Head style name in the Define Styles dialog box.

2 Click the Edit button. Without making any changes, click OK in the Define Styles dialog box, and then click OK in the Define Styles dialog box.

The style is converted to a PageMaker style, and the asterisk next to the name in the Styles palette disappears.

In the next step, you convert another imported style, using a slightly different technique to perform exactly the same function.

3 To change the Sidebar Text style to a PageMaker style, press Command (Macintosh) or Control (Windows) and click the Sidebar Text style name in the Styles palette. Click OK without making any changes.

4 Save *02Work.pm6*.

BULLETS AND NUMBERING

This publication contains several lists that have stars as bullets. The sidebar text that you just placed on page 7 has several paragraphs that need to have starred paragraphs like those on page 3. You use the Bullets and Numbering plug-in to create these.

Adobe PageMaker comes with a variety of plug-ins that help you to perform complex procedures easily, or to perform special tasks. You can also acquire additional plug-ins created by independent developers. If you have access to the Internet, see Adobe's Web page at http://www.adobe.com.

1 Zoom in on the text you just placed onto page 7 and click an insertion point in the paragraph that begins "Le français Jacques Anquetil."

2 Choose PageMaker Plug-ins from the Utilities menu and Bullets and Numbering from the submenu.

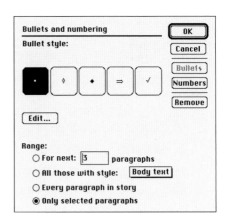

The Bullets and Numbering plug-in inserts consecutive numbers (*autonumbering*) or a bullet character of your choice, along with a tab, at the beginning of each designated paragraph. You can specify that they should be added to selected paragraphs, to paragraphs that have a specific style, to a specific number of paragraphs based on the location of your cursor, or to every paragraph in the story. In this example, you begin by editing the bullet style.

3 Click the button for All Those with Style, and choose Hanging indent from the pop-up list of defined paragraph styles.

4 Click the Edit button.

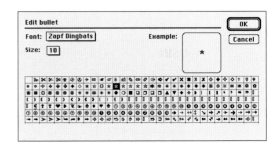

5 Choose the Zapf Dingbats font, set the size to 10 point, choose any star character, and click OK. Click OK again to exit the Bullets and Numbering dialog box.

Note: To see a character more clearly, set the size to something large, like 36 point, and click the character. It displays in the sample box at the chosen size. When you have identified the character you want, return the size to 10 point.

PageMaker adds bullets to all text in the story that has the Hanging indent style, using the character that you chose.

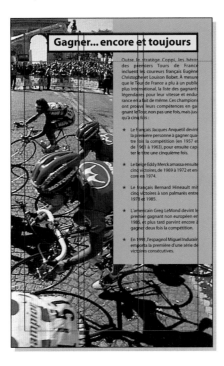

USING THE DROP CAP PLUG-IN

The initial character of a paragraph is sometimes enlarged and lowered to act as a design element on the page. The resulting character is called a *drop cap.*

1 To add the drop cap to the first body paragraph on page 7, click an insertion point in the first paragraph of the body text. Choose PageMaker Plug-ins from the Utilities menu and Drop Cap from the submenu.

2 Click OK to accept the default drop cap size of three lines.

Now that you have completed the layout, you're ready to build the booklet by using the Build Booklet plug-in.

Time out for a movie

If your system is capable of running Adobe Teach movies, play the movie named *Make Booklet* to see a preview of Adobe's Build Booklet plug-in. For information on how to view Adobe Teach movies, see "Watching Adobe Teach Movies" at the beginning of this book.

BUILDING A BOOKLET

The Build Booklet plug-in lets you create a copy of your current publication in which pages are arranged for printing multipage spreads or signatures. This publishing technique is known as *page imposition.* For this project, two pages are printed on each sheet of paper. When the paper is folded, the book pages are in the correct order. In your booklet, the first and last pages will be printed on one page, the second page on the same sheet as the second-to-last page, and so on.

Before building the booklet, you want to make sure that your text and layout are finished. Major changes may change the pagination and require that you rebuild your booklet.

1 Browse through your publication, making sure that everything is in order.

2 Choose PageMaker Plug-ins from the Utilities menu, then choose Build Booklet from the submenu. The Build Booklet dialog box appears.

3 Choose 2-up Saddle Stitch from the Layout menu. This option is for standard booklet printing, whereby double-sided pages are folded once and fastened along the fold.

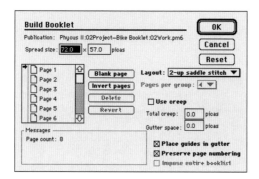

The 2-up Perfect Bound option creates a series of folded booklets that are bound with adhesive along the spine. With this option, you select the number of pages per booklet. The 2-, 3- and 4-up Consecutive options create multipage spreads. The sets of 2, 3, or 4 pages are combined side-by-side onto a single page. These options work well for creating multipanel brochures.

After you choose a layout, PageMaker calculates the spread size for you. You can adjust this size if you want to print crop marks or to adjust for bleeds. The spread for our booklet is 72 picas by 57 picas.

The Build Booklet plug-in gives you several additional options for arranging your booklet. You can delete extra pages, insert blank pages, and rearrange pages.

The Use Creep option allows you to adjust page placement to account for paper thickness. You should check with your commercial printer to determine the value for Creep. The Gutter Space option allows you to add space between pages, adjusting the spread size automatically. For this project, you don't need to adjust for creep or to specify a gutter.

4 Leave the Place Guides in Gutter option checked. This option adds nonprinting ruler guides to the booklet.

The Preserve Page Numbering option retains the page numbering specified in the original document's pages. Since this publication doesn't contain page numbers, this option has no effect.

5 Click OK to create the booklet.

6 When the query box appears, choose to save your original document. The Build Booklet command saves and closes the current document and opens a new, untitled document that has the new spread size and the new sequence of pages.

A status box appears as the document is reformatting.

7 Click OK when the booklet is completed. Save the new file as *02Booklt.pm6* in *Projects*.

8 Notice that page 1 of the booklet is a 72 pica by 57 pica page that contains the objects from page 1 and page 8 of the original publication.

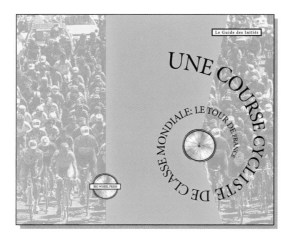

9 Go to page 2. This page contains the images from pages 2 and 7 of the original publication. The Build Booklet plug-in cuts and separates graphics, such as the photograph that originally appeared on pages 6 and 7.

Occasionally some graphics may appear on the wrong layer. On the right of the new page 2, you can see that the large background graphic has come to the front of the other objects.

10 To fix this, select the photograph on the right side of the booklet's page 2 and choose Send to Back from the Arrange menu.

11 Continue to page through your document, examining each page and making sure that no other graphics have been moved.

Page 3 of the booklet contains images from pages 3 and 6, and booklet page 4 contains images from the original pages 4 and 5.

If you wish, you can compare your booklet with example, *02FnlBkt.pm6* to see if they are the same.

12 When you have finished browsing through the booklet, close all open files and quit the Adobe PageMaker application.

OUR ANNUAL BEST BUYS

Gear

Utah

Top Gear for Tough Travel
The Best from Utah Gear

• UNITED STATES •

3

You complete the first three pages of a catalog for Utah Gear, a fictional company specializing in recreational equipment. This company produces a catalog every month,

RECREATION CATALOG

and a "Best of" catalog once a year. This project is the first few pages of the annual "Best of" collection. The design is an eye-catching combination of attractive fonts, high-quality photographs, and shapes in earth tones of green, blue, putty, and yellow. Design details include inline graphic icons embedded in the introductory paragraph, a distinctive orange-and-white table of contents, and bold black rules. ■ Thank you to REI: All text and props for this project were supplied by Recreational Equipment Inc. Some text has been modified slightly for teaching purposes. Adobe Systems extends its warm thanks to REI.

This project focuses on working with a variety of imported graphics, including scanned photographs, illustrations, and Kodak Photo CD images. Design details include inline graphic icons embedded in the introductory paragraph, a dis-

RECREATION CATALOG

tinctive orange and white table of contents, and bold black rules. You'll work with links, inline graphics, and various file formats. After completing the layout, you explore several different printing scenarios and finally create an Adobe Acrobat PDF file so that the catalog can be distributed online as well as in paper form.

In this project you learn how to:

- Work with text on the pasteboard

- Insert inline graphics

- Replace graphics while retaining formatting

- Create designer rules

- Create a custom text wrap

- Manage linked graphics

- Import a Photo CD image

- Use the Find/Change command in the Story Editor to make a global format change

- Prepare files for a service bureau

This project should take you about 1.5 hours to complete.

BEFORE YOU BEGIN

As before, you delete the existing PageMaker preferences or configuration file to return all settings to their defaults and make sure that lesson fonts are installed. Then you open and inspect a copy of the final document that you create in this project.

1 Return all settings to their defaults by deleting the *Adobe PageMaker 6.x Prefs* file from the *Preferences* folder (Macintosh) or by removing *\pm6\rsrc\usenglish\pm6.cnf* from the drive containing PageMaker (Windows).

2 Make sure that the Minion, Minion Semibold, Minion Semibold Italic fonts, and the Myriad Multiple Master family of fonts are installed on your system.

3 Launch the Adobe PageMaker application, then open the *03Final.pm6* file in *03Project*.

4 To see a "slide-show" presentation of the catalog, hold down the Shift key and choose Go to Page from the Layout menu. Click the mouse button to stop turning the pages.

5 Leave the final file open so you can use it as a visual reference as you work through the project.

EXAMINING THE TEMPLATE

Since this is a catalog that Utah Gear publishes on a monthly basis, you begin by opening a template that provides you with the basic layout.

1 In *03Project*, open the *03Begin.pt6* file.

Because *03Begin.pt6* was saved as a template, the file opens as an untitled document. It consists of the cover, opening page, and several empty pages where you will position catalog pictures and item descriptions.

2 Browse through the document template.

The empty pages have the major graphic elements already in place. The template has text styles defined in the Styles palette, and custom colors defined in the Colors palette. The document master consists of a simple three-column grid with a one-half-inch gutter. Before you begin, save and name the file.

3 Save the untitled document in *Projects* as *03Work.pm6*.

Time out for a movie

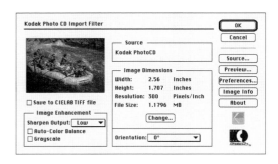 If your system is capable of running Adobe Teach movies, play the movie named *Placing a Photo CD* to see an overview of how to place graphics of this type. For information on how to view Adobe Teach movies, see "Watching Adobe Teach Movies" at the beginning of this book.

PLACING A KODAK PHOTO CD IMAGE

You start work on the catalog by placing a graphic on the cover. The image comes from a Kodak Photo CD. Files of this type contain several default resolutions. The original image is in the landscape orientation of its source. When you import a Kodak Photo CD image, you are given the opportunity to change the size and resolution of the image. You can save these settings in the original Kodak Photo CD file, or you can save them to a CIE Lab TIFF file. The original Kodak Photo CD files are enormous and slow to access because of the amount of information they contain. Saving the image as a CIE Lab TIFF produces a much smaller file that is faster to access. This kind of TIFF file contains accurate color information that is device independent: color fidelity is maintained on any PostScript Level 2 printer.

Note: When you place a Kodak Photo CD image, PageMaker automatically turns on the Kodak Color Management System. To turn it off when you are finished placing the graphic, display the Preferences dialog box, click the CMS Setup button, and set Color Management to Off.

1 In *03Work.pm6*, go to page 1—the cover—of the catalog. Display the Place Document dialog box, select *03IMG14.PCD* in *03Project*, and click OK.

Note: On a Windows platform, choose All Files from the Files of Type pop-up menu if the file doesn't appear in the list.

Because you selected a Kodak Photo CD image, PageMaker displays the Kodak Photo CD Import Filter dialog box.

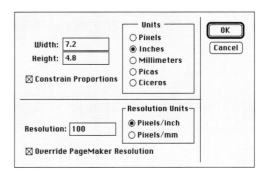

2 Enable Save to CIELAB TIFF File.

Enabling this choice means that your image size and resolution will be saved to a new TIFF file, rather than stored in the original Kodak Photo CD file. A Kodak Photo CD file can never be stored inside a PageMaker publication. If you choose the Save to CIELAB TIFF option, however, the resulting TIFF file is like any other TIFF file. You have all your options.

3 In the Image Enhancement portion of the dialog box, set Sharpen Output to Medium and enable Auto-Color Balance. If Auto-Color Balance is already enabled, click it twice, to disable and then re-able it. Click OK when the Note appears.

Note: Auto-Color Balance is useful only when the lightest point in a picture is pure white.

4 Click the Change button to set the desired dimensions and resolution. Enable Constrain Proportions, and set the Units to Inches.

5 Enter 7.2 for the width. Enable Override PageMaker Resolution, and set the Resolution to 100 pixels per inch.

For real-world production, the rule of thumb is a resolution of twice the screen frequency—lines per inch (lpi)—that will be used to print the image. Therefore, you would probably choose a resolution of between 200 and 266 for this setting. For this project, however, a resolution of 100 is sufficient and uses less disk space and memory.

6 Click OK to return to the main dialog box, and click OK again to exit the main import dialog box.

Because you specified that you wanted to create a new TIFF file, PageMaker displays a dialog box in which you specify a name and location for the new file.

7 Save the file as *03Photo.tif* in *Projects*. When a window appears asking if you want to include the graphic inside the publication (Macintosh only), click No. This creates a link to the external file instead of copying the file into the publication.

PageMaker creates the new TIFF file and presents you with the loaded graphic icon. As you move the icon, a hairline moves in both the top and side rulers to show its exact position.

8 To place the TIFF image, position the loaded icon so that it is ¼ inch to the left of the page and ¾ inch above the top of the page. Click to place the image.

9 With the image selected, choose Send to Back from the Arrange menu.

The part of the image that hangs out over the edge is called a *bleed* and is necessary for printing images that come all the way to the edge of the paper. To judge the composition of the page, however, you want to crop the bleed. When it is finally time to print, you'll pull the bleed back out again.

10 To crop the bleed, choose the cropping tool from the Toolbox. Position it over the upper left corner of the image, and pull inward until the edges of the image are even with the edges of the page.

11 Save *03Work.pm6*.

Your cover page should now match the one in *03Final.pm6*.

REPLACING TEXT AND GRAPHICS

One advantage to working with a template is that you can use existing text and graphics as placeholders. Using placeholders ensures that each version of the publication is consistent and saves you the time it takes to position design elements precisely. On page 2 of the catalog, you first replace the text of last year's opening paragraph with new text, then you replace the graphic with a new graphic.

Replacing text

1 Go to page 2 and zoom in on the text in the lower left quadrant of the page. Use the text tool to click an insertion point in the word *ready*. (It could actually be anywhere except the drop cap.)

2 Display the Place Document dialog box, navigate to *03Project*, and select *03Intro.doc*. Deselect the Retain Format option.

Replacing the story without retaining the format ensures that the new text will pick up the formatting of the text it is replacing.

3 Enable Replacing Entire Story, and click OK.

The new text flows into the publication, replacing the template's original text. The positioning and formatting remain the same.

Replacing an image

Now you use a similar technique to replace the picture on page 2.

1 With the pointer tool, select the photo in the top right corner of the page.

2 Display the Place Document dialog box, and click once on *03Mtn.tif*. Enable Replacing Entire Graphic and Retain Cropping Data. Click OK (Macintosh) or Open (Windows).

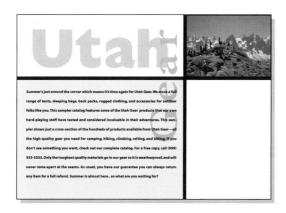

The new image replaces the original graphic. It is in the same position as the original and like the original, it is behind the heavy vertical and horizontal lines that are a dominant design feature of the page. Enabling Retain Cropping Data ensures that the new image is also the same size as the cropped original.

Note: If you replace an image with one whose proportions are different, the new image will distort to match the proportions of the original image.

INLINE GRAPHICS

The introductory paragraph on page 2 is going to contain several inline graphics that break up the monotony of the large text block. *Inline graphics* are images that are inserted into a text block and that then follow along with the text as the text is edited. In the following steps, you explore two methods of placing inline graphics.

Placing an inline graphic

1 Zoom in on the block of text that you just placed on page two. Use the text tool to click an insertion point right after the phrase "range of tents" in the second line.

2 Display the Place Document dialog box, and click *03TentIc.tif*.

Because you have an insertion point, the As Inline Graphic option is enabled. This is what you want.

3 To place *03TentIc.tif*, double-click it or click OK.

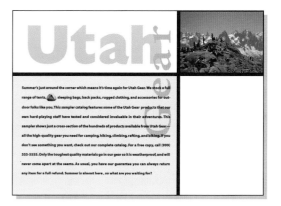

PageMaker places the image at the insertion point. The graphic is now attached to the text. If you move or edit the text, the inline graphic will follow along with the text.

4 To place the second inline graphic, click an insertion point after the comma at the end of the phrase "gear you need for camping" in the sixth line. Display the Place Document dialog box once more, be sure that As Inline Graphic is enabled, and double-click *03Boot.tif.*

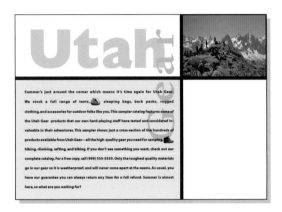

Pasting an inline graphic

In the previous steps, you used the Place Document command to insert inline graphics. You can achieve the same thing by using the Paste command. This works well when you have placed material on the pasteboard prior to inserting it in the publication.

To create an inline graphic by pasting, click an insertion point at the place where the graphic should be, and then paste a graphic which has been previously cut or copied.

1 With the pointer tool selected, display the Place Document dialog box. Be sure that As Independent Graphic is enabled, and then double-click *03BagIcn.tif.*

2 Click the loaded graphic icon on the pasteboard to the left of page 2 to place the image on the pasteboard.

3 Select the graphic that you just placed, and cut it.

4 With the text tool, click an insertion point after the phrase "you have our guarantee" in the ninth line of the paragraph, and paste.

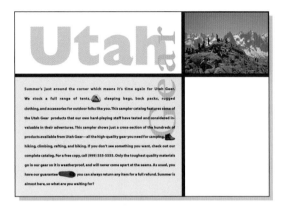

Adding some letterspacing

The small bold type of this paragraph now looks rather tight, so you are going to use the Control palette to add a little overall spacing between the letters. If you used this paragraph style in many places in the document, you would adjust the Track setting in the style definition to achieve the same result. Since this style occurs only once, the Control palette is the appropriate tool.

1 With the text tool, select all of the paragraph except the first letter.

You have to exclude the first letter from the selection because you are going to apply a drop cap to the paragraph. PageMaker can't apply a drop cap to a kerned letter.

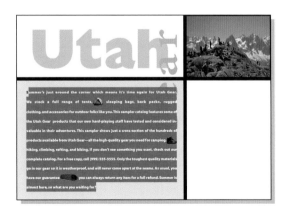

2 Choose Control Palette from the Windows menu to display the control palette. In the Character view of the Control palette, enter **0.02** in the Kerning box. Click the Apply button or press Return (Macintosh) or Enter (Windows) to apply the setting.

Kerning box

Adding fixed spaces

You now need to add some space around each inline graphic. You placed each graphic immediately after a phrase, so each one currently has a word space after it, but not before it. You want to have an en space (and only an en space) before and after each inline graphic.

1 Click to the left of the first inline graphic, and put in an en space. To type an en space, type Command Shift **N** (Macintosh) or Ctrl Shift **N** (Windows). Now click to the right of the graphic, delete the word space, and type another en space.

2 Add an en space before and after each of the other two inline graphics, being sure to remove or replace the word space that follows each one.

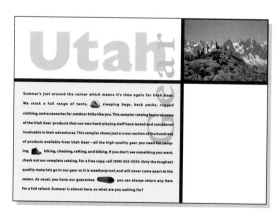

APPLYING A DROP CAP

The final design element of the introductory paragraph is a three-line drop cap, which you add by using PageMaker's Drop Cap plug-in.

1 Use the text tool to place an insertion point anywhere in the paragraph. Choose PageMaker Plug-ins from the Utilities menu and Drop Cap from the submenu.

2 Make sure that the line size is set to 3, then click Apply.

PageMaker turns the first letter of the paragraph into a three-line drop cap.

3 Click Close to dismiss the Drop Cap dialog box.

Note: Apply the drop cap only after all other paragraph formatting, such as kerning and inline graphics, has been completed. If you try to apply other formatting after PageMaker has inserted the drop cap formatting, the commands will conflict, and you may not get the results you expect.

ATTACHING RULES TO TEXT

In addition to attaching graphic images to text, you can attach lines or rules to text to create a variety of effects. Take a look at page 2 of the final file. Notice that the table of contents is placed in front of an orange-striped background. The orange stripes are not individual graphic elements but rules that are defined as part of the paragraph style applied to the table of contents text.

To format the table of contents, you first place the contents text. Then you define a paragraph style that places the orange band behind alternate entries.

1 Select the pointer tool, and then display the Place Document dialog box. Choose *03Toc.doc*, be sure that As New Story is selected, and deselect Retain Format.

In a previous step, you checked the position of the loaded icon by positioning the hairlines in the rulers. Another way to see the position of the icon is to look at the values in the Control palette.

Note: You can pan a page even when you have a loaded text or graphic icon. The icon remains loaded and ready to place the text or graphic.

2 Position the loaded text icon so that the X value in the Control palette is approximately 5.7 and the Y value is near 2.5. Place the text on the lower right quadrant of page 2 by dragging between the black vertical line and the right edge of the page, then down about 2 inches.

3 Select all of the newly placed text with the text tool, and then use the Character view of the Control palette to set the font to MyriadMM 830 Black 600 Norm, the font size to 17 points, and the leading to 36 points.

4 Change to the paragraph view of the Control palette, enter .25 for the left indent, and apply the setting.

— Left indent

5 Display the Colors palette, and with the text still selected, apply the color Deep Teal.

6 Double-click the word *Introduction*. Notice that the selection highlight extends above and below the word. The highlight reflects the amount of leading, also called the *leading slug"*

Leading slug —

7 Choose Paragraph from the Type menu. The Paragraph Specifications dialog box appears.

8 Click the Rules button. A *rule* is a line that you can set to appear above or below each paragraph in a selection of text. You can also make this part of a style definition.

9 Click the check box for Rule Above Paragraph. Choose Custom from the Line Style pop-up menu and enter 36 points (the size of the leading slug) in the Line Weight box. Click OK.

10 Select Orange for the Line Color, leave the option for Width of Column selected, and leave the Tint set to 100%.

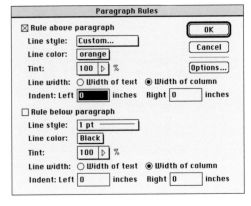

11 Click the Options button to display the Paragraph Rule Options dialog box.

This is where you set the vertical placement of the rule. Rules can be positioned relative to either the top or the bottom of the leading slug. The thickness (Line Weight) of the rule always starts at the top of the rule and grows downward.

12 Enter .306 into the Top box. Hold down the Option key (Macintosh) or the Shift key (Windows) and click OK to exit the nested dialog boxes.

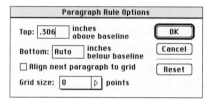

An orange 36-point rule is now attached to the text. The rule starts .306 inches above the baseline and hangs down, allowing the text to appear in the middle of the rule. Now you define a style based on the text that you just formatted.

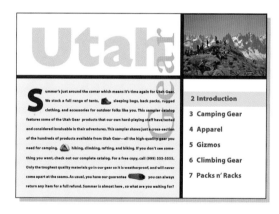

Creating a style based on formatted text

1 Be sure the line of type for which you defined the rule is selected. Choose Define Styles from the Type menu.

2 Make sure the word *Selection* is highlighted in the Define Styles dialog box, and click the New button.

3 Name the new style TOC Rule. For Based On, choose No Style from the pop-up menu. You can leave Next Style set to TOC Rule. Exit from both dialog boxes.

Note: Next Style is the style that is automatically chosen when you press Return or Enter. If you wanted to create the table of contents by typing it rather than importing text, you could make use of the Next Style feature as follows: Create a second style—No Rule—that is identical to this one but without the orange rule. Set the Next Style to be TOC Rule. Then change the Next Style for TOC Rule to be the No Rule style. As you type the table of contents, each new line will automatically have the correct style applied to it. You'll get your alternating bands of white and orange without having to do anything but type the text.

4 Apply the TOC Rule style to the lines "Introduction," "Apparel," and "Climbing Gear."

5 Make sure that the bottom of the text block windowshade is dragged all the way down to the bottom margin of the page. With the text tool, click in the empty line below "Packs n' Racks," and apply the TOC Rule style to this blank paragraph.

6 Now select the table of contents text block with the pointer tool and examine it. If necessary, adjust the position of the text block so that it exactly fills the width between the heavy vertical line and the edge of the page. Position the bottom of the last orange rule on the bottom of the page.

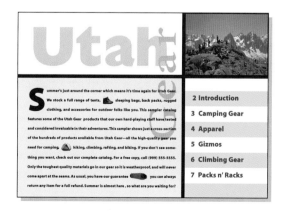

7 With the text block still selected, choose Send to Back from the Arrange menu.

8 Save your work. You should save at regular intervals as you work on the project.

Note: An interim file is provided with the steps completed up to this point. If you want to complete the rest of this project without having to do the earlier steps, go to 03Project, *open* 03Inter1.pt6, *and save it in* Projects.

WORKING WITH TEXT ON THE PASTEBOARD

Now that the second page is completed, you are ready to import the descriptive text for the catalog items. Since all the item descriptions are entered in a single text file, you work by placing the text onto the pasteboard and then cutting and pasting individual item descriptions next to placed images. Placing the text onto the pasteboard gives you access to the text from all the pages in the publication.

1 Go to page 3, and view the page at Actual Size. Then pan the page to the right so that you can see the pasteboard area at the left of the page.

2 Display the Place Document dialog box. Highlight *03Text.doc*, and be sure that As New Story and Retain Format are enabled. Click OK.

The text file *03Text.doc* is typed in Microsoft Word with styles whose names match exactly the style names used in the PageMaker template. The definitions of the styles are not the same in Word and PageMaker, but the *names* are. Because the style names are identical, the Retain Formats option performs a special function: it applies the corresponding PageMaker styles to the text at the time the text is placed. Compare this with how you placed *03Intro.doc*, where you were replacing text instead of placing a new story. There, you retained the PageMaker formatting by deselecting Retain Format.

3 Click the loaded text icon on the pasteboard to the left of the page. Because the style names were applied in Word, the text is fully formatted when it flows onto the pasteboard. The width of the text block is determined by the publication page margins if there is room, but if you click to the left of the page, the text block does not overlap the page.

If you have access to Microsoft Word, you can open *03Text.doc* in Word and notice that the text does not look at all the way it does after being placed into PageMaker. This is because the style names are the same but the style definitions are different.

MODIFYING A TEXT STYLE

The catalog entries are formatted with four styles: Prod. Name, Body, Item Info, and Price. This special "best of" issue of the catalog uses a font for the Prod. Name style different from that in the template, so you need to modify the definition of that style.

In the previous steps, you use the Style palette to access the Edit Styles dialog box. In the following steps, you use the Control palette to do exactly the same thing.

1 Use the text tool to click in the phrase *Blue Kazoo*.

2 Display the paragraph view of the Control palette.

Notice that the Prod. Name style is applied to the selected text.

3 Hold down the Command key (Macintosh) or the Control key (Windows) and click the Prod. Name style name in the Control palette.

4 In the Edit Style dialog box, click the Type button, then set the font to MyriadMM 830 Black 600 Norm and the size to 18 points. Hold down Option (Macintosh) or Shift (Windows) and click OK to exit from both dialog boxes.

You have changed the definition of the Prod. Name paragraph style. All the text that has the Prod. Name style applied to it changes to the new definition, including text that is not displayed.

Note: You can also modify a style definition by Command-clicking (Macintosh) or Control-clicking (Windows) the style name in the Styles palette.

The text is formatted and ready to be positioned on the layout.

POSITIONING THE TEXT

In the next steps, you cut and paste the product descriptions onto page 3 of the catalog, breaking text threading as necessary and positioning individual text blocks. Before you begin, it may help you to look at *03Work.pm6* to see where each text block should go.

Note: The process of cutting, pasting, and positioning the following pieces of text requires a lot of switching back and forth between the text tool and the pointer tool. You can switch tools quickly by using the keyboard shortcut: Command-spacebar on Macintosh or Control-spacebar on Windows. Begin by clicking on the text tool, and then use the keyboard to switch back and forth.

1 If the guides are not visible, display them by choosing Show Guides and Rulers from the Layout menu and Show Guides from the submenu.

2 Choose Guide and Rulers from the Layout menu, and make sure that Snap to Guides is enabled.

3 On the pasteboard, select the text for the first item, starting with *Blue Kazoo* and ending with the price. Cut the selection. Click between the margins of the first column near the top, and paste the text. Use the pointer tool to position the text block so that the top of the block rests against the top margin.

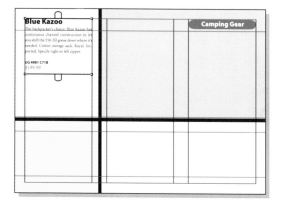

When you click between margins or within a column to paste, the text block fills the area exactly. However, if your pointer touches a margin when you click, PageMaker may see your pointer as being outside the area, and the text block expands beyond the margins.

4 Next, select all the text for the REI Trail Dome item, cut it, and paste it between the margins at the top of the second column. Position it so that the top of the text block aligns with the top page margin.

5 Select the text for the "Z-Rest and Therm-a-Rest®" item. Cut it, and paste it between the margins of the first column in the yellow rectangle at the bottom. Position it so that the first headline baseline is on the guide line that is at 4 inches.

6 Select and cut the text for the Kelty Trekker. Place it into the second column below the heavy black horizontal line. Place the first baseline ("Kelty Tracker") on the guide at 4 inches, and then use the pointer tool to adjust the windowshade so that the last visible line is the one that begins "and a full-strap waistbelt."

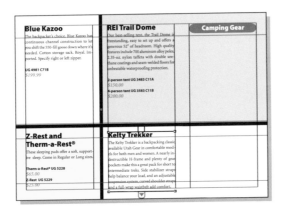

7 To place the remaining text for this item into the third column, click the red arrow at the bottom of the windowshade. With the loaded text icon, place the remaining text into the third column below the heavy horizontal black line. Position the text block so that the first baseline is on the guide line that is at 4.188 inches.

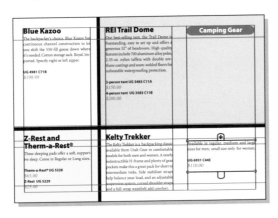

The text for each item is now a separate story, even though the text was originally a single story when you placed it onto the pasteboard. The two text blocks for the Kelty Trekker are a single story in two threaded blocks.

You've now placed all the text for page 3. If you want extra practice, you can place the remaining text on pages 4 and 5 by cutting and pasting it from the pasteboard and using *03Final.pm6* to show you where to place it.

8 Save *03Work.pm6*.

LINKING GRAPHIC IMAGES

Now that the text is positioned on page 3, you are ready to begin placing graphics. When you place a text or graphic file into your publication, PageMaker automatically creates a link between the placed file and the original file. You can choose whether or not to copy a graphic into the publication. If you leave it outside of the publication, you keep the publication from getting too large. If you copy the graphic into the publication, you can choose to update it automatically if it changes. As a rule, it's better to leave large graphics outside the publication. In the following steps, you place several graphic images and explore linking options.

As you place the following images, refer to *03Final.pm6* or to the illustrations in this chapter to see precisely how to position them.

1 Display the Place Document dialog box, and choose to place *03Tent1.tif* as an independent graphic.

A dialog box appears notifying you that the image will add 333K to the size of the file if it is copied into the publication.

2 Click No to prevent the graphic from being copied into the publication.

If you don't choose to copy the file into the publication, PageMaker creates a **pointer** that references the external file. It creates a link to the original file whether you copy it into the publication or not.

TIP: TO INCLUDE ALL NECESSARY FILES WHEN COPYING A PUBLICATION, CHOOSE SAVE AS FROM THE FILE MENU AND EN-ABLE FILES FOR REMOTE PRINTING.

If you choose to copy images into your publication when you place them, the result can be an extremely large PageMaker file. Large files take a long time to open and to print and are generally unwieldy. On the other hand, if you decide not to include images inside your publication, you need to make sure that all the placed image files are available when you are ready to print the publication. If you copy the publication to another system, you must be sure that you copy the external linked graphic files with it.

3 Click the loaded graphic icon in the top of the right column to place the tent image. Click the upper left reference point of the proxy in the Control palette, and drag, nudge, or type values in the Control palette so that the X value is 5.456 and the Y value is 1.128.

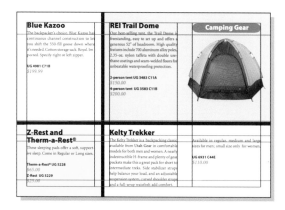

ABOUT CLIPPING PATHS

The tent image that you just placed is a photograph that was scanned and then saved from Adobe Photoshop as TIFF file. Click the image to select it, and notice that although the handles show that the image is rectangular, the image's background appears to be transparent. The rectangular shape doesn't show when the image isn't selected. This is because the image has a *clipping path* that was applied in Photoshop.

In the past, clipping paths could be applied only to EPS images. Adobe Photoshop 3.0 and higher can save clipping paths on TIFF files.

In this catalog, each image that appears on a colored background has been provided with a clipping path in Photoshop. This hides the image's background so that it does not obscure the colored background of the PageMaker page design.

Note: In Photoshop EPS graphics with 8-bit preview images, clipping paths display as black in Windows 95. They print correctly, however, on PostScript printers. As a workaround, try saving the images with a 1-bit preview, or as TIFFs.

SETTING LINK OPTIONS

Since you didn't copy the tent image into your PageMaker publication when you placed it, a low-resolution preview image is displayed in the document. This preview image allows you to position, resize, rotate, and crop the graphic. These changes are also applied to the original when the publication is printed. If you open the original graphic in Photoshop again, however, you will find it unchanged.

In the following steps, you set the link option default to automatically prevent images from being copied into the publication. That way you don't get the query box each time you import an image.

1 Click the pasteboard to be sure no graphic is selected.

If a graphic is selected, the next step will set the option for only that one graphic, rather than set a new default.

2 Choose Link Options from the Element menu. The Link Options: Defaults dialog box appears. This dialog box controls how placed objects are stored and updated.

3 In the Graphics section, turn off the option for Store Copy in Publication, then click OK.

Note: Text files are always copied into a publication. You have the "copy/don't copy" option only for graphics.

Now all placed images will automatically remain outside the PageMaker document. If you are taking your file to a service provider, you need to include all the linked graphic files when you hand the job off to your printer. If you don't include them, the file will be printed using the low-resolution preview images, which do not include enough information for high-quality printing.

4 Place *03Tent2.tif*. No warning appears because the file is automatically stored outside the publication. Click to place the image to the left of and below the first tent, as pictured in *03Final.pm6*.

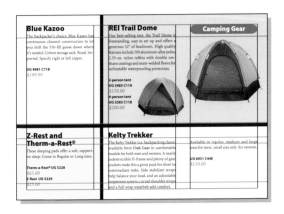

5 Save your work. You should be saving often.

ABOUT FILE FORMATS

PageMaker supports a variety of different graphic file formats. The two graphic file formats most often used for high-end color work are EPS (Encapsulated PostScript) and TIFF (Tagged Image File Format). TIFF is the format of choice for saving scanned images. TIFF files are bitmap images that consist of a grid of bits or pixels with a specific resolution (pixels per inch). TIFF and other bitmap formats are created by scanners and by image editing and paint programs such as Adobe Photoshop. The TIFF graphic format is capable of extremely accurate color reproduction.

The file format determines the type of changes you can make to the image once it is placed into Adobe PageMaker. When you are working with bitmap images (such as TIFF), the best strategy is to finalize the size within the original application. If you resize or rotate a bitmap image after it has been placed into PageMaker, the image may distort or acquire moiré patterns.

EPS images are object-oriented (vector) files that are typically created in a high-end drawing program such as Adobe Illustrator. EPS files can be resized and rotated without distortion. The drawback is that a monitor cannot display an EPS file directly. An EPS file must include a preview image to display. These preview images may not be viewable on all platforms.

Some applications, such as Adobe Photoshop, allow you to save your bitmap files in EPS format. The resulting EPS file still contains the bitmap image and must be treated as such. The only way to convert a bitmap image to a true vector format is to use an application that is specially designed to perform this task, such as Adobe Streamline.

PLACING THE REMAINING IMAGES

The following steps provide instructions for placing the rest of the images on page 3.

The next image to place is the backpack. It is stored in the *03Lib.pml* library and has a text wrap already applied to it. The text wrap pushes text out of the way and makes it flow around the graphic. Later in this project, you get to create a text wrap of your own.

1 To display the *03Lib.pml* library, choose Library from the Windows menu. In the Open Library dialog box, navigate to 03Project and choose 03Lib.pml.

Note: If you have opened a library previously in the current PageMaker session, that library appears directly. If it is not the one you want, click on the Options triangle and Open 03Lib.pml.

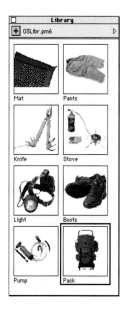

2 Drag the image labeled "Pack" from the library to the lower part of the right column on page 3. Release the mouse button to place the image.

3 Move the image a little with the pointer, and notice that it is surrounded by two rectangles: one dotted and one solid. The dotted line is the text wrap.

4 Position the image so that the solid rectangle nestles into the lower right corner of the page.

5 Drag *03Mat.tif* from the library to the bottom of the left column on the page. Move it so that the lower left corner of the mat is exactly in the lower left corner of the page.

6 Display the Place Document dialog box, choose *03Bag.tif*, and click OK (Macintosh) or Open (Windows). Place the image in the right half of the column containing the "Blue Kazoo" text. It's all right that part of the text is covered up. You fix that by creating a text wrap. The right side of the bag itself (not the shadow) should just touch the right column margin. Place the top selection handles against the top page margin.

7 If you haven't saved recently, save *03Work.pm6* now.

SETTING TEXT WRAPS

To finish page 3, you learn how to apply a custom text wrap to a graphic. You can apply a text wrap to either a bitmap or a vector graphic.

To preserve the shadow that falls on the background, the blue sleeping bag has not had a clipping path applied to it. It was photographed against a white surface that blends with the white area of the page. The shadow adds depth and impact to the image.

1 Select the *03Bag.tif* image and choose Send to Back from the Arrange menu. With the image still selected, choose Text Wrap from the Element menu. Select the center Wrap option, leave the right Text Flow option selected, and then enter **0** on all four sides for the Standoff. Click OK.

Choosing the center Text Wrap option causes the text to flow around the graphic instead of over it. The *standoff* is the distance between the edge of the wrap and the text.

The graphic is now surrounded by a dotted line that is the wrap boundary. There are handles at the corners and in the middle of each side, but to create the shape you want, you need to add some more handles.

2 To create additional handles, click the boundary with the pointer tool. Click two extra handles on the left side: one between the middle and top handle and one between the middle and bottom.

3 Now use the pointer to move each of the four handles on the left side so that they are roughly ¼ inch from the bag. Slide the next-to-bottom one up slightly to match the illustration below.

FORMATTING TEXT WITH THE FIND/CHANGE COMMAND

The Utah Gear company wants its name to appear in boldface in the Deep Teal color wherever it appears in the text. PageMaker's Find and Change utility lets you search for text and apply a format to the found items rather than replace them with different text. In the following steps, you find each instance of the phrase "Utah Gear" and decide for each occurrence whether it should receive the special formatting. You apply the boldface and Deep Teal color to all the instances except the one on the cover.

1 Select the text tool, and click in the first word of the introductory paragraph on page 2 ("Summer's just around…"). Choose Edit Story from the Edit menu.

2 Choose Change from the Utilities menu. Type **Utah Gear** in the Find What box, and leave the Change To box empty. Under Search Story, enable All Stories.

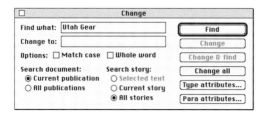

Since each item is a separate story, you must enable All Stories to search your whole file.

3 Click the Type Attributes button. In the Change Type Attributes dialog box, go to the Change To section, and select Deep Teal from the Color pop-up menu and Bold from the Type Style menu. Leave all the other settings at Any.

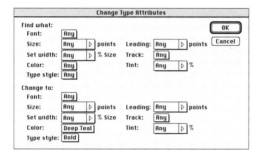

4 Click OK to set the Change To attributes, and then click Find. The first occurrence PageMaker finds is in the introductory paragraph ("Summer's just around…"). Click Change & Find to apply the new attributes and find the next occurrence. The next three occurrences also receive the formatting, so click Change & Find for each of them. The fifth occurrence is on the cover. If you made it Deep Teal, it wouldn't be visible against the dark background, so click the Find button to go to the next occurrence without making a change. That's the last occurrence of the name, so click OK to dismiss the Search Complete box and close the Change dialog box.

Now you are ready to return to the Layout window. PageMaker opened a separate Story Editor window for each story in which it found an occurrence of the search item.

5 To close all of the open Story Editor windows, hold down Option (Macintosh) or Shift (Windows) and choose Close Story from the Story menu.

6 Save *03Work.pm6*.

COMPLETING PAGES 4 AND 5

If you'd like more practice assembling text and graphics, you can complete pages 4 and 5 of the catalog. These pages currently have the background design elements on them, just as the template would have if you were doing this job in real life. Each graphic has been provided for you in the library (*03Lib.pml*), complete with text wraps where needed. You can complete the two pages by cutting and pasting text from the pasteboard and then dragging the art from the library, just as you did on page 3.

To see how the pages should look, check the illustrations below or look at *03Final.pm6*.

Page 4

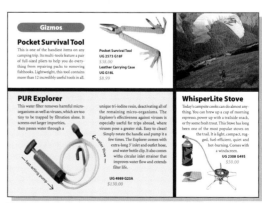

Page 5

The items in *03Lib.pml* have the necessary text wraps already applied to them. If you want to practice making your own text wraps, you can place the original graphic files and apply the wraps.

To find the filename of a graphic that's in the library, drag the graphic into *03Final.pm6* (or any PageMaker publication), click it to select it, and choose Links from the Element menu. The filename appears at the top of the dialog box.

MANAGING LINKS

As you work on a PageMaker file, you may occasionally move, rename, or update one of the graphic files that you have placed. When you do so, the link to that file becomes outdated.

You can use the Links dialog box to see the status of all the linked files in a document and to update the links.

Viewing the status of links

1 In *03Final.pm6*, choose Links from the File menu.

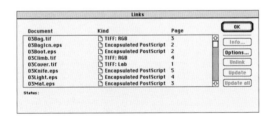

The Links dialog box displays a list of the text and graphic files in your publication, along with file format information and page locations. Status indicators in the left column show the current status of the files. The files that you are now viewing should all be up to date, so there are no symbols in the leftmost column. Notice as you highlight each item that a message below the list says "This item is up to date."

2 Click OK.

In the following steps, you move one graphic file and simulate updating another file by replacing it with a copy that has a newer date. Then you look at the links list again to see the results.

Changing the links

Macintosh:

1 Go to the Application menu in the top right corner of your screen and choose Finder. Open the *03Project* folder, and double-click the *Save* folder and the *Links* folder to display them in separate windows.

Displaying the folders in separate windows makes it easier to move files around.

Windows 95:

1 Click Start. Mouse down to Programs and choose Windows Explorer. Navigate to the *03Project* directory.

Both platforms:

2 Drag *03Tent2.tif* from *03Project* into the *Links* folder.

You have moved the file, so PageMaker's pointer to that file is now out of date.

3 To simulate updating the pants image, drag *03Pants.tif* from the *03Project* folder into the *Save* folder. Then drag the copy of *03Pants.tif* that's in the *Links* folder into *03Project*.

Be sure to begin by dragging the file that's in *03Project*, not the one in *Links*. By placing it in the *Save* folder instead of in the trash or recycle bin, you can easily return the project to its original state when you have finished, so that the sequence can be recreated at another time.

Since the copy that you moved into *03Project* has a more recent date than the one that you moved from *03Project*, you have simulated updating the *03Pants.tif* file in another application, such as Adobe Photoshop.

4 Return to *03Final.pm6* and choose Links from the File menu.

Notice that there is an open diamond symbol (Macintosh) or a tick mark (Windows) next to *03Pants.tif* and a question mark next to *03Tent2.tif*. The diamond or tick mark indicates that the file has been modified, and the question mark indicates that PageMaker can no longer find the file. If the graphic is not included in the publication and the link is not updated by the time the publication is printed, PageMaker prints the low-resolution preview that is included in the PageMaker file. If the file is included inside the PageMaker publication, it will print, but will not include any changes made to the file using other applications.

Relinking a file

The tent graphic was moved, so you need to create a link to the file in its new location.

1 Click *03Tent2.tif* in the list of links.

A message appears at the bottom of the dialog box, indicating that the file is missing; moving the file modified the link.

2 To create a link to the file in its new location, click the Info button, then open the *Links* folder, highlight *03Tent2.tif*, and click Link.

PageMaker updates the link to reference the new location of the file and the question mark disappears from the item in the link list.

Updating a link

The pants graphic still has the same name and location, but you have simulated editing the file in another application. If the graphic were stored outside PageMaker, you wouldn't have to do anything. PageMaker would automatically read

the current version of the file. This graphic has been stored inside the publication, however, so you need to tell PageMaker to re-read (update) the file so that it is storing the latest version.

1 Select *03Pants.tif* in the links list.

2 Click the Update button to update the link to the file and the preview image in the publication. Close the Links dialog box.

PUBLISHING A DOCUMENT

For a high-end project such as this catalog, the final step is to take the collection of files to a prepress service provider. For this project, we assume that the service provider is handling issues such as bleeds, trapping, and imposition. You explore some of these topics for yourself in Project 4.

Preparing files for a service bureau

The PageMaker file for the catalog contains pointers to many linked graphic files. When you are preparing files for a service provider, it is critical that you include all the linked graphic files that were not actually copied into your publication. In this project, that includes all the graphic files except the three small inline graphics. In addition, PageMaker needs the tracking values file if you have used the Expert Tracking command to modify tracking values. This file is called *Tracking Values* on a Macintosh and *Trakvals.bin* on a Windows machine. PageMaker's Copy Files for Remote Printing feature ensures that all required files are included when you take a PageMaker publication to a service bureau.

1 In *03Work.pm6*, choose Save As from the File menu.

The Save As dialog box appears.

2 Enable Copy: Files for Remote Printing.

When this is enabled, PageMaker copies all external linked files and the tracking values file, as well as the publication file itself.

3 Navigate to Printing in *03Project*, name the file **03Pub.pm6**, and click OK (Macintosh) or Save (Windows).

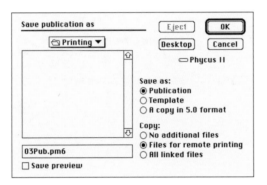

PageMaker saves a copy of the publication and of all the necessary accompanying files to the location you specify. In the real world, you would typically copy these files to some sort of removable high-density medium that you could take to the service provider.

Note: You need at least seven megabytes of free space on your hard drive to complete this step.

To take a look at the files, hide PageMaker 6, switch to the Finder (Macintosh) or Explorer (Windows 95), and open the Printing folder in *03Project*. You'll see the *03Pub.pm6* file, all the linked graphic files, and the tracking values file. You do not see any file that was stored inside the publication, including the text files and inline graphic files.

4 Close all open publications and quit Adobe PageMaker.

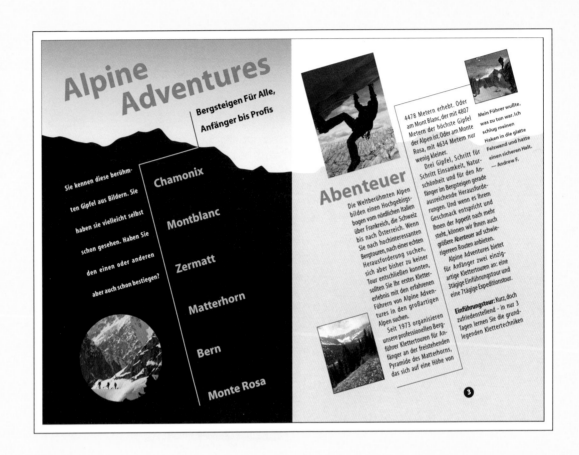

Alpine Adventures

Bergsteigen Für Alle, Anfänger bis Profis

Sie kennen diese berühmten Gipfel aus Bildern. Sie haben sie vielleicht selbst schon gesehen. Haben Sie den einen oder anderen aber auch schon bestiegen?

Chamonix

Montblanc

Zermatt

Matterhorn

Bern

Monte Rosa

Abenteuer

Die Weltberühmten Alpen bilden einen Hochgebirgsbogen vom nördlichen Italien über Frankreich, die Schweiz bis nach Österreich. Wenn Sie nach hochinteressanten Bergtouren, nach einer echten Herausforderung suchen, sich aber bisher zu keiner Tour entschließen konnten, sollten Sie Ihr erstes Klettererlebnis mit den erfahrenen Führern von Alpine Adventures in den großartigen Alpen suchen.

Seit 1973 organisieren unsere professionellen Bergführer Klettertouren für Anfänger an der freistehenden Pyramide des Matterhorns, das sich auf eine Höhe von 4478 Metern erhebt. Oder am Mont Blanc, der mit 4807 Metern der höchste Gipfel der Alpen ist. Oder am Monte Rosa, mit 4634 Metern nur wenig kleiner.

Drei Gipfel, Schritt für Schritt Einsamkeit, Naturschönheit und für den Anfänger im Bergsteigen gerade ausreichende Herausforderungen. Und wenn es Ihrem Geschmack entspricht und Ihnen der Appetit nach mehr steht, können wir Ihnen auch größere Abenteuer auf schwierigeren Routen anbieten.

Alpine Adventures bietet für Anfänger zwei einzigartige Klettertouren an: eine 3tägige Einführungstour und eine 7tägige Expeditionstour.

Einführungstour: Kurz, doch zufriedenstellend - in nur 3 Tagen lernen Sie die grundlegenden Klettertechniken

> Mein Führer wußte, was zu tun war. Ich schlug meinen Haken in die glatte Felswand und hatte einen sicheren Halt.
> — Andrew F.

3

4

This six-panel brochure is a market-
ing piece for a Swiss company that
offers a variety of alpine recreational
activities throughout the Alps, including backpacking, mountain

SIX-COLOR BROCHURE

climbing, cross-country skiing, and
hang gliding. The company is in the
process of completing a series of
brochures highlighting each type of
activity. The brochure features a
die-cut front panel with a circular
masked graphic; a tinted varnish
finish adds luster to the entire production. The mountain image that
is a recurring motif throughout the
piece is enhanced using Adobe Gallery Effects, one of PageMaker 6's
new offerings. ■ To create a high-
quality proof, you use PageMaker's
Create Adobe PDF command to create a full-color PDF file using Adobe
Acrobat Distiller.

In this project, you finish a three-panel brochure for a company that organizes mountaineering trips and activities. The design of the brochure features a die cut using a photograph of the Alps as the cutting edge. For the illustrations, you

CLIMBING BROCHURE

create a red spot color and a tinted varnish for use as spot colors in addition to the standard process colors.

This project focuses on color printing issues including spot and process color separations, trapping, preparing a file for an imagesetter, and specifying a die cut. You also work with Adobe Gallery Effects.

This project covers:

• Creating a new master page

• Applying a Gallery Effect filter

• Using a mask

• Using Trapping Options

• Setting objects to overprint

• Printing color separations

• Proofing using an Acrobat PDF document

• Using the Build Booklet plug-in to prepare a six-color, three-page spread

• Preparing a die cut

This project should take you about 1.5 hours to complete.

BEFORE YOU BEGIN

1 Return all settings to their defaults by deleting the *Adobe PageMaker 6.x Prefs* file from the *Preferences* folder (Macintosh) or by removing *\pm6\rsrc\usenglish\pm6.cnf* from the drive containing PageMaker (Windows).

2 Make sure the Myriad Multiple Master family of fonts is installed.

3 Make sure that Adobe Acrobat Distiller is installed on your system.

Acrobat Distiller 2.1PE (Personal Edition) and Acrobat Reader are both distributed with the Adobe PageMaker software. The Personal Edition version of Distiller converts only files created by Adobe products. You must install Acrobat Distiller and Acrobat Reader separately if you are using the ones that come with PageMaker. They're not part of the regular PageMaker installation sequence. *See "What You Need to Know" at the front of this book for more about installing these applications.*

Important: If you have not used Distiller before beginning this project, you must open it once and then close it. Otherwise, you can't invoke it from the PageMaker File menu .

3 Launch the Adobe PageMaker application, and open the *04Final.pm6* file in *04Project* to view the final image.

SETTING UP THE PUBLICATION

This series of brochures uses a consistent format with rotated text and images. Each new brochure has a different cover, background, type color, and die cut. In this project, you will open a publication that has the text and graphics already placed, then you'll set up the master pages and put the finishing touches on the brochure.

1 Open the *04Begin.pm6* file in *04Project*.

Each page of the publication is 5.5 inches wide and 8 inches tall.

2 Double-click the pointer tool in the Toolbox to display the Preferences dialog box, then set the units for Measurements and Vertical Ruler to Picas. Click OK.

Next, you set a Link Option so that images are not copied into the publication when they are placed. This keeps the publication file at a manageable size. If you don't set this option, PageMaker displays a query window each time you place a large image, asking whether to include it in the publication.

3 With the pointer tool, click on the pasteboard to be sure nothing is selected. Then choose Link Options from the Element menu. In the Graphics section, deselect Store Copy in Publication, and then click OK.

4 Save the file in *Projects* as *04Work.pm6*.

SETTING UP MASTER PAGES

The final publication contains two sets of master pages. The Document Master pages are the basic page masters, but page 2 needs a different background, so you create a second pair of master pages to use for the 2–3 page spread. The master pages contain the background mountain image and the distinctive line that runs between the two text columns on each page.

1 To display the Master Pages palette, choose Master Pages from the Window menu.

2 In *04Final.pm6*, click on page 1 and notice that Document Master is highlighted in the Master Pages palette to show what master pages are in use. Now click on page 2 and notice that 2nd Master Page is highlighted in the Master Pages palette, showing that a different master page spread is in use for the 2–3 page spread.

3 In *04Work.pm6*, click the master page icon in the lower left corner of your screen.

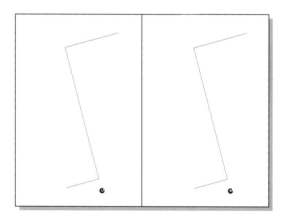

Placing the mountain image

PageMaker displays the master pages that underlie the current page spread—in this case, Document Master. The decorative ruling lines and page numbers are present, but you need to add the background mountain images. Since this image is an EPS file created in Adobe Illustrator, you can drag-place the file. This allows you to place and size the graphic at the same time.

4 Double-click the upper left-hand corner of your document window, right where the vertical and horizontal rulers meet. This ensures that the horizontal zero point is at the meeting of the two pages and the vertical zero point is at the top of the pages.

5 Zoom out enough so that you can see all of the left page.

Next you place an EPS graphic on the master page. Because this graphic contains a color not currently in the Color palette of the PageMaker publication, the new color will be added to the list of colors in the Colors palette. The PS symbol next to the new color name indicates that it is a color brought in by an EPS graphic.

6 Choose Colors from the Window menu to display the Colors palette. Notice that the palette contains two greens, two blues, red, yellow, and orange, in addition to Registration, Paper, and Black.

7 Display the Place Document dialog box and choose to place *04Mtn1.eps* as an independent graphic.

8 Position the loaded icon so that the top of it is even with the bottom of the left master page at the left corner, then drag up and to the right. Drag so that the rectangle exactly fills the width of the page and the tick mark in the vertical ruler is at 11 picas.

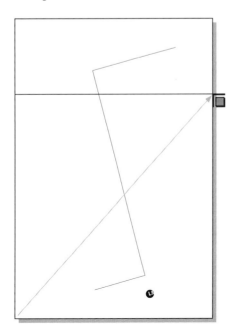

A rectangle is visible as you drag, showing where the boundaries of the image will be if you release the mouse button at that point. There is also a small tick mark in each ruler, showing where the boundary of the image will be.

9 Release the mouse button to place the graphic.

10 Zoom in on the bottom of the page and adjust the graphic if necessary so that it sits exactly on the bottom of the page and the width fills the page width exactly.

11 Choose Send to Back from the Arrange menu.

This graphic is based on the original photograph of the Alps. The photo was imported into Adobe Illustrator, then traced with the pen tool, and finally colored with a PANTONE Warm Gray. Later in this project, you override the imported color with a tint that you define in PageMaker.

12 Look in the Colors palette again and notice that the Warm Gray color has been added to the Colors palette. When you import an EPS file from an illustration program such as Adobe Illustrator, any colors in the EPS file are added to PageMaker's Colors palette by default. Each one has a PS symbol next to it in the palette.

You have several options for changing this default behavior. You can choose whether to add colors to the palette when you import an EPS graphic. You can also convert spot colors to process colors as you import the graphic. To see how to make these choices, display the Place Document dialog box again. This time, hold down the Shift key as you double-click on *04Mtn1.eps*. The EPS Import Filter dialog box appears. Look over the options, and then click Cancel to dismiss the dialog box without reimporting the image.

Copying and reflecting the image

The mountain image needs to be reflected to the opposite page of the spread, so you copy the mountain graphic, paste it, and then reflect the image onto the right master page.

1 Select the mountain image that you just placed, and copy it.

2 Use Power Paste to place a copy of the graphic exactly on top of the original. Power Paste is Command-Option-V on the Macintosh and Control-Shift-P in Windows.

3 With the pasted graphic still selected, click any one of the right-hand reference points on the proxy in the Control palette, and then click the Horizontal Reflection button in the Control palette.

Horizontal reflection button

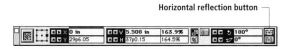

Because you chose a reference point on the right side of the proxy, PageMaker "flips" the copy of the mountain around an imaginary axis on the right side of the original image. If you choose a point on the left side of the proxy, the image will flip to the left.

4 With the flipped mountain image selected, choose Send to Back from the Arrange menu to move the mountain behind the other elements on the right-hand page.

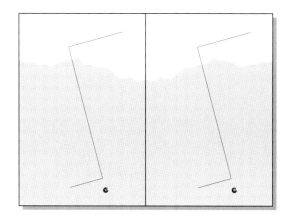

5 Save *04Work.pm6*.

6 To see the effects of your work, display pages 4 and 5, and notice that the mountain images now appear behind the type.

DUPLICATING THE MASTER PAGE

The master elements on page 2 are slightly different from those on 3 , 4, and 5, so the 2–3 page spread needs to have a different pair of master pages than do the remaining pages of the document. You create the new master page spread by copying the Document Master pages and then editing them.

1 Go to the page 2–3 spread and look at the Master Pages palette. Document Master is highlighted, indicating that these are the master pages in use by the currently displayed spread of document pages.

2 Click the master page icon in the lower left corner of your screen to display the Document Master master pages.

When you click the master page icon, PageMaker displays the master pages that are applied to the currently displayed document pages.

3 With Document Master selected in the Master Pages palette, choose Duplicate from the palette pop-up menu. Name the new master page **2nd Master** and click Duplicate.

Duplicate Master Page	
Duplicate:	Document Master
Name of new Master:	2nd Master
	Cancel Duplicate

PageMaker creates and displays the new pair of master pages.

4 Select all the elements on the new left master page, and delete them.

5 Click the page 2-3 icon, then click 2nd Master in the Master Pages palette to apply the new master pages.

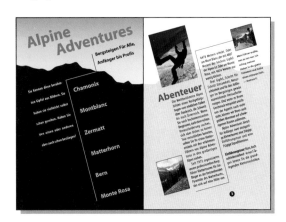

WORKING WITH COLORS

You set up your colors palette by deleting unused colors and then defining two process colors and one spot color.

Removing colors

Unused colors clutter up your Colors palette, but it's easy to get rid of them.

1 Choose Colors from the Window menu.

PageMaker displays the Colors palette. This palette stores the default colors and any other colors that you define, as well as ones that are brought into the publication when EPS graphics are imported. The default colors include None, Black, Paper, Registration, Red, Green, Blue, Cyan, Magenta, and Yellow.

2 Choose Define Colors from the Element menu.

The Define Colors dialog box appears. It contains a number of colors besides the default colors. The first thing you do is delete Green and Blue, since you won't be using them.

Note: The colors that appear within brackets ([ ]) cannot be removed. Process colors appear in italics, and spot colors appear in roman (nonitalic) letters.

3 Select Green and click Remove, Then select Blue and click Remove.

Notice that Green and Blue have disappeared from the list of colors in the Colors palette.

Defining new colors

This brochure is going to be printed using six color plates. Four of them will be the standard process colors: cyan, magenta, yellow, and black. One plate will be a PANTONE red that you define as a spot color, and the last plate will be a glossy varnish with a delicate 10% tint. In the next steps, you define first the spot color for the varnish and then the PANTONE red spot color.

1 With the Define Colors dialog box still open, click New. The Edit Colors dialog box appears.

2 Make sure that Spot is selected in the Type pop-up menu, and press the Library pop-up menu.

The library contains a large selection of electronic color swatch books that are included with PageMaker 6.

3 Select the PANTONE® Coated library, then type **Warm Gray** to highlight PANTONE Warm Gray 1 CVC. In Windows, click on the highlighted color once and the full name will appear in the name box. Click OK once, and type **Varnish/10%413C** in the Name box. Click OK again to return to the main Define Colors dialog box.

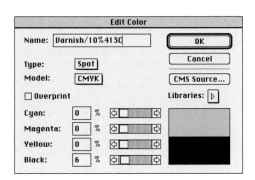

The color name is an indication of the type of varnish tint that the printer will mix when the job is finally printed. You must always discuss such special ink treatments with the printer. Spot colors are inks that are hand mixed. In this case, you will tell the printer to use a high-gloss varnish with a 10% mix of PANTONE 413. Choosing Warm Gray is only a way of approximating the look of the varnish on the screen.

Now you create the PANTONE Red spot color.

4 Click the New button again. Make sure that the Type is still Spot and choose the PANTONE Coated library again.

5 Begin typing **Red 032** until PANTONE Red 032 CVC is highlighted. Then click OK three times to add the color to the Colors palette, and exit the Define Colors dialog boxes.

Applying the colors

Now you want to return to the Document Master master pages. If you just click the master page icon, you will go to the 2nd Master master page, because that is the one in use by the current 2–3 page spread. You could then click Document Master in the Master Pages palette to display the ones you want, but there's an easier way: you can pop up a list of available master pages from the master page icons.

1 Press and hold with the mouse button (Macintosh) or right-click (Windows) on the master page icons to display a pop-up menu of available master pages. Choose Document Master.

Now you apply a 10% tint of the varnish color that you defined earlier to both images.

2 Select the left mountain image, and then Shift-click the right mountain image to add it to the selection. Click the Fill button in the Colors palette, click Varnish/10%413C, and choose 10% from the Tint pop-up menu.

Because you are applying color to EPS images, you usually don't see any change in the screen display, but the selected color will print.

3 Click on 2nd Master in the Master Pages palette and apply a 10% tint of the same varnish color to the mountain image on the right-hand page.

Next, you change the paragraph style definition to change the color of the heading text from green to the PANTONE spot red that you just created.

4 Command-click (Macintosh) or Control-click (Windows) on Section Heading in the Styles palette.

PageMaker displays the Edit Style dialog box.

5 Click the Type button, then select PANTONE Red 032 CVC from the Color pop-up menu. Option-click (Macintosh) or Shift-click (Windows) to exit the nested dialog boxes.

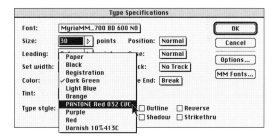

All the heading text is now colored red.

IMPORTING THE COVER IMAGE

Page 1 and page 6 of this two-fold piece are back to back. The paper is die cut along the mountain horizon in the image that appears on page 1 and reversed on page 6, so that the die cut follows the image's horizon on both sides of the paper. You begin by placing the mountain image onto page 6. Then you apply a Photoshop Gallery Effect to the image, copy it, paste it onto page 1, and reverse it from right to left.

1 Go to page 6, display the Place Document dialog box, choose *04Cover.tif*, and click OK. In Windows, if this file does not appear in the list, choose All Files from the Files of Type pop-up menu.

2 Click anywhere on the page with the loaded graphic icon to place the image. To position the image, click the lower left reference point on the Control palette proxy and set X to −33 picas and Y to 48 picas, and click the Apply button.

You can apply Photoshop Effects only to files that are in RGB TIFF or CMYK TIFF format. For demonstration purposes, this file has been altered slightly. Most of the pixels above the die cut line are converted to white pixels, so the file is easier to work with. The file was scanned at 72 dpi.

3 Make sure the mountain image is still selected, then choose Image from the Element menu and Photoshop Effects from the submenu.

You can apply any Adobe Photoshop-compatible plug-in (including Photoshop filters, third-party plug-ins, and Adobe Gallery Effects) by using the Photoshop Effects command.

Note: If you have Adobe Photoshop 3.0.4 or later installed on your computer, you can access additional plug-ins from within PageMaker. Copy the Photoshop plug-ins to the Plug-ins *folder within the* PageMaker RSRC *folder. Alternatively, you can create a shortcut (Windows) or alias (Macintosh) to Photoshop's* Filters *folder and store it in the* Plug-ins folder.

4 In the Photoshop Effects dialog box, click the Save As button and navigate to *Projects*. Then type **04Effect.tif** for the name of the new file and save it.

PageMaker copies the original image and applies the effect to the copy, leaving the original image intact.

5 Select GE Spatter from the Photoshop Effect menu, then click OK.

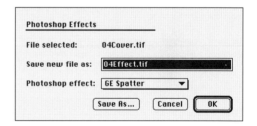

PageMaker processes the image information and then opens the Adobe Gallery Effects dialog box. The entries are specific to the effect that you selected.

6 For this image, set the Spray radius to 9 and the Smoothness to 13, then click OK.

7 To see the effect of your settings, position the small white square over the part of the image you want to see previewed and click the Preview button.

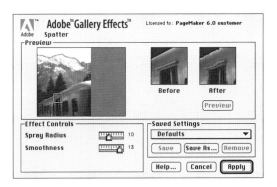

8 Click Apply to apply the settings to the copied image.

It takes a moment for PageMaker to duplicate the image and apply the filter. When the process is completed, your document is linked to the new image.

COPYING THE IMAGE

Now you copy the image from page 6 to page 1 and flip it from right to left. Because the image is reversed on the two sides of the paper, the die cut line will follow the line of the mountain tops on both sides of the page.

1 Select and copy the image on page 6 and then go to page 1. Zoom out so that you can see the whole page and part of the pasteboard to the left.

2 Press Command-Option-V (Macintosh) or Control-Shift-P (Windows) to Power Paste the image.

Because the image was copied from a left-hand page, the Power-Pasted copy appears on the pasteboard to the left of page 1, which is a right-hand page.

3 Click any right-hand reference point on the Control palette proxy, then click the Horizontal Reflection button to flip the image.

The image now appears correctly positioned on page 1.

4 Save *04Work.pm6*.

CREATING MASKS

Page 2 of the final file contains a circular graphic that was created by using a mask. You import a photograph and then draw an oval to create a mask on the image.

TIP: TO SELECT ONLY
THE MASKING CIRCLE,
DESELECT BOTH IMAGES,
THEN CLICK EXACTLY
ON THE BORDER OF
THE CIRCLE.

1 Go to page 2, display the Place Document dialog box, choose *04Mask.tif,* and click OK.

2 Click in the lower left corner of the second page to place the image.

The exact position isn't important right now.

Next you draw a circle, place it over the image, and use it to create a mask. Masks are used to cover part of an image so that only a portion of it is visible. You draw the shape of the mask by using the oval, rectangle, and polygon tools.

3 Select the oval tool, then hold down Shift to draw a circle of any size on the pasteboard.

4 Set the fill of the circle to None by clicking the Fill button in the Colors palette and then clicking None.

5 In the Control palette, make sure the Proportional Scale option (the button to the right of the Width scale box) is activated, then enter 11p1 for width, and apply the setting.

6 Use the pointer tool to drag the circle over the small mountain image. Position it roughly as shown below. The part of the image outside the circle will be hidden and will not print.

7 With the pointer tool, click on the edge of the circle to select it, and Shift-click to add the small image to the selection. Choose Mask from the Element menu.

PageMaker creates a mask from the circle. You can change what part of the image is visible by dragging it with the pointer tool or by selecting it and using the arrow keys. Position the image so the part that is visible in the circle matches the illustration and *04Final.pm6.*

Once you have the image positioned inside the mask, you group the image and mask into a single object and drag the object to its final location.

8 If the image is not still selected, click anywhere in the center of the circle to select the underlying image, then hold down Command and Shift (Macintosh) or Control and Shift (Windows) and click exactly on the edge of the circle to add it to the selection. You should see two sets of selection handles.

9 Make sure both objects are selected, then choose Group from the Arrange menu.

10 Look at *04Final.pm6* to see where the circle image should be placed, and use the pointer tool to drag the masked, grouped circle to that position.

11 Just a reminder: save *04Work.pm6*.

Note: An interim file is provided with the steps completed up to this point. If you want to complete the rest of this project without having to do the earlier steps, go to 04Project, *open* 04Inter1.pt6, *and save it in* Projects.

Time out for a movie

If your system is capable of running Adobe Teach movies, play the movie named *Trapping Hints* to hear prepress professionals talk about PageMaker's trapping options. For information on how to view Adobe Teach movies, see "Watching Adobe Teach Movies" at the beginning of this book.

PREPARING THE BROCHURE FOR SEPARATIONS

When you print separations, you create a separate set of paper or film images for each color used in the publication. A commercial printer uses these separations to create the plates used to print the job—one plate for each color. Since this publication has six colors—cyan, magenta, yellow, black, PANTONE Red 321, and the tint varnish—you will create six sets of output when you print separations.

When you print separations, Adobe PageMaker automatically creates a knockout where objects overlap. *Knockout* means that the color underneath has a cutout where the color on top occurs. In the brochure, the orange text knocks out the black background. On the black separation, the orange text appears as white letters on a black background.

Printed text   *Knocked-out text*

If the orange ink were to overprint the black, the two inks would mix and the result would not be orange, but black. PageMaker creates knockouts automatically, but there are two resulting issues that you need to be aware of—trapping and overprinting.

The Adobe PageMaker *Print Publishing Guide* is an excellent source of information on printing processes.

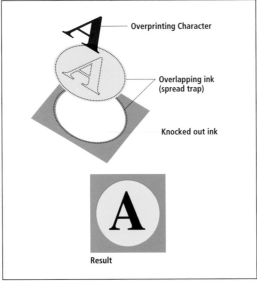

Trapping and overprinting

TRAPPING AND OVERPRINTING

When a file is printed by a commercial printer using printing plates, the paper passes between rollers for each ink used in the publication. Each time the paper passes a roller, there is the possibility of misalignment or misregistration, if the paper is stretched or compressed by the printing press. Misregistration can cause thin gaps of white (often called *light leaks*) or color shifts between adjacent objects on the page.

Misregistration

To compensate for this misregistration, you can use a technique called *trapping*, which overlaps adjoining color areas slightly, preventing gaps between colors.

The trapping process has many variables. Light objects on dark backgrounds are trapped differently from dark objects on light backgrounds. There are special considerations for text, black objects, and imported files. The amount of trap varies, depending on the paper, print quality, and printing press.

Trapping can be daunting for even the most experienced user. It is essential that you work closely with your printer or service bureau if you decide to take trapping on yourself.

Adobe PageMaker provides the Trapping Options command, which you can use to set automatic trapping for your publication. Always consult with your commercial printer to find the correct values for these settings. They depend upon many factors, such as type of paper and inks being used and the type of press. In the following steps, you set trapping for the mountaineering brochure.

1 Choose Trapping Options from the Utilities menu.

2 Click the check box for Enable Trapping for Publication.

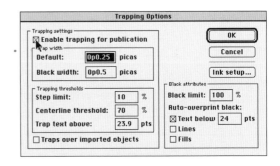

3 In the Trap Width area, leave the Default set to ¼ point (0p0.25).

This is a common trapping value. The Default option specifies the trap (amount of overlap) for all colors except black. PageMaker applies traps based on a set of internal parameters. Usually, lighter colors will expand or spread into adjacent darker colors. When you set trapping you don't see the results on the screen, nor will color composites accurately represent traps.

4 Leave Black Width set to ½ point (0p0.5).

The Black Width option specifies trap for colors next to or under black. Usually, black width is 1.5 to 2 times the default trap. Again, get this number from your printer or service bureau.

5 Leave the three Trapping Thresholds options set to their default values.

The Step Limit sets the threshold at which a trap will be applied. The higher the number, the more extreme the color difference needs to be before PageMaker applies an automatic trap.

Centerline trapping is used when colors have similar *neutral densities*, meaning neither color is much darker or lighter than the other. The Centerline Threshold value determines when PageMaker uses centerline trapping placement. Higher numbers use centerline trapping only for very similar colors. Lower numbers use it for a greater relative range of colors.

PageMaker traps only text above the point size indicated in the Trap Text Above box. Smaller point sizes typically overprint if specified to do so in the Black Attributes options.

6 In Black Attributes, enable the Lines and Fills options.

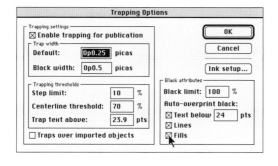

This causes the lines and fills of objects that you draw with the PageMaker tools to overprint if they are black. In the mountaineering brochure, this will prevent the thin line elements on the master page from knocking out the tinted mountain silhouette. Black objects are usually overprinted.

7 Leave Black Limit set to 100%.

The 100% value for Black Limit tells PageMaker that only colors containing 100% black should be counted as black. The Black Limit option is useful when compensating for extreme *dot gain*, in which the porous surface of the paper causes the halftone ink dots to spread. This most often occurs when printing on newsprint or other low-grade paper stock.

8 Leave Traps Over Imported Objects unchecked.

This option is used only in the rather unusual case that you need to trap an object that has been drawn in PageMaker and that lies under an imported graphic.

The Ink Setup button allows you to change the neutral density of specific inks. The default values are based on industry standards. A commercial printer would use a densitometer to measure a particular ink's density percentage, then change the number in this dialog box to reflect the findings. Changing this number will change the way PageMaker traps colors.

Again, for more information on any of these options, see the Adobe *PageMaker User Guide* or the Adobe *Print Publishing Guide*.

9 Click OK to apply trapping.

Trapping Options affect only elements created in Adobe PageMaker—lines, rules, and text. You cannot specify traps within imported photographs or illustrations. Any trapping for imported files must be applied within the application that created the image or by using a product such as Adobe TrapWise.

Your commercial printer or service bureau may be using a trapping program such as Adobe TrapWise for complex trapping needs. Adobe TrapWise is a professional-quality trapping program that requires a PageMaker publication to be converted to an EPS file. TrapWise applies trapping to all elements in the EPS publication, including files imported from a variety of applications. It also allows for manual adjustments and will trap difficult areas such as gradients and partial objects. If your printer is using a trapping program, you should *not* use PageMaker's Trapping Options. Always discuss trapping with your printer or service bureau.

PRINTING SEPARATIONS

In this section, you explore printing separations to an imagesetter.

Checking and installing PPDs

PageMaker creates separations based on the characteristics of the selected printer, so in a real-world situation, you would select and install a PPD (PostScript Printer Description) that is appropriate for the printer—usually an imagesetter—on which the separations will be output. PageMaker's installation application allows you to select additional PPDs at any time.

You need your original PageMaker installation media to complete the following steps. If they are not available, just select a PPD that is appropriate for your current printer, or select the Color General PPD. This will not produce output that is actually usable, but it will allow you to complete the steps in the "Setting up Separations" section.

1 To check your PPDs, choose Print from the File menu.

2 Click on the PPD pop-up menu to see a list of available printer descriptions.

You must choose a PPD that is appropriate for the imagesetter to which you will be outputting. The printer for that PPD does not have to be attached to your system. The PPD that you choose determines the default settings in the Print dialog boxes.

For this project, you install a PPD for an Agfa Imagesetter and one for a Fiery. The Agfa Imagesetter would be a typical choice for printing separations, and the Fiery is a popular color composite proofing device.

3 In the Install (Macintosh) or PM6 (Windows) folder, double-click the PageMaker 6 Installer/ Utility (Macintosh) or Setup.exe (Windows).

4 Click the appropriate language button, and then choose Custom Install.

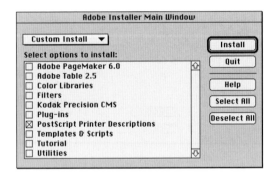

5 Make sure Adobe PageMaker 6 is deselected.

You don't want to reinstall the whole program.

6 Choose PostScript Printer Descriptions, and click the Install button.

The Installer displays a list of available PPDs.

7 Choose the Agfa SelectSet 5000 and the Fiery 200i-R1. Click OK, then click Install. When the installation is complete, click Quit to exit the Installer utility.

You do not need to restart the system after installing a PPD.

Setting up separations

Next you tell PageMaker which colors should be output as separate files, and select select some other useful options, such as crop marks and registration marks.

1 In *04Work.pm6*, display the Print Document dialog box, and choose the Agfa SelectSet 5000 PPD.

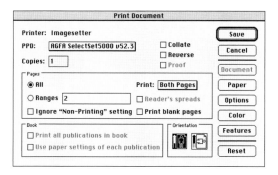

2 Click the Paper button. In the Paper Options dialog box, click the buttons for Printer's Marks and Page Information.

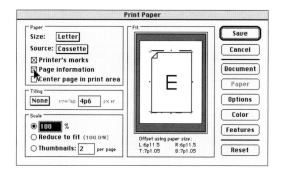

These options place crop marks, registration marks, density control bars, and color control bars on the output. All of these help your commercial printer and service bureau align separations and check color accuracy. The Printer's Marks option adds ¾-inch to the size of the paper that is required. The Page Information option prints the filename, page number, current date and color separation name in the lower left corner of each separation.

3 Examine the Fit area of the dialog box.

It shows the relationship between the page size of your document and the physical paper size available in the printer you have specified (the PPD). Use this dialog box to check whether crop marks, registration marks, and other page information such as color and density, will fit on the paper. These items are all printed outside of the document page, so the physical paper must be larger than the document size to allow for these. If the publication and selected marks are too large for the printable area of the paper, the values appear in red in the Fit area.

4 Click the Color button. In the Color Options dialog box, click the Separations button.

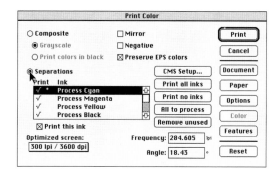

The Ink column lists the names of each spot and process color ink needed to print the colors in your publication. These inks are the spot and process colors that have been defined in the Colors palette or imported with your placed EPS files.

5 Scroll through the list to examine the inks that are available. Notice that the four process colors have a check mark next to them, indicating that they will be output as separations.

A complete set of separations will be printed for each color selected. To select a color for separation, click the box next to the color name, and then click the Print This Ink check box.

6 Click PANTONE Red 032, and click the checkbox for Print This Ink. Similarly, specify that Varnish/10%413C should be printed.

7 Save *04Work.pm6*.

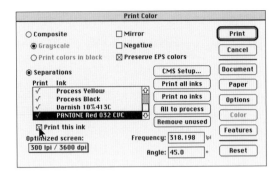

8 At this point in a real-world scenario, you would click Print to output the six sets of pages—one set for each selected color. Each set of pages contains the output for only one color. If you have a printer attached to your system, and you'd like to see the separations, choose a PPD appropriate for your local printer, make the settings, and click Print. If you are not going to print, press Escape or click Cancel to dismiss the Print dialog box.

PREPARING A DIE CUT

The front panel of this piece is going to be a die cut. The printer will cut the paper so that the top edge of the front panel follows the line of the mountain tops. You need to give the printer a separate file that indicates exactly the final shape of the paper. This shape will be two complete pages, side by side, plus the shape of the mountain image.

1 Open a new file. Set the Page Size to Tabloid, the Orientation to Wide, and deselect the Double-sided option. Click OK to accept the settings and create the new publication.

2 Double-click the pointer tool in the Toolbox to display the Preferences dialog box. Set the Measure In and Vertical Ruler Units to Picas.

3 Display the Place Document dialog box, and choose *04Mtn2.eps* as an independent graphic. Click anywhere on the page to place the image.

4 With the image still selected, click the lower left reference point on the proxy in the Control palette. Set X to 1p6 and Y to 55, and apply the settings.

5 Select the rectangle tool, and draw a rectangle of any size. Keep the lower left corner of the proxy selected, and set Width to 66, Height to 48, X to 34p6, and Y to 55. Apply the settings.

6 With the rectangle still selected, click the Both button in the Colors palette, and click Black.

The rectangle is the size of two panels, and the black mountain image defines the shape of the third panel. It is a duplicate of the color mountain image that appears on both sides of the front panel, so the three panels together are the shape of the die cut.

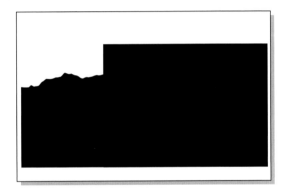

7 Save the new file in *Projects* as *04Diecut.pm6*. Close *04Diecut.pm6* and return to *04Work.pm6*.

USING BUILD BOOKLET TO PRINT SPREADS

Commercial printers generally print on large paper, with several publication pages on each sheet. For any two-sided job, both sides of the paper are printed. The large sheets of paper are then folded and trimmed. Figuring out how to arrange the publication pages on the sheet of paper so that the pages are in the right order and right side up after the printed paper is folded and trimmed is a task called *imposition*. If you've ever tried to figure out even a greeting card or a two-fold flyer, you know that imposition isn't easy. PageMaker's Build Booklet plug-in performs the imposition task for you if you are printing a two-, three-, or four-page spread. In the following steps, you use the Build Booklet plug-in to perform the imposition for this three-panel brochure.

Talk to your commercial printer or service bureau about whether you should attempt imposition before submitting the job. Whether you perform imposition for the final printing or not, PageMaker's Build Booklet feature allows you to print proofs that will replicate the final project without having to cut and paste pages.

When you use PageMaker's Build Booklet feature, PageMaker closes the original file, creates a new file, and copies the pages from the original to the new file in the necessary order and orientation.

1 Review *04Work.pm6* to make sure all your pages look correct.

2 Choose Document Setup from the File menu and turn off Facing Pages. Click OK.

3 Choose PageMaker Plug-ins from the Utilities menu, then choose Build Booklet from the submenu. The Build Booklet dialog box appears.

The 2-, 3-, and 4-up Consecutive layout options create multipage spreads. Each set of 2, 3, or 4 pages is combined side by side onto a single page. These options work well for creating multi-panel brochures.

4 Choose 3-up Consecutive from the Layout pop-up menu.

After you choose a layout, PageMaker calculates the spread size for you. If you are imposing the piece for a commercial printer, you should add about 6 picas to each dimension to allow space for crop marks, page information, and bleeds.

5 Leave the Spread Size set to 99 by 48 picas. Leave Total Creep and Gutter Space set to zero, and leave Place Guides in Gutter and Preserve Page Numbering unchecked.

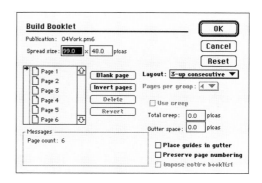

Creep is an adjustment that compensates for the accumulated thickness of several sheets of paper being folded together. *Gutter Space* is space that you leave between pages to allow for folding and trimming. None of these settings applies to this project.

6 Click OK to begin the imposition process. When you are queried about whether to save the original file, choose Save.

PageMaker saves and closes the original brochure, then copies all the elements in the publication to a new document with the new size. Each page of the new publication contains three pages of the original publication.

PageMaker posts a dialog box announcing its progress. When the "Operation completed" message appears, click OK. Don't worry about the messages that items are crossing gutters. That's just the design of the piece.

7 Save the untitled file in *Projects* as *043Up.pm6*.

At this point, you would typically want to see a high-quality color proof of your piece before sending it to the commercial printer. If you didn't have a high-end color composite printer attached to your system, you would take your files to a service bureau for output on a proofing device such as the Canon Fiery. You would check with the service bureau in advance to see what printer PPD to select for the following steps.

8 With *043Up.pm6* active, choose Document Setup from the File menu. Set the Orientation to Tall and click OK.

9 Display the Print Document dialog box. Choose the Fiery 200i-R1 PPD.

The Fiery would be a common real-world choice. If you have a color printer with a tabloid-size paper tray attached to your system, and you wish to actually output this piece, choose an appropriate PPD instead of the Fiery.

10 Click the Paper button to display the Print Paper dialog box, and look at the Fit window. Notice that the image does not fit on the currently selected paper, and that some of the numbers below the image are in red.

The red numbers indicate that the output dimensions won't fit on the currently-selected paper.

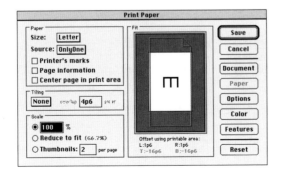

11 Choose Tabloid from the Paper Size pop-up menu, and notice that the page now fits on the paper and all the numbers at the bottom of the Fit area are black. Make sure that Printer's Marks and Page Information are all deselected.

12 Click the Options button, and choose Optimized from the Send Image Data pop-up menu to ensure a high-quality proof.

13 The Data Encoding option determines how the file is sent from the computer to the printer. The binary option results in smaller files and faster transmission. Most Macintosh systems support binary transfer. Windows systems may not support binary transfer. If the binary option is available, that means that the currently selected printer driver supports it.

14 If you do not have a color composite printer attached to your system, click Cancel to dismiss the Print dialog box. Otherwise, click print to output your color composite proof.

USING AN ACROBAT PDF FILE TO PROOF A PUBLICATION

In the next steps, you create a PDF file from your publication. This file can be viewed online by any of the Adobe Acrobat family of products. It can also be printed out to provide another form of color proof.

You could distill either the *04Work.pm6* file or the *043Up.pm6* booklet file. In the latter case, Distiller preserves the three panels in their side-by-side position. This is an accurate representation of the finished piece, but difficult to view onscreen. The following steps tell you to distill *04Work.pm6* instead. Feel free to distill the booklet if you prefer.

1 Open *04Work.pm6*.

2 Choose Create Adobe PDF from the File menu. PageMaker asks if you wish to save the document first. Answer Yes.

PageMaker displays the Create Adobe PDF dialog box.

3 Be sure than that Acrobat is chosen as PageMaker's Printer Style. This ensures that Distiller uses the special Acrobat PPD. Enable Distill Now.

Creating a PDF document is a two-step process. First Distiller writes a PostScript file from the original. Then it "distills" this PostScript file into a PDF file. If you choose Distill Now, it performs both steps. If you choose Prepare PostScript File for Distilling Separately, it creates the PostScript file and stops. You can then use Acrobat Distiller as a separate application to open the PostScript file and convert (distill) it to an Acrobat PDF file.

4 Enable View PDF Using, and choose Acrobat Reader 2.0.1 from the pop-up menu.

Enabling this means that the PDF document will display in Acrobat Reader as soon as Acrobat Distiller has created it. If your system has insufficient RAM to run PageMaker, Acrobat Distiller, and Acrobat Reader simultaneously, you will receive insufficient memory messages when you attempt to distill. There are two possible solutions. If your system supports virtual memory, enable it. PageMaker works well with virtual memory. The other solution is to choose Prepare PostScript file for Distilling Separately in Step 4. You can then close PageMaker and use Acrobat Distiller as a separate application. This option is described in the Distilling Later section.

5 Do not select Include Downloadable Fonts.

You need this option only if you are going to create a PostScript file that will then be distilled on another system that may not have the necessary fonts.

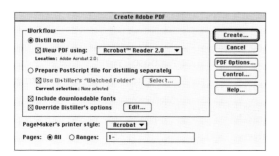

6 Click the Edit button next to Override Distiller's Options. Be sure that Embed All Fonts is enabled. If this option is off, the fonts are not included in the PDF file. Instead, Distiller includes some generic serif and sans serif fonts that it will use when the PDF file is displayed on systems that don't have the original fonts. When you enable Embed All Fonts, the PDF file will always look exactly like your original PageMaker file.

7 Leave the defaults for text and graphics compression and Downsample to 72 dpi. Enable Convert CMYK Images to RGB.

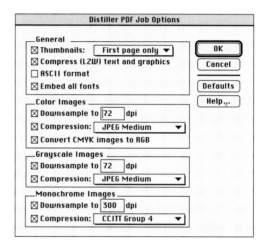

These settings are appropriate if the document is going to be distributed electronically but not printed on paper. Screens display at about 72 dpi, so there is no need to take up space with higher-resolution graphics. Also, screens display using the RGB (red-green-blue) color model, so you want Distiller to convert your CMYK (cyan-magenta-yellow-black) colors to RGB colors. If you were going to print the Acrobat document out on paper, you would want to choose a higher dpi, and to disable the "convert to RGB," since paper printing uses the CMYK color model.

For this project, you don't need to set any of the Options or Controls. The Options allow you to create indexes, tables of contents, notes, and to add file information. Some of the Controls are discussed in the Create PDF section at the end of Project 5.

8 Be sure Pages: All is chosen, and click Create.

PageMaker displays a dialog box for you to specify a name and location for the PDF file. By default, the name is the original filename with *pdf* on the end of it. If the original file name ended in *pm6*, the *pdf* replaces the *pm6*.

9 Navigate to *Projects* and click Save to save *04Work.pdf*.

PageMaker first creates a special PostScript file and then launches Acrobat Distiller, which creates the PDF file from the PostScript file. When this process is completed, Acrobat Reader opens and displays the new PDF document.

10 Click the arrows at the top of the Acrobat Reader window to move through the document.

Distilling later

If your system cannot run PageMaker, Acrobat Distiller, and Acrobat Reader simultaneously, follow these steps:

1 Display the Create Adobe PDF dialog box and choose Prepare PostScript File for Distilling Separately.

2 Deselect Use Distiller's Watched Folder. Follow the other instructions above and save the file in *Projects* as *04work.ps*.

3 Close PageMaker. Launch Acrobat Distiller and open *04Work.ps*.

4 Click Save to save *04Work.pdf* in *Projects*.

5 When Distiller has finished its work, close Acrobat Distiller and open Acrobat Reader. Open *04Work.pdf* to view it.

FINISHING UP

Close all open documents and quit Acrobat Reader, Acrobat Distiller, and PageMaker.

CAMPEONATO 1998

ABRIL 17-25

CAMPEONATO 1998

Acompañe a sus héroes favoritos del fútbol ya retirados cuando los once equipos regionales de profesionales del antaño jueguen la primera ronda del 1997 International Senior Soccer League a través de Europa y Asia. Marque en su calendario de Abril 17 al 25.

calendario

DÍA	PARTIDO DE DESEMPATE	CIUDAD
ABRIL 17	Centro América vs. Europa del Oeste	Bogotá, Columbia
ABRIL 17	Europa de Este vs. Africa	Buenos Aires, Argentina
ABRIL 19	Europe del Norte vs. Europa del Sur	Montevideo, Uruguay
ABRIL 19	Nortemérica vs. Sur América	Cayenne, Guayana Frances
ABRIL 21	Caribe vs. Europe del Este	Georgetown, Guyana
ABRIL 21	Oeste de Europa vs. Oceania	Quito, Ecuador
ABRIL 23	Europa del Sur vs. Norteamérica	Lima, Peru
ABRIL 23	Asia vs. Centro América	Rio de Janeiro, Brazil
ABRIL 25	Africa vs. Europe del Norte	Asunción, Paraguay
ABRIL 25	Oceania vs. Caribe	Santiago, Chile
ABRIL 25	Sur América vs. Asia	Caracas, Venezuela

• ARGENTINA •

5

This 16-by-24-inch poster makes use of PANTONE's new Hexachrome colors which provide a greater range and depth of color than are possible with conventional four-color pro-

SOCCER SCHEDULE POSTER

cess printing. The soccer schedule table, created with Adobe Table 2.5, is an embedded OLE object, so it can be updated from within PageMaker by double-clicking on it. This project also provides the opportunity to begin working with the Kodak CM color management system that comes with PageMaker 6. You learn to create source profiles for imported graphics, to preseparate them, and to use the Create Adobe PDF command to produce a file for online viewing with Adobe's Acrobat Reader or Acrobat Exchange.

The starting point for this project is last year's poster, which was created using QuarkXPress®. You have decided that PageMaker 6 is a better tool for the job, so you are going to convert last year's poster from QuarkXPress to Adobe

SOCCER SCHEDULE POSTER

PageMaker 6 by using Adobe's new QuarkXPress® Converter. The next thing you learn in this project is how to set PageMaker's Color Management System so that you can apply a source profile to a bitmap graphic and separate it into PageMaker's new high fidelity colors.

After replacing and separating the large graphic, you delete last year's schedule table and create a new table by using PageMaker's Insert Object command to access Adobe Table 2.5. This creates a table that is an embedded OLE object, editable from within PageMaker. You perform the routine tasks of replacing the text in the text block and editing the title text and then create three new high fidelity colors to apply to selected items in the poster. To proof the poster, you use PageMaker's print tiling feature to print it out on your letter-size printer in pages that you can piece together into a full-size image.

There's one more step: You decide to make an Acrobat version of the poster by using PageMaker's new Create Adobe PDF feature to make the poster available online.

In this project you learn how to:

• Use the QuarkXPress Converter

• Create and format an OLE embedded table

• Use the PageMaker Kodak Color Management System to assign a source profile to an image and create a separation file for it

• Define PANTONE Hexachrome spot colors

• Create six-color high-fidelity separations for a bitmap image

• Print an oversize document on a printer that doesn't accommodate oversize pages

• Convert a PageMaker document to Adobe's PDF format for viewing with the Acrobat family of products

This project should take you about 1.5 hours to complete.

BEFORE YOU BEGIN

1 Return all settings to their defaults by deleting the *Adobe PageMaker 6.x Prefs* file from the *Preferences* folder (Macintosh) or by removing *\pm6\rsrc\usenglish\pm6.cnf* from the drive containing PageMaker (Windows).

2 Make sure that Birch and Myriad Multiple Master fonts are installed.

3 Make sure that Adobe Acrobat Distiller and Adobe Acrobat Reader are both installed on your system. Acrobat Reader 2.0.1 and Acrobat Distiller 2.1 or 2.1PE (Personal Edition) are distributed with Adobe PageMaker 6 on the CD-ROM. The Personal Edition of Distiller converts only files created by Adobe products. See "What You Need to Know" at the front of this book for more information about installing these applications.

Important: If you have not used Distiller before beginning this project, you must open it once as a separate application and then close it. Otherwise, you can't invoke it from the PageMaker File menu as a plug-in. Similarly, if you have never used the Adobe Table 2.5 application, you must open it once as a separate application in order to use it to Insert Object from within PageMaker. Double-click the icon and then close it. The Adobe Table 2.5 icon is located within the Adobe Table folder that is within the PageMaker 6 folder. Or you can access it from the Adobe menu under Programs (Windows). Adobe Table 2.5 works only on Macintosh and Windows 95 systems. Those using an older version of Windows must use Adobe Table 2.1 as a separate application. Table 2.1 is not an OLE server.

5 Launch the Adobe PageMaker application and open the *05Final.pm6* file in *05Project* to see how the poster will look when you have completed the steps in this lesson.

WORKING WITH RAM

This project makes use of the Adobe Table 2.5 application, and of the Create Adobe PDF plug-in. Both of these applications are memory-intensive. You may run into out-of-memory problems if you have less than 20 MB of RAM on your system. PageMaker 6 works well with virtual memory, however, so you may be able so solve memory problems using that resource.

CONVERTING LAST YEAR'S POSTER TO PAGEMAKER

PageMaker comes with a separate application that converts Macintosh QuarkXPress® 3.1, 3.2, and 3.3 files to PageMaker files. In the first part of the project, you use it to convert last year's poster, which was done in QuarkXPress, to a PageMaker 6 file.

If you are working on a Windows platform and have an early release of PageMaker 6 that does not yet include the QuarkXPress Converter utility, skip to "Opening the PageMaker File."

1 In the PageMaker 6 application folder, open first the Utilities folder and then the QuarkXPress Converter folder. Double-click on QuarkXPress Converter icon to launch the application.

QuarkXpress® Converter

2 Choose Select File from the File menu to display the Select Files to Convert dialog box.

3 Navigate to the *05Project* folder, highlight the *05Postr.Qrk* file in the upper scroll list, and click Add to place it in the lower scroll list of files to convert.

If you want to convert several files, you can add them all to the conversion list at this point.

4 Click Done. The Select Files window closes.

5 In the main Converter dialog box, click Choose Destination in the Options menu. To choose a location, enable Folder Designated Below, navigate to *Projects*, and open it. The line below the file list should say "Destination: Projects." Click Select to return to the main QuarkXPress Converter dialog box.

Note: Enabling Convert White Box in the Options menu converts Quark boxes that have white backgrounds to boxes with clear backgrounds. If the creator of the Quark file forgot to make some of the text boxes transparent in Quark, this feature prevents opaque white boxes from appearing in your PageMaker file.

6 Click Convert.

The Converter converts all selected Quark files to PageMaker 6 files. Each PageMaker file has the original name with *.PM6* added to the end of it.

Note: To see a record of the converter's activities, click the View Log button in the upper right corner of the main Converter dialog box. For each graphic it converts, the Converter places a line in this log identifying the original name, the new name, and each activity performed. Some graphic formats are converted to a PageMaker-compatible format. A line stating that a graphic has not been converted means only that the format of the graphic is unchanged.

7 Close the QuarkXPress Converter by choosing Quit either from the File menu or from the keyboard.

OPENING THE PAGEMAKER FILE

1 In *Projects*, open *05Postr.Qrk.PM6*—the converted PageMaker version of the poster—just as you would any other PageMaker file.

If you don't have the QuarkXPress Converter: Open the interim file *05Inter1.pt6* in *05Project*. This file was created by using the Converter.

2 When PageMaker asks you for the location of the first graphic file (probably *05Soc97.eps*), navigate to *05Project*, highlight the required filename, and click Link.

PageMaker links to the file and then looks in *05Project* to find and link to the rest of the graphic files that are in the publication.

3 Save the file as *05Work.pm6* in *Projects*.

Note: The file 05Postr.Qrk.PM6 is no longer needed; you may want to get rid of it to avoid confusion later.

TIP: WHEN YOU ARE IN A COLOR LIBRARY, YOU CAN SELECT SEVERAL COLORS AT ONCE BY HOLDING DOWN COMMAND (MACINTOSH) OR CONTROL (WINDOWS) AS YOU CLICK EACH ADDITIONAL COLOR.

SETTING UP THE DOCUMENT

2 Double-click the pointer tool to display the Preferences dialog box.

3 Set picas as the unit for both the measurements and the vertical ruler.

4 Be sure the rulers are displayed, and double-click on the corner where the vertical and horizontal rulers intersect. This ensures that the zero point of each ruler is at the upper left corner of the page.

REPLACING THE BACKGROUND IMAGE

The first step in updating the poster is to delete last year's large background image and to replace it with a new one.

1 With the pointer tool, click on the large background graphic to select it.

Note: Click just above the table. That should ensure that you select the large graphic and not one of the smaller items on top of it. The position of the selection handles shows you the size and shape of the object you have selected.

2 Display the Place Document dialog box, and highlight *05Soc98.tif.* Select Replacing Entire Graphic, and be sure that Retain Cropping Data is selected. Click OK (Macintosh) or Open (Windows).

Because you selected Replacing Entire Image, PageMaker replaces the old image with the new one without going through the step of presenting you with a loaded graphic icon. Choosing Retain Cropping Data causes the new image to appear in the same position and at the same size as the old one, including being behind all the other objects.

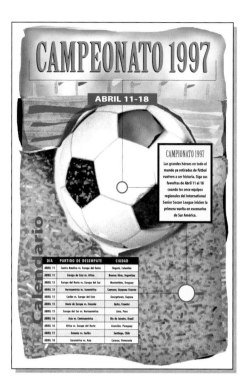

3 Save *05Work.pm6.* Continue to save often throughout this project. We remind you only occasionally.

Time out for a movie

If your system is capable of running Adobe Teach movies, play the movie named *Hexachrome Color* to hear prepress professionals talking about the pros and cons of PANTONE Hexachrome™ color. For information on how to view Adobe Teach movies, see "Watching Adobe Teach Movies" at the beginning of this book.

DEFINING NEW COLORS

When you converted this document from Quark-XPress, two colors that were created in Quark—Pale Yellow and Dark Blue—were brought over into the PageMaker document. The current design uses three new ones, in addition. This year's poster is going to be printed on a press that can handle the new high-fidelity colors, so you decide to use the new PANTONE Hexachrome colors that are available in PageMaker 6. Later in this project, you're going to convert the background image to Hexachrome colors as well.

What is high-fidelity color?

In the past, process colors were printed using four standard inks: cyan, magenta, yellow, and black (CMYK). A more recent technology allows up to eight process colors to be used in order to achieve a greater range and depth of printed color. This requires not only specially designed printing presses but a new set of color standards as well.

PANTONE Hexachrome colors

Pantone has established a set of color standards called PANTONE Hexachrome colors, so named because they are printed by using six process inks rather than the traditional four. The Hexachrome inks are cyan, magenta, yellow, black, orange, and green. The cyan, magenta, yellow, and black inks are subtly different from those used in standard CMYK printing.

These Hexachrome colors are available for both coated and uncoated paper stocks, just as PANTONE's other process colors are. The entire PANTONE Hexachrome color library is included with PageMaker 6.

Defining a PANTONE™ Hexachrome color

1 Choose Define Colors from the Element menu. In the Define Colors dialog box, click the New button. PageMaker displays the Edit Color dialog box.

2 Click and hold on the Libraries arrow and drag down to the PANTONE Hexachrome Coated choice.

PageMaker displays the Color Picker dialog box. You can explore the whole range of PANTONE Coated colors by using the scroll bar below the display area. You can also go directly to any color by typing its number in the box at the top of the display.

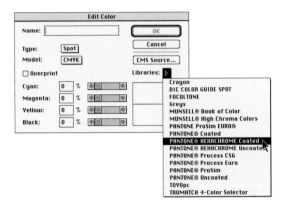

3 To choose your first color, type **H 455-3** in the PANTONE box. Be sure to type a space after the H. Look at the highlighted color to be sure it's the one you want, and then click OK twice to return to the main Define Colors dialog box.

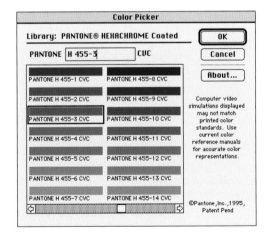

Note: You must click OK twice to return to the Define Colors dialog box after selecting each color. If you return only to the Edit Color dialog and then reenter the library to select another color, your new selection replaces the previous one.

4 Click New again, and choose the PANTONE Hexachrome Coated library once more.

5 To select the next color, drag the slider button at the bottom of the color display area all the way to the left. Click PANTONE Hex, Magenta to select it, and then click OK to return to the Edit Color dialog box. Click OK again to return to the Define Colors dialog box.

6 To define the third and last color, click New once more, and choose the PANTONE Hexachrome Coated color library again. Type **H 340-1** in the Name box to select the dark blue color. You are finished defining colors, so click OK until you have exited all the way out of the Define Colors dialog boxes.

Making a color library

Once you have created a set of colors, you may want to use them again for related projects. The Copy feature in the Define Colors dialog box allows you to copy colors from another PageMaker document, but for color collections that you use often, you may find it easier and more convenient to save the colors in a color library.

1 Choose PageMaker Plug-ins from the Utilities menu, and choose Create Color Library from the submenu.

2 Type **Sports Hex** for the new library name. This is the name that will appear in the list of color libraries.

3 In the File Name box, replace the word *Custom* with *05Colors*. Leave the *.bcf* extension. This is the name of the file in which PageMaker stores the library information.

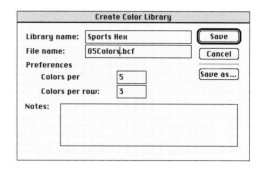

Although you could save the library to another location by clicking the Save As (Macintosh) or Browse (Windows) button, the file must be in the default location to be available to PageMaker. On a Macintosh, this location is the Color folder which is in the RSRC folder in the PageMaker folder. In Windows, the location is the \PM6\ RSRC\USENGLSH *(or other language)*\Color] directory.

4 Click Save to create the library.

5 To see your new library appear in the list of library choices, display the Define Colors dialog box again, click New, and click and hold the Library button. You should see Sports Hex in the list of available libraries. Cancel out of the dialog boxes when you are finished.

UPDATING THE HEADLINE

To begin, you apply one of your newly defined PANTONE Hexachrome colors to the headline at the top of the poster. Then you change the year from 1997 to 1998 and change the text of the underlying shadow type as well.

1 To work at a comfortable size, select the zoom tool and draw a selection marquee around the headline at the top of the poster.

2 Use the text tool to select the "Campeonato 1997" text. Display the Colors palette if it's not already out, and click PANTONE Hex, Magenta CVC.

3 With the text tool still selected, highlight the *7* in *1997* and replace it with an *8*.

4 Change to the pointer tool and drag on one of the right-hand handles to widen the text block a little so that the line no longer breaks.

You've fixed the main text, but it's now obvious that the drop shadow is a separate object that still needs to be changed.

FIXING THE DROP SHADOW

There are many ways to move objects in PageMaker. The nudge technique described in the next steps is a very accurate way to move something out of the way and then move it back again.

1 Display the Preferences dialog box again. (Remember that you can just double-click on the pointer tool in the Toolbox.) Set the Vertical Nudge to 8 picas, and click OK.

2 With the pointer tool, click the headline text block to select it. Press the Down Arrow key twice. Since vertical nudge is set to 8 picas, the headline text block moves down 16 picas, revealing the type block for the shadow beneath it.

3 With the text tool, change the date of the shadow type from 1997 to 1998. Widen the text block enough to keep the text on one line.

4 Return to the pointer tool, select the magenta headline text block, and press the Up Arrow key twice.

PageMaker nudges the text block up 16 picas to return it to its former position. In the next step, you group the two text blocks so that the shadow won't accidentally be disarranged as you work on the rest of the poster.

5 Click the headline with the pointer tool. Hold down the Command (Macintosh) or Control (Windows) and Shift keys and click again to add the underneath text block to the selection. Choose Group from the Arrange menu.

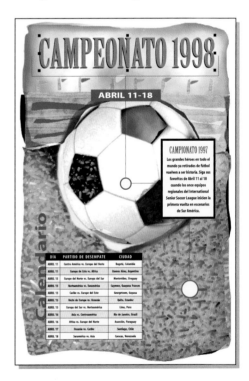

The two text blocks are now a single unit. If you need to separate them later, select the grouped object and choose Ungroup from the Arrange menu.

6 Return to the Preferences dialog box, and set the vertical nudge back to 0p1 so that you can use it to make delicate adjustments in the future. Tiny nudges are the common way of using this feature.

UPDATING THE BORDERED BOX

This year's poster has different text in the small bordered box on the right and uses a different border on the box. The steps used in updating this bordered box and its contents are all familiar and serve as a review.

Placing the new text

Next you drag down a ruler guide and then re-place the text that's in the bordered box on the right.

1 Choose View from the Layout menu, and choose Fit in Window. Drag a horizontal guide from the top ruler, and position it at 55p6, using the Y value in the Control palette to determine when it's where you want it.

2 With the text tool, click an insertion point anywhere in the text that's inside the bordered box.

3 Display the Place Document dialog box, navigate to *05Project*, and highlight *05Camp98.doc*. Enable Place: Replacing Entire Story, and be sure that Retain Format is selected. Click OK (Macintosh) or Open (Windows).

PageMaker replaces the original text in the box with the new text. Choosing Retain Format does not pick up the formatting of PageMaker styles as it did in Project 3, because the PageMaker text was formatted with local formatting rather than with paragraph styles. You'll have to format this text yourself.

4 Select the text block with the pointer tool, and drag the side handles out so that the text block is exactly the same width as the rectangle that lies under it. Look in the Control palette to be sure that the width of the text block is at least 23p9.

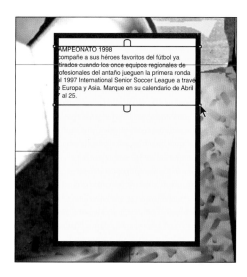

Formatting the new text

1 Display the Control palette if it's not displayed already. Zoom in on the bordered text box. With the text tool, click anywhere in the boxed text and Select All.

2 In the Control palette, click the Paragraph-view button. Click the Center Alignment button, and then set both the right and left paragraph indents to 1p10. Apply the settings.

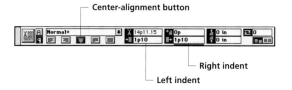

Center-alignment button

Right indent

Left indent

3 Change to the Character view in the Control palette, and select the top line of text ("Campeonato 1998"). Choose Birch as the typeface. Then set the size to 46 point and the leading to 52 points.

4 To create the small line that separates the heading from the body text, display the Paragraph Specifications dialog box and click the Rules button. Enable Rule Below Paragraph, and make the following settings:

Line Style > 4 pt
Line Color > PANTONE H 340-1
Line Width > Width of Column
left and right indents each > 8 picas.

Note: Be sure to make the settings in the Rule Below Paragraph section in the bottom half of the dialog box, not in the Rule Above section.

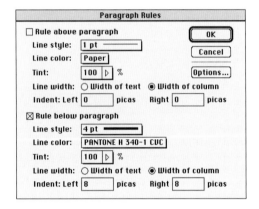

5 Still in the Paragraph Rules dialog box, click the Options button and set the Bottom Picas Below Baseline value to 1p4. Then Option-click (Macintosh) or Shift-click (Windows) OK to exit the nested dialog boxes.

6 With the top line still selected, apply PANTONE H 455-3 from the Colors palette.

7 With the text tool, triple-click in the single paragraph of body text to select it, and use the Control palette to apply the following attributes: typeface MyriadMM 700 Bold 300 Cond, size 22, and leading 32.

8 With the pointer tool, drag the text block so that the baseline of the top line ("Campeonato 1998") sits on the horizontal guide at 55p6.

Applying the new border

1 Select the bordered rectangle that lies under the paragraph text block.

2 Choose Line from the Element menu, and then choose the 6-point dashed line from the submenu.

The border of the pale yellow rectangle that underlies the paragraph changes from solid to dashed.

3 Shift-click the text block to add it to the selection, and then once again choose Group from the Arrange menu to make the text block and background a single unit.

CHANGING THE DATE

1 Zoom in on the small blue box just below the "Campeonato 1998" headline, and use the text tool to change the date from *Abril 11-18* to *Abril 17–25*. Replace the hyphen between the two numbers with an en dash. An en dash is Option-hyphen on Macintosh and Control-equal sign in Windows.

An en dash is always used to indicate a range. If you would express something by saying "from __ to __," then you should use an en dash rather than a hyphen between the two parts.

2 Use the pointer tool to select the blue rectangle behind the date, and apply PANTONE H 455-3 from the Colors palette. Look at the selection handles to be sure that you selected the rectangle rather than the text block on top of it.

The rectangle should turn green. This is another of the PANTONE Hexachrome colors that you defined earlier.

ONE MORE COLOR

1 Select the large rotated word *Calendario* with the text tool.

2 Apply the color PANTONE H 340-1 from the Colors palette.

3 If you have not been saving your work regularly, now is a good time to do so.

Note: An interim file is provided with the steps completed up to this point. If you want to complete the rest of this project without having to do the earlier steps, go to 05Project, *open* 05Inter2.pt6, *and save it in* Projects.

CREATING AN EMBEDDED TABLE

The next steps tell you how to create an OLE-embedded table that can be updated from within PageMaker.

Before you begin working on this year's table, look at the table in *05Final.pm6* to remind yourself of what you'll be creating as you follow these steps.

Deleting last year's schedule

1 With the pointer tool, select the table and delete it.

2 Select and delete the pale yellow rectangle that was behind the table.

Creating the table

1 From the Edit menu, choose Insert Object. PageMaker shows you a list of the types of things you can insert. Click New (Macintosh) or Create New (Windows), and double-click Adobe Table 2.5 to open the application.

You are now working in the Adobe Table application, but you are creating a table that is part of your poster file ("embedded" in it) rather than a separate file. You cannot save your work while you are working in this way. If you look at the File menu, you'll see that there is no Save entry. When you have completed your work in Adobe Table, you'll return to your poster file by choosing Quit & Return (Macintosh) or Exit (Windows) from the File menu.

This technique creates a table that is an embedded OLE object. You can edit the table later by double-clicking it to invoke Adobe Table 2.5 from within PageMaker.

2 Specify 12 rows and 3 columns in the Table Setup dialog box. Click OK.

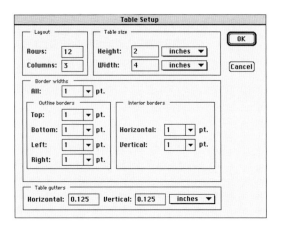

Don't worry about any of the other settings for now.

3 To import the text into the table, begin by selecting all the cells in the table.

You can do this by dragging through the cells with the pointer, but there's an easier way. Adobe's Table Editor offers a special set of tools for selecting table cells: the Selection buttons. The Selection buttons are gray buttons along the top and left of the table. If you don't see them, go to the View menu and choose Show Selection Buttons. Click the small Selection button in the upper left corner of the table—the Select All button—to select all cells in the table.

In the next step, you import a text file that has been prepared in a word processor. The text has been entered so that the contents of each cell are separated by a tab (*tab-delimited*). Each row ends with a line return.

4 Choose Import Text from the File menu. In the Import Text dialog box, be sure that the Delimiter Format is Tab-delimited. Navigate to *05Project,* and double-click *05Sched98.doc.* The text flows into the table.

Note: Instead of selecting the whole table, you could place an insertion point in the upper left cell. If you use this technique, you must be careful to have an insertion point and not to accidentally select the cell. The cell becomes selected when you touch a border of it with the pointer.

Formatting the table

1 If the rulers are not already displayed, turn them on by choosing Show Rulers from the View menu.

2 To set the width of the first column, move the mouse pointer over the right end of the Selection button at the top of the column. When the pointer turns into a double-headed arrow, drag the column border to the 1-inch mark on the ruler. Now use the same technique to drag the right side of the second column to the 4.5 inch mark, and drag the right side of the third column to 7.5 inches.

Dia	Partido de Desempate	Ciudad
Abril 17	Centro América vs. Europa del Oeste	Bogotá, Columbia
Abril 17	Europa de Este vs. Africa	Buenos Aires, Argentina
Abril 19	Europe del Norte vs. Europa del Sur	Montevideo, Uruguay
Abril 19	Norteamérica vs. Sur América	Cayenne, Guayana Frances
Abril 21	Caribe vs. Europe del Este	Georgetown, Guyana
Abril 21	Oeste de Europa vs. Oceania	Quito, Ecuador
Abril 23	Europa del Sur vs. Norteamérica	Lima, Peru
Abril 23	Asia vs. Centro América	Rio de Janeiro, Brazil
Abril 25	Africa vs. Europe del Norte	Asunción, Paraguay
Abril 25	Oceania vs. Caribe	Santiago, Chile
Abril 25	Sur América vs. Asia	Caracas, Venezuela

3 You want all the rows in the table to be the same height, so be sure the whole table is still selected, and choose Row/Column Size from the Cell menu. Type .5 in the Row Height box to set the height of each row to a minimum of one-half inch. Be sure that the unit is Inches, and click OK.

Adobe Table—the application you're working in right now—provides two palettes to make formatting tables easy. The Text palette is already displayed. The other one is the Table palette.

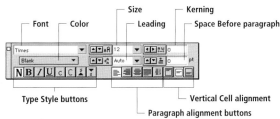

Text palette

4 To display the Table palette, choose Show Table Palette from the Window menu.

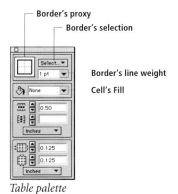

Table palette

5 To apply the correct font to the table text, select all the cells in the table once again and choose MyriadMM 700 Bold 300 Cond from the pop-up font list in the Text palette.

6 With all of the table cells still selected, click the Center-Align button in the Text palette to center the text in each cell.

The text in the left column and top row should be in all caps. You don't need to retype it to change it.

7 Click the Selection button to the left of the top row to select the row, and then Control-click the Selection button above the left column to add the column to the selection. Click the All Caps button in the Text palette.

Adobe Table changes the selected text to all caps.

DÍA	PARTIDO DE DESEMPATE	CIUDAD
ABRIL 17	Centro América vs. Europa del Oeste	Bogotá, Columbia
ABRIL 17	Europa de Este vs. Europa del Sur	Buenos Aires, Argentina
ABRIL 19	Europe del Norte vs. Europa del Sur	Montevideo, Uruguay
ABRIL 19	Norteamérica vs. Sur América	Cayenne, Guayana Frances
ABRIL 21	Caribe vs. Europe del Este	Georgetown, Guyana
ABRIL 21	Oeste de Europa vs. Oceania	Quito, Ecuador
ABRIL 23	Europa del Sur vs. Norteamérica	Lima, Peru
ABRIL 23	Asia vs. Centro América	Rio de Janeiro, Brazil
ABRIL 25	Africa vs. Europe del Norte	Asunción, Paraguay
ABRIL 25	Oceania vs. Caribe	Santiago, Chile
ABRIL 25	Sur América vs. Asia	Caracas, Venezuela

8 Select the top row only. Choose White from the Color list in the Text palette, and choose Solid from the Fill list in the Table palette. This creates the reverse effect for this row. Leave the row selected so that you can apply the correct type size in the next step.

9 The top row should be 22-point type. You won't find this size in the pop-up list of preset sizes in the Text palette, so double-click the Size box to select the contents and type in 22. Press Enter/Return to apply the setting. You can leave the leading set to Auto.

10 Before you deselect the top row, there's one last thing to do. To add some letterspacing, double-click the Kerning box in the Text palette to select the contents, type in **.08**, and apply the setting.

DÍA	PARTIDO DE DESEMPATE	CIUDAD
ABRIL 17	Centro América vs. Europa del Oeste	Bogotá, Columbia
ABRIL 17	Europa de Este vs. Africa	Buenos Aires, Argentina
ABRIL 19	Europe del Norte vs. Europa del Sur	Montevideo, Uruguay
ABRIL 19	Norteamérica vs. Sur América	Cayenne, Guayana Frances
ABRIL 21	Caribe vs. Europe del Este	Georgetown, Guyana
ABRIL 21	Oeste de Europa vs. Oceania	Quito, Ecuador
ABRIL 23	Europa del Sur vs. Norteamérica	Lima, Peru
ABRIL 23	Asia vs. Centro América	Rio de Janeiro, Brazil
ABRIL 25	Africa vs. Europe del Norte	Asunción, Paraguay
ABRIL 25	Oceania vs. Caribe	Santiago, Chile
ABRIL 25	Sur América vs. Asia	Caracas, Venezuela

11 Select all of the left column except the top cell. The easy way to do this is to click the Column Select button at the top and then Control-click the top cell to deselect it. Use the Text palette to make the text size in this column 17 point.

12 Next, you need to apply the correct size to all the cells that are not part of the top row or left column. One way to do this quickly is to click the Select All button and then Control-click the Row Select button for the top row, and Control-double-click the Column Select button for the left column.

This selection sequence above might sound odd, but it's actually quick and easy, and it makes sense when you realize that the buttons toggle the selection state of the whole row or column.

13 Use the Text palette to make the text in the selected cells 16 point.

In the next step, you apply a 20% fill to alternate rows of the table.

14 Click the selection button next to the third row of the table ("Europa de Este vs. Africa"). Hold down the Control key and click the Select button for the fifth, seventh, ninth, and eleventh rows to select each of them. In the Table palette, choose 20% from the Fill list.

DÍA	PARTIDO DE DESEMPATE	CIUDAD
ABRIL 17	Centro América vs. Europa del Oeste	Bogotá, Columbia
ABRIL 17	Europa de Este vs. Africa	Buenos Aires, Argentina
ABRIL 19	Europe del Norte vs. Europa del Sur	Montevideo, Uruguay
ABRIL 19	Norteamérica vs. Sur América	Cayenne, Guayana Frances
ABRIL 21	Caribe vs. Europe del Este	Georgetown, Guyana
ABRIL 21	Oeste de Europa vs. Oceania	Quito, Ecuador
ABRIL 23	Europa del Sur vs. Norteamérica	Lima, Peru
ABRIL 23	Asia vs. Centro América	Rio de Janeiro, Brazil
ABRIL 25	Africa vs. Europe del Norte	Asunción, Paraguay
ABRIL 25	Oceania vs. Caribe	Santiago, Chile
ABRIL 25	Sur América vs. Asia	Caracas, Venezuela

15 From the File menu, choose Quit & Return (Macintosh) or Exit (Windows). Adobe Table closes, and your table appears in the center of the poster.

16 With the table still selected, look at the Control palette, and be sure that the Height and Width are both at 100%. If they are not, be sure that the Proportional mode is on, and then set the Width to 100%.

Finishing the table

Next, you use the keyline feature to create a yellow background for the table. Since the unshaded rows of the table are transparent, this yellow background shows through and creates the illusion that the table is colored. Finally, you position the table by dragging it into place .

You could create the table background by drawing a rectangle and placing it behind the table, but using the keyline technique is easier and results in a background that is an integral part of the table. The background is automatically grouped with the table.

Keylines are most often used to create automatic borders around objects.

1 With the table selected, choose Utilities and then choose Keyline from the PageMaker Plug-ins submenu.

2 In the Keyline dialog box, set the line to extend 1 point outward and enable Send keyline behind object.

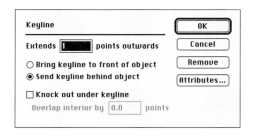

3 Click the Attributes button, and make the following settings in the Fill and Line dialog box:

Fill > Solid
Color > Pale Yellow
Line > 2 pt

Leave the other settings at their defaults and click OK. Click OK again to exit the Keyline dialog box.

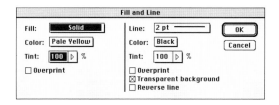

These steps have created a solid pale yellow background that shows through the transparent parts of the table, simulating the effect of a colored table.

4 Drag the table so that its left side is flush with the baseline of the word *Calendario* and its top aligns with the top of the letter *d*. This is an instance in which visual positioning is adequate and appropriate. You don't always need to use a lot of numbers.

5 Be sure to save *05Work.pm6* now if you haven't been saving your work regularly.

Editing the table

To edit an OLE-embedded table, double-click on it with the pointer tool. If the table has been grouped with another object, as in this project, you must ungroup it and deselect all other objects first.

DÍA	PARTIDO DE DESEMPATE	CIUDAD
ABRIL 17	Centro América vs. Europa del Oeste	Bogotá, Columbia
ABRIL 17	Europa de Este vs. Africa	Buenos Aires, Argentina
ABRIL 19	Europe del Norte vs. Europa del Sur	Montevideo, Urúguay
ABRIL 19	Nortemérica vs. Sur América	Cayenne, Guayana Frances
ABRIL 21	Caribe vs. Europe del Este	Georgetown, Guyana
ABRIL 21	Oeste de Europa vs. Oceania	Quito, Ecuador
ABRIL 23	Europa del Sur vs. Norteamérica	Lima, Peru
ABRIL 23	Asia vs. Centro América	Rio de Janeiro, Brazil
ABRIL 25	Africa vs. Europe del Norte	Asunción, Paraguay
ABRIL 25	Oceania vs. Caribe	Santiago, Chile
ABRIL 25	Sur América vs. Asia	Caracas, Venezuela

You might want to take a look at *05Final.pm6* again to see if your work matches it.

CREATING HEXACHROME SEPARATIONS FOR THE LARGE GRAPHIC

In the next part of this project, you use the Kodak Color Management System (CMS) to convert the large background image to PAN-TONE Hexachrome colors. The Kodak Color Management System, together with PageMaker's Save for Separation feature, creates a file that contains the separation information for the six Hexachrome colors. This provides the dual benefits of saving time later when printing separations and of increasing your control over the process.

About Color Management

As color has become more available to graphics professionals and novices alike, it has become painfully obvious to us all that different devices render colors in different ways. The RGB technology of monitors, for example, is capable of showing a different range of colors from the

CMYK color space of classical process printing. In addition, the way a particular scanner interprets color may be different from the way other scanners see it, and more different still from the ways monitors display it and printers print it. Each scanner, monitor, and printer has its own particular limitations and characteristics.

The real-world result of all this has been that when a color job came off the press, it was all too likely that the colors were not those that were scanned in, and not those that appeared on the monitor as the piece was worked on.

To meet this challenge, the graphics industry has created a number of color management systems that describe the color capabilities of many different devices and that accurately translate the rendered colors of one device into those of another. PageMaker provides its users with the Kodak Color Management System but can work with other available systems as well.

A color management system needs to "know" three things to display and output colors accurately: what device created the image (which monitor or scanner), what kind of monitor is displaying it now, and what device is ultimately going to output the image. In the case of color images today, that last part usually has several possible answers. There is typically a composite printer used for proofing and another device used to create separations for printing. In many cases, images are also going online, which is a third answer to the output question.

Enabling color management

Before you can save an image for separation, you must assign it a *source profile*, meaning that you must tell PageMaker something about where the image came from. To assign a source profile, you must turn on a color management system. In this case, we are using the Kodak CM, which ships with PageMaker.

Enabling Kodak CM means that you will be seeing a more accurate representation of the image's colors on your screen. However, enabling it will slow down your work at certain points because it is calculation intensive. You may want to wait until close to the end of your work cycle to turn it on, or you can turn it on long enough to check the color quality of your images and then turn it off again.

Whatever your work pattern, you should use Kodak CM or another installed color management system to assign a source profile to each image in order to get maximum benefit from the system; the source profile helps PageMaker make more accurate separations.

1 In the File menu, choose Preferences and then click the CMS Setup button.

2 For this project, make the following settings:

Color Management > **On**
Monitor Simulates > **Separations printer**
New Items Use > **None**
Monitor > **Generic: Monitor**
Composite Printer > **Generic: CMYK**
Separations Printer > **PANTONE: Hexachrome CMYKRG** (*see the Note below*)
RGB Image Source > **Generic: Monitor**
CMYK Image Source > **Generic: CMYK**

3 Click OK to exit CMS Preferences and OK again to exit Preferences.

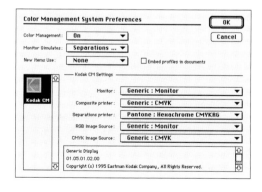

Note: Hexachrome CMYKRG appears twice in the Separations Printer list. The first occurrence is optimized for light, bright colors, and the second one is optimized for darker, saturated colors.

The settings above are generic settings, meant to work approximately on a wide range of systems. They won't really be precise for any system. For any of the settings, if you find a device listed that matches the system you are actually using, feel free to select it.

The Monitor and Monitor Simulates settings: For Monitor, choose the device that is closest to the monitor you are using to display the PageMaker publication. For Monitor Simulates, choose whether you'd rather have the monitor try to simulate printer chosen in the Composite Printer setting, or the printer chosen in the Separations Printer setting. PageMaker then attempts to match the output of the selected printer on your monitor.

To assign a source profile automatically to each image at the time it is placed in PageMaker, enable the New Items Use setting. PageMaker then automatically assigns a source profile to any image that doesn't already have a profile. PageMaker can detect whether the incoming image is RGB or CMYK, and it then tags the image with the RGB Image Source or CMYK Image Source that you specify here. Some images have source profiles assigned to them by the application that created them.

Enabling color management means that it takes a little longer to import each image, but the image is automatically given a source profile, which is the first step in color management. You probably want to turn color management off when you're not using it, because it does slow down the display of images somewhat.

Assigning a source profile to a placed image

The next step is to assign a source profile to the background image. Then you'll be able to make the Save for Separation choice from the Image submenu. Without a source profile assigned to an image, PageMaker can't perform this function.

1 Select the large background image.

2 In the Element menu, choose CMS Source from the Image submenu.

3 Choose Kodak CM from the pop-up menu next to This Image Uses.

4 Choose Generic: Monitor from the Source Profile list. Click OK.

Note: If you see the monitor you are actually using on the pop-up list, feel free to choose it.

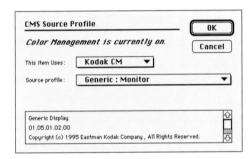

You can use this technique to assign a source profile to any placed image. Choose the Source Profile that most closely matches the device that created the image. If the image was scanned, that would be the scanner. If the image was created in an application such as Adobe Illustrator, that would be the monitor of the system on which the image was created.

Preseparating the background image

When you preseparate an image, PageMaker creates a new file that contains the CMS separation information.

1 Be sure that the large image is still selected.

2 In the Element menu, choose Save for Separation from the Image submenu.

3 Navigate to *Projects*, and name the new image file *05Work2.tif*.

4 Choose Best as the Screen Preview, and enable Relink to New Image.

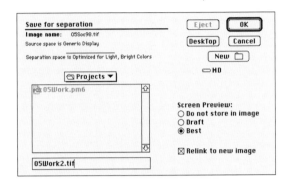

Choosing to create a screen preview increases the size of the new file. In some work situations, you may create the separations only at the end of the work cycle, so you could omit the screen preview. You can also choose the smaller Draft preview, or you can create a preview but choose not to link to the separation file at this time.

5 Click OK (Macintosh) or Save (Windows).

PageMaker creates a file containing CMS separation information for the printer that you selected as the Separations Printer in CMS Setup. When it is finally time to make the color separations for the whole file, printing is much faster because PageMaker uses the information in this file instead of calculating at print time.

VIEWING YOUR WORK

You have now completed the poster.

1 To see your work, choose Guides and Rulers from the Layout menu and then disable Show Guides.

2 Choose View from the Layout menu, and choose Fit in Window from the submenu.

3 To see the contrast in appearance when color management is off, display the Preferences dialog box. Click the CMS Setup button, and turn Color Management off. Click OK twice. Notice the change in the appearance of the large background image.

PRINTING A TILED DRAFT

To see a detailed draft of this large poster, you can print it at full size on your desktop printer's standard-size paper by using PageMaker's print tiling feature.

1 Choose Print from the File menu. In the Print Document dialog box, choose a PPD that is appropriate for your desktop printer.

2 Click the Paper button, or click Options if you've chosen a non-PostScript printer. Choose Auto from the Tiling list. Type 3 in the Overlap box to set a 3-pica margin around the image on each tile. For this single-page project, you don't need to change any other settings.

The Overlap setting must be at least equal to your printer's minimum margin. That figure varies from printer to printer, but ¼-inch is a common figure for PostScript printers. Non-PostScript printers sometimes have wider margins. *Minimum margin* means an area around the edge of the physical piece of paper where the printer just won't print, no matter what you do. (To determine the minimum margins for your printer, create a new one-page document and fill the page completely with a gray rectangle. Then print the page, and see how wide the white margins are.)

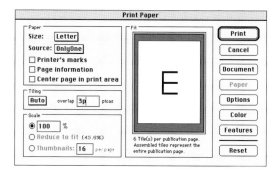

3 Click Print if you wish to print now. PageMaker outputs the poster on as many pieces of paper as necessary. The images are positioned so that you can fasten them together to form a complete, full-size image.

CREATING AN ACROBAT FILE

As a final step, you want to put the poster on a Web page that lists sporting events. You decide to post it as a PDF file (Adobe's Portable Document Format) to preserve all the design and formatting of the publication. PDF files are viewable by both Acrobat Reader and Acrobat Exchange.

To complete the following steps, you must have Acrobat Distiller and Acrobat Reader installed on your system. Both of these applications ship with PageMaker 6. For more information about installing them, see "What You Need to Know" at the font of this book.

Creating a PDF document is a two-step process. First Distiller writes a PostScript file from the original. Then it "distills" this PostScript file into a PDF file. If you choose Distill Now in the following procedure, it performs both steps. If you choose Prepare PostScript File for Distilling Separately, it creates the PostScript file and stops. You can then use Acrobat Distiller as a separate application to open the PostScript file and convert (distill) it to an Acrobat PDF file.

The Distill Now option specified in the following steps is memory-intensive because it requires that PageMaker, Acrobat Distiller, and Acrobat Reader all be open at the same time. If you receive notices of insufficient memory when you attempt to distill *05Work.pm6* into a PDF document, there are two possible solutions. If your system supports virtual memory, enable it. PageMaker works well with virtual memory. The other solution is to use

Create Adobe PDF only to prepare a PostScript file and to then use Acrobat Distiller as a separate application. This option is described in the Distilling Later section at the end of Project 4.

1 Choose Create Adobe PDF from the File menu. PageMaker asks if you wish to save the document first. Answer Yes.

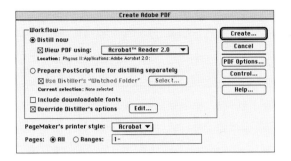

PageMaker displays the Create Adobe PDF dialog box.

2 Be sure than that Acrobat is chosen as PageMaker's Printer Style.

This ensures that Distiller uses the special Acrobat PPD.

3 Enable Distill Now, and enable View PDF Using. Choose Acrobat Reader 2.0.1 from the pop-up menu.

Distill Now instruct Distiller to perform both parts of the operation: create a PostScript file from the PageMaker publication, and then distill it into a PDF file. The View PDF Using choice instructs the plug-in to automatically open and display the new PDF document in Acrobat Reader as soon as distillation is complete.

Acrobat Distiller is a separate application in which you can set a number of options. The Edit button next to Override Distiller's Options allows you to change these Distiller settings from within PageMaker.

The Options are all truly optional, but to get an idea of what you can do, the next steps tell you how to add Document Information to the PDF file and how to add a Note.

4 Click the PDF Options button. Click the Add Document Information box if it's not already checked. When it's checked, click Edit Info.

5 In the Document Information dialog box, fill in the Title, Subject, Author, and Keywords boxes with any information that you would like to make available to those who view the document in Acrobat Reader. Click OK.

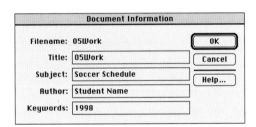

6 Still in the PDF Options dialog box, click Add Note to First Page.

This creates a note in a window that opens with the PDF file. If you choose Display Opened, the window containing the note is open when the PDF document opens. It can then be closed just like any other window. If you choose Display Closed, a small note icon appears in the upper left corner of the Acrobat document. The viewer can double-click the icon to open the Note window and view your information. The text on the title bar of the Note window is whatever you type in the Label box. Material that you type in the Note box appears in the Note window in the PDF file.

7 Click OK to return to the Create Adobe PDF dialog box.

8 Click Create. The Create Adobe PDF plug-in displays a dialog box in which you can navigate to the folder where you want to put the new file. By default, the new filename will be the old file name with *pdf* replacing the *pm6* extension at the end. You are free to change this name if you want to, but it's a good idea to keep the *pdf*. The extension identifies the file type.

11 Click Save. Create Adobe PDF first writes a PostScript file from the PageMaker original and then Acrobat Distiller creates the PDF file. If you enabled View PDF Using Acrobat Reader—and if Acrobat Reader is installed on your system—the newly created PDF document appears. Your note is in a window on the upper left. To see the document information that you entered, choose Document Information, General from the File menu.

FINISHING UP

Close all open files, and quit or exit Acrobat Distiller, Acrobat Reader, and PageMaker 6.

Welcome to World Wide Sport!

Finally there is space where sports fans all over the world can get up-to-the-minute event schedules, information and statistics. World Wide Sport provides the information you need to track sporting events around the globe. While you're here, check out the photographs and biographical profiles of players and teams as well as all the latest scores and stories.

Click the buttons below to find World Wide Sports info

SportsLink

World Wide Sport is pleased to bring you SportsLink, the best collection of sports information on-line. Access up to the minute sports reporting and information with the World Wide Sport web page. Link to other international sports updates, and U.S. college sport pages. Below is a list of other web locations of interest to sports fans. Each is updated at least weekly. Click on a hot link to go to the home page of your choice.

> Boxing Federation of America
> Cambridge University Rowing
> Danish World Cup
> Eurosport Race Report: Formula One Favorites
> German Grand Prix: Hockenheim, the Track
> Italian World Cup Info Page
> Jai-Lai Center/ Mexico City

6

PageMaker's new HTML Author plug-in means that you can now create a publication in PageMaker and then export it to HTML format, the file-type used as the source of

WORLD WIDE WEB PAGE

pages on the World Wide Web. This project includes a discussion of issues you face when designing for the Web and then takes you step by step through the whole process. You assemble a PageMaker publication that meets the requirements of a Web page and add active areas—links and anchors—that allow the end user to jump to different documents. Then you use the HTML Author plug-in to generate the HTML file, including a note and file description that are accessible to the end user in separate windows.

In this project, you create a home page for the World Wide Web. Your client is a sporting goods company that wants to promote goodwill and a positive image for itself by using its Web page to provide sports scheduling information.

WORLD WIDE WEB PAGE

This project is designed to teach you something about the constraints and opportunities involved in designing for the World Wide Web. You create two pages in PageMaker and then use PageMaker's new HTML Author tool to convert them into the HTML files that Web browsers use as their source.

In this project you learn:

- HTML design issues

- How to use the HTML Author plug-in to create anchors and links

- How to export the PageMaker file to HTML

This project should take you about 1 hour to complete.

BEFORE YOU BEGIN

1 Return all settings to their defaults by deleting the *Adobe PageMaker 6.x Prefs* file from the *Preferences* folder (Macintosh) or by removing *\pm6\rsrc\usenglish\pm6.cnf* from the drive containing PageMaker (Windows).

2 Launch the Adobe PageMaker application.

3 Choose Preferences from the File menu, and then select Millimeters as the units for Measurements In and Vertical Ruler.

By setting the preferences when no document is open, you are setting the PageMaker defaults.

4 Open *06Final.pm6* in *06Project* to see how the Web page will look when you have completed the steps in this project.

5 Choose Guides and Rulers from the Layout menu, and make sure Snap to Guides is enabled.

ABOUT DESIGNING FOR THE WEB

When you design for the HTML (hypertext mark-up language) files that underlie World Wide Web pages, you have less control over the appearance of the text than with other media. The font, font size, measure, and indents that you choose will be replaced by other specifications when the file is viewed online. This is because people who are "surfing the Web" use Web browsers to display the HTML files.

An HTML file is a text file that includes the text that the reader will see, plus several kinds of codes. There are many HTML codes, but they fall into three general categories: codes that identify types of text (for example, header or numbered list); codes that display graphics; and function codes that jump the reader to another location or invoke an online utility such as a mail program.

A Web browser controls the typeface and point size used to display each type of paragraph. The size of the window on the user's computer determines the measure (the text width). In most browsers, the user can set the font and type size that the browser uses to display Web pages. There are default settings that are in wide use: typically, 12-point Times Roman for body type and lists, and larger sizes of Times Roman for heads. Most people don't change these defaults. Some do.

Paragraph codes

When you use PageMaker 6 to create an HTML Web page, you first use PageMaker to create a document, and then you use the HTML Author plug-in to create an HTML file from the PageMaker file. HTML 2.0 has a limited inventory of paragraph types. There is a very specific list of possibilities. A paragraph can be a title, one of six levels of heading, a body paragraph, an indented block, a numbered (ordered) list, a bulleted (unordered) list, or an address. There are a few other paragraph types on the basic HTML list. Some Web browsers, such as Netscape, offer enhancements to the basic list. That means that there are more possibilities. However, these possibilities are specific to each browser. If you use a style option in one browser, and view the file from another browser that doesn't support that option, the text reverts to one of the default types. PageMaker's HTML Author plug-in supports only the basic HTML 2.0 codes.

Web pages can—and usually do—include links. The user clicks on an active ("hot") area of text or on a linked graphic and sees some other text or graphic that is linked to that spot. The link can be another place in the file, another file on your system, or a file anywhere on the Internet.

Acrobat and the Web

Although your HTML files will look different to different viewers, depending on the settings they have made in their Web browsers, you can link to Adobe Acrobat PDF files whenever you have material whose formatting you want to preserve. You do this by creating links to these PDF files in your HTML document or you can post the PDF files as independent documents. Older Web browsers view PDF files by invoking Acrobat Reader when they encounter a PDF file. The "Amber" release of Acrobat works more closely with Web browsers, however. With the "Amber" release of Acrobat, users will be able to view PDF documents directly from "Amber"-enabled Web browsers. PDF files are therefore a good option for maintaining creative control over your Web pages.

Authoring for the Web

What does all this mean to you as a writer and designer? It means that for HTML files, your designs must be flexible. They have to accommodate the possible range of typefaces and sizes that a browser may use. You can't specify tabs, indents, or paragraph alignment because the browser does that for you. Lists, for example, are always indented. Body text never is.

Designing for the HTML files presents you with possibilities as well as with limitations. For example, you don't have to pack everything into one linear sequence the way you do on paper. The ability to link files greatly enhances the range of things you can do. You just have to learn to "think link."

The typical arrangement in an HTML Web page is an alternating sequence of text and graphics. Use lists, indented text, and graphics to break up the text and keep the viewer involved and interested.

Graphics on the Web

It's important that graphics files be as small as possible when they're going to be viewed online, because a large graphic loads very slowly. JPEG and CompuServe's GIF are graphic file formats that are popular for online use because they are compact and look good on-screen. Neither one is a particularly good choice for high-end paper output, because they don't contain enough color information. In this project, we use GIF (also called GIFF on Macintosh and Unix platforms). It is currently the most widely used graphic format on the Web.

CREATING THE PAGEMAKER SOURCE DOCUMENT

The first step in creating your Web page is to create the source document in PageMaker.

1 Start a new document. In the Document Setup dialog box, leave the page size set to Letter. Make sure the Tall orientation is selected, deselect the Double-sided option, and set the Number of Pages to 2. Specify right and left margins of 25.4 millimeters and top and bottom margins of zero. Click OK to accept the settings.

2 Save the document in *Projects* as *06Work.pm6*.

3 To place the text, display the Place Document dialog box and choose *WebText.doc*. Click on page 1 between the margins near the top of thek page to flow the text into the document.

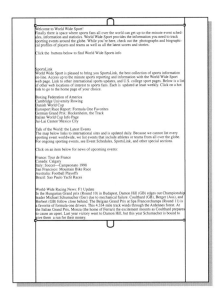

The text fills the area between the margins. You'll adjust the vertical position of the text block after applying some paragraph styles to the text.

4 Zoom in on the first few paragraphs. Click an insertion point at the beginning of the first line "Welcome to…" and press Return or Enter to create a blank line above it.

5 Put the insertion point in the blank line and display the Place Document dialog box. Double-click *WWSport.gif* to place it in *06Work.pm6* as an inline graphic.

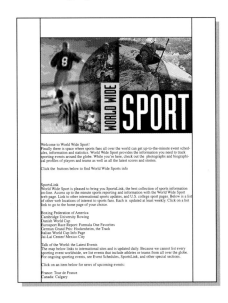

Because you had an insertion point at the time you placed the graphic, it was automatically placed as an inline graphic in the publication.

APPLYING HTML STYLES

Now you want to apply paragraph styles to the text. You have two options. One is to create and apply any PageMaker styles that you want to and then specify the correspondence between these styles and the HTML styles that the HTML Author uses. The second option, described in the following steps, is to import the HTML styles into your document and apply them directly.

1 Display the Styles palette, and notice that only the PageMaker default paragraph styles are present. Choose PageMaker Plug-ins from the Utilities menu, and choose HTML Author from the submenu.

2 Click the Preferences tab, leave all the settings as they are, and then click OK.

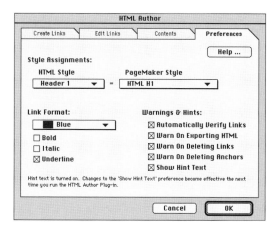

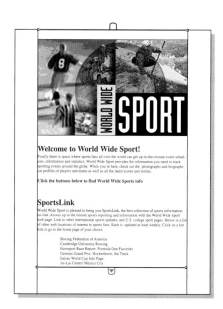

You don't have to do anything other than open and close the dialog box to import the styles. We'll take a closer look at the HTML Author dialog box a little later in this project.

Your Styles palette now contains 20 or more styles that begin with the letters *HTML*.

Next, you apply HTML Body Text style to all of the imported text. Then the only remaining text formatting is to apply the nonbody styles.

3 Select the text tool, and click an insertion point anywhere in the text you just placed. Select All, and apply the HTML Body Text style.

4 Go to page 1 and zoom in on the first few paragraphs under the graphic. Apply HTML H1 to the first paragraph ("Welcome to…").

5 Use the pointer tool to select the text block on page 1. Place the pointer over text—not over the graphic—and drag the text block so that the top of it is as close as it can get to the top of the page without actually touching the top. If the text block touches or crosses the top of the page, the page won't get converted to HTML. Be sure the text block remains positioned between the right and left margins.

6 Apply HTML H3 to the third paragraph ("Click the buttons…"). Skip the blank paragraphs and apply HTML H1 to the paragraph that begins with *Sports Link*.

7 Skip the next paragraph, and select the six lines of the list that begins with *Boxing Federation* and ends with *Jai-Lai Center*. Apply HTML Unordered List.

This style creates automatic bullets in the final document, but you don't see them in the PageMaker file.

8 Select the text block with the pointer tool and roll up the windowshade so that the last visible line is the *Jai-Lai Center* one.

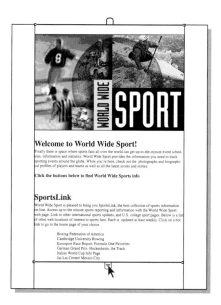

9 Click on the bottom windowshade handle to load the text cursor and turn to page 2. Click between the margins near the top of the page to flow the text onto the page.

10 Continue applying HTML styles. The line that begins *Talk of the World* gets HTML H1. Apply HTML H2 to the *Click on an item* line. The next six paragraphs (France to Brazil) should be HTML Ordered List.

The Ordered List style produces autonumbering in the online document.

11 Finally, apply HTML H2 to the paragraph that begins with *World-Wide Racing*.

12 Now is a good time to save *06Work.pm6*.

ADDING GRAPHICS

1 Return to page 1. There are three blank lines below the line that begins *Click the buttons*. Place an insertion point in the first blank line and display the Place Document dialog box. Double-click *MapBtn.gif* to place it in the blank line as an inline graphic.

2 Move the insertion point down one line so that it's in the second blank line. Display the Place Document dialog box and double-click on *EventBtn.gif* to place it as an inline graphic.

3 Look at the bottom of page 1 and make sure that the *Jai-Lai Center* line is still visible. Lengthen the text block if necessary.

4 Go to page 2. Place the insertion point in the blank line that's right above the *Talk of the World* line, display the Place Document dialog box, and place *WWMap.gif* as an inline graphic.

TIP: AN EASY WAY
TO ACCESS THE HTML
AUTHOR IS BY CHOOS-
ING SCRIPTS FROM THE
WINDOW MENU TO
DISPLAY THE SCRIPTS
PALETTE. THEN OPEN THE
PLUG-INS MENU TO
DISPLAY THE LIST, AND
DOUBLE-CLICK ON
HTML AUTHOR.

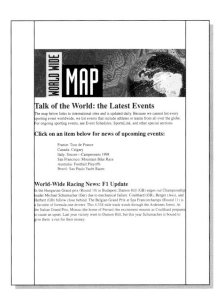

Note: If there's no blank line above Talk of the World, *return to the bottom of page 1 and roll the text block up a little so that the blank line pops to page 2.*

5 Use the pointer tool to position the page 2 text block so that its top is as close as possible to the top of the page without actually touching it, just as you did on page 1. If necessary, drag the bottom handle of the windowshade so that all the text is visible.

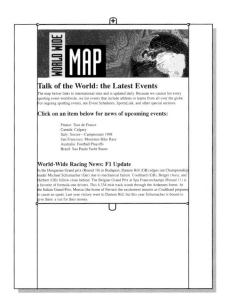

6 With the text tool, click an insertion point in the blank paragraph that precedes the *Click on an item* line. Place *Map.gif* as an inline graphic in the blank line.

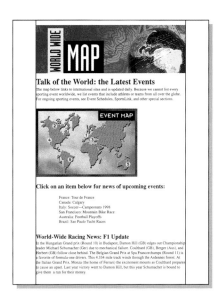

Your final step before invoking the HTML Author plug-in is to set the margins to zero. The HTML Author plug-in will issue messages if anything, including a text block, is touching a margin. You no longer need the margins because you've completed the source document, so the easiest solution is to set all margins to zero before using the HTML Author plug-in to create the HTML document.

7 Choose Document Setup from the File menu, and set the right and left margins to zero. Click OK.

8 Save *06Work.pm6*.

That's it. You've placed and formatted all the text and graphics in the PageMaker file that is the source of your Web page. Take a look at *06Final.pm6* to see if your two pages look like the example.

Note: An interim file is provided with the steps completed up to this point. If you want to complete the rest of this project without having to do the earlier steps, go to 06Project, *open* 06Inter1.pt6, *and save it in* Projects.

Time out for a movie

 If your system is capable of running Adobe Teach movies, play the movie named *HTML Author* to see a preview of how to create links and anchors in HTML documents using Adobe PageMaker's HTML Author plug-in. For information on how to view Adobe Teach movies, see "Watching Adobe Teach Movies" at the beginning of this book.

LINKS AND ANCHORS

To a person viewing a Web page, a link is a place they can click on that will then show them new text or graphics. A link is also known as a *hot spot.* In most browsers, the mouse pointer indicates that it is over a hot spot by changing to a pointing-hand symbol.

A link can jump to another point inside the current document, or it can jump to another document. To jump to a place inside the current document, you must designate the point to jump to by placing an *anchor*.

The fascinating thing about links is that users never know whether they're going to stay in the same location or be jumped to some place on the other side of the world. You, as the Web page author, get to make this magic happen.

Creating an anchor

The first link in your Web page will be a link between the World Map button on the first page and the Event Map on the second page. When an active area links to a point inside the same document, the spot that it should link to must be identified with an *anchor.* You begin by creating an anchor for the map.

1 On page 2, select the Event Map inline graphic (*Map.gif*) with the text tool.

Next, you display the HTML Author plug-in again, but this time you use the Scripts palette to access it. It doesn't matter whether you use the menu or the palette to access it. Using the Scripts palette is a little easier.

2 Choose Scripts from the Window menu. In the Scripts palette, click the triangle (Macintosh) or plus sign (Windows) next to Plug-ins to display the list, and then double-click HTML Author.

3 Choose Anchor from the Create pop-up list and type **world map** in the Enter Anchor Label box.

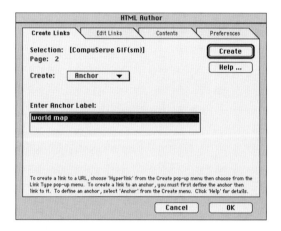

4 Click the Create button, and then click OK.

You've now named an anchor point that you can refer to later when creating a link. There's no change in the appearance of the graphic.

Note: This procedure sometimes magnifies the page image. You may need to zoom out to a more comfortable view

Creating a link to an anchor

1 Display page 1 and select the World Map button graphic with the text tool.

2 Display the HTML Author dialog box by choosing it from the menu or from the Scripts palette.

3 This time, choose Hyperlink from the Create pop-up list. Then click the Link Type pop-up list and choose Link to Anchor from the bottom of the list.

4 Highlight *world map* in the Choose Anchor list. (If you had created other anchor points, they would all be listed here.) Click the Create button. Click OK.

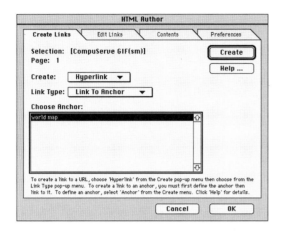

You've just created a link between the World Map graphic on page 1 and the map itself on page 2. Notice that the World Map graphic on page 1 now has a thin blue line around it, showing that it is an active, or linked, area.

4 Save *06Work.pm6*.

Creating hyperlinks to other documents

Now you want to link the Event Schedules graphic button on page 1 to an HTML document that displays a schedule.

1 Use the text tool to select the Event Schedules graphic on page 1.

2 Display the HTML Author dialog box again, and choose Hyperlink from the Create pop-up menu (or leave it chosen—PageMaker remembers your last choice).

3 Choose the blank from the top of the Link Type pop-up menu.

You choose the blank because you are linking to a local file. To link to a site on the Internet, you could choose one of the list entries to place the appropriate code in the URL (uniform resource locator) box.

4 In the Enter URL box, type **Schedule.htm.** Click Create, and then click OK.

Schedule.htm is the file you are linking to.

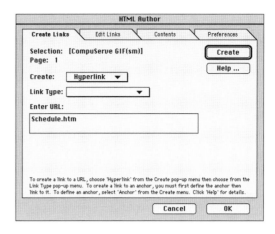

To link to a file on the World Wide Web, select http:// or http://www. from the Link Type list and then include the entire path (location and name) of the file. You are using the plain form here (without the http://) because you are linking to a local file. This means that you will be able to view your work in an HTML viewer without actually being connected to the Internet.

5 Go to page 2 of *06Work.pm6,* and zoom in on the list that's under the Event Map.

In the next two steps, you link the line of text that references the Tour de France to a GIF file that shows a map of the race course. Then you link the line about soccer in Italy to a GIF file that displays a schedule of soccer games.

6 Highlight the first line of the list (France…) with the text tool. Display the HTML Author dialog box, and leave Create set to Hyperlink and the Link Type set to blank. Enter **TourMap.gif** for the URL. Click Create and then click OK.

7 Highlight the third line on the list (Italy…) and display the HTML Author dialog box again. Leave Create set to Hyperlink and the Link Type set to blank. Type **Soccer.gif** into the Enter URL box. Click Create and then click OK.

This creates a link between the highlighted text and a file named *Soccer.gif.*

Editing a link

That last link (*Soccer.gif*) was wrong. The filename that you want to link to is actually *SocPostr.gif*. You need to edit the link.

1 With nothing selected, display the HTML Author plug-in again. Click the Edit Links tab at the top of the dialog box.

2 In the list of links, highlight the one you need to change ("Italy: Soccer..."). Click the Modify button.

3 In the box next to Link to URL, change *Soccer.gif* to *SocPostr.gif*. Click OK and then click OK again to exit the HTML Author dialog box.

4 Now save *06Work.pm6*, spell check it, and compare it to *06Final.pm6*.

If you're not familiar with spell checking, Project 7 contains detailed steps for spell checking a publication.

EXPORTING HTML

The final step in this process is to use the HTML Author tool to export an HTML file.

The HTML Author plug-in adds the HTML codes that Web browsers require to display a page.

1 Make sure nothing is selected in the PageMaker file, and display the HTML Author dialog box once again. This time, click the Contents tab.

2 Click the New button. In the New HTML Document dialog box, enable PageMaker Pages.

This ensures that the HTML document will display page by page just as it appears in the original PageMaker document. Choosing the Stories option would cause a story to be displayed in one contiguous chunk, even if it had threaded through several non-contiguous pages in the original PageMaker document.

3 In the Document Title box, enter **World Wide Sport**.

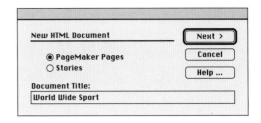

This is the name that will appear in the title bar of the window when the file is displayed in a Web browser or HTML viewer.

4 Click the Next button. In the Assign dialog box, click the Add All button to specify that the HTML document should include all the pages in the PageMaker document.

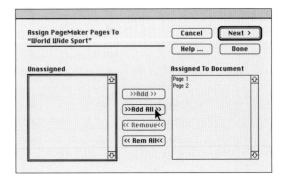

If you wanted to create an HTML document that included only some of the PageMaker pages, this is where you would select which pages to include.

5 Click the Next button. You now need to specify a name and location for the HTML file that you are creating. Navigate to *06Project* and enter *06Web.html* (Macintosh) or *06Web.htm* (Windows) for the file name.

You need to put the HTML file in *06Project* rather than in *Projects* so that the links are in the right place when you view the file.

6 Enable Export HTML Now and click OK (Macintosh), or click Export HTML (Windows).

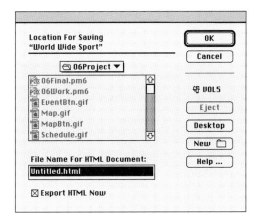

PageMaker informs you of its progress as it creates the HTML file. If any graphics are too close to the edges, you get a warning about "crossing margins." It's okay, so just click OK.

7 When the process is finished, you are still looking at the main HTML Authoring window, so click OK one more time to exit.

VIEWING THE WEB PAGE

To view your newly created HTML file, you need a Web browser or HTML viewer. Web browsers let you view HTML documents on your local system as well as documents on a network. We use Netscape in the following example. You will find similar functionality in any Web browser or HTML viewer that you may have available.

1 Launch Netscape, and choose Open File from the File menu.

If you were looking for something located on the Internet rather than a local file, you would choose Open Location. At that point, Netscape would look to see if you were connected to the Internet and would dial your Internet access provider if necessary.

2 Navigate to *06Project*, and choose *06Web.html* (Macintosh) or *06Web.htm* (Windows). Netscape opens your HTML file.

3 To experience the functionality of the links, click each of the places where you created a link. When you are done viewing the link, click the Back button.

Most Web browsers operate in a similar fashion. Text that is linked is in a different color and is often underlined. (You set this appearance in your Web browser options or preferences.) Linked graphics usually have a colored line around them or are visually distinguished in some way. Every browser has a Back command that returns you to the previous screen after you have clicked a link.

4 Close all open files. Quit PageMaker.

ADOBE ON THE WEB

If you have Internet access and a Web browser, be sure to visit Adobe's home page at http://www.adobe.com/

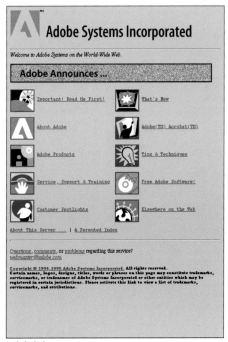

Adobe's home page

You will find information about Adobe products (including information about HTML Author as it evolves), free software and upgrades, tips and tricks from experts, links to other Web sites, and information about how to configure your Web browser to view Adobe Acrobat PDF files. New goodies are added frequently, so don't miss it!

Volume 23

SUMMER 1998

Frenetic **Fun** for the **Physically** Fit

Adventure

Special Issue

Travel

Bungee Jumping in Mexico

For a honeymoon it was a bit of a stretch, but for travel and adventure, bungee jumping is the way to go

Let me say first thing that I've never been suicidal, that I get vertigo if I look down while waiting on the curb to cross the street, and that my idea of adventure is eating two scoops of ice cream instead of one scoop of fat-free frozen yogurt.

But then I got married and went to Mexico with my new husband. In Mexico, we thought, there would be romantic nights in resort rooms reeking of vanilla. Yes, vanilla. More of an amateur chef than a wild woman, I find my thrills in cooking concoctions that make people drool. In some of my culinary research, I'd read how vanilla originated in El Tajín, an area in the northern state of Veracruz in Mexico along the Gulf. Better yet, the Totonacs—the dominant native tribe there—regard vanilla as an aphrodisiac.

My husband-to-be had okayed this destination because he was interested in the spectacular archaeological ruins in the area. Settled at least 2,000 years ago, El Tajín boasts the Pyramid of the Niches

among its many excavations. Also, being a chocoholic, he asked that our route include a few days in Tabasco, the adjacent southern Mexican state that made chocolate a survival food around the world.

We flew into Mexico City, then on to Poza Rica, where we caught a local taxi to our hotel in Papantla. The scent of vanilla perfumed the air, wafting from the dried seed pods and bottles of extract being sold by Totonacs wandering the streets. In our own wanderings through the museums and cultural center, we learned that Totonac men are renown polygamists, lusty men who usually die before reaching age fifty. Inhaling the ubiquitous vanilla, I could understand why.

The vanilla affected me, too, but my impulses took a different turn.

One day, near the entrance of the archaeological zone, we watched a traditional Totonac ceremony now performed for tourists: what's called Indian flying and looked to me like the original bungee

Continued on page 2

EDITOR'S NOTE

How was my vacation? I thought you'd never ask. Frankly, it was fantastic—and sometimes frightening. That means it was thrilling, too, and I crave adrenaline rushes the way most people need chocolate. So would I do it again? You betcha.

When world-class rafting expert Jon Benson invited me on his whitewater rafting trip down the Yangtze River in China, I blurted yes even before he'd finished wrapping his lips around the question. The chance to raft with someone of Jon's daredevil attitude on one of the world's wildest rivers promised too many exciting chills and spills to miss.

Reluctantly, I'm back behind my desk, feeling the same kind of letdown that action addicts feel when the intensity ends. You know what I mean, I'm glad to be back—sort of.

This issue of Adventure Travel features real-life stories by me and other outdoor maniacs who've forsaken luxury resorts for the thrill of rugged challenges in remote locations. Keep your eyes open for our next issue and as we like to say...happy trails to you!

Britta Munstead, Editor,
Adventure Travel

This project is a newsletter published by a consortium of companies that provide travel-related services. Although it is small enough to be called a newsletter, the

ADVENTURE NEWSLETTER

variety and complexity of its layout are those of a magazine. It is a professional publication with excellent typography and design. The focus of this project is on issues of professional-level typography and layout. Many of the elements are provided for you in a library, so that you can skip over more mundane tasks and concentrate on mastering professional layout skills.

In Project 7, you lay out two pages of a periodical newsletter. To maintain the professional appearance of this highly designed publication, you create a leading grid to ensure that the pieces align in an ordered way so that the complex page re-

ADVENTURE NEWSLETTER

tains a unified and harmonious overall appearance. You also employ a number of PageMaker's typographic controls and use the Story Editor for tasks such as spell-checking and replacing certain characters.

In this project you learn how to:

- Create a leading grid to align both type and graphics to a common grid

- Use the Guide Manager

- Use Partial Autoflow

- Apply Expert Kerning

- Create a page that has different column layouts on different parts of the page

- Use paragraph settings to control column breaks

- Use the "Add Cont'd Line" plug-in

- Use the Story Editor to find and replace characters

- Perform a spell check

- Use more of PageMaker's image-control features

- Force-justify a line

- Control hyphenation and widows

This project should take you about 2 hours to complete.

BEFORE YOU BEGIN

1 Return all settings to their defaults by deleting the *Adobe PageMaker 6.x Prefs* file from the *Preferences* folder (Macintosh) or by removing \pm6\rsrc\usenglish\pm6.cnf from the drive containing PageMaker (Windows).

2 Make sure that the Myriad Multiple Master family of fonts is installed, as well as Corvinus Skyline, AGaramond, and AGaramond Semi bold Italic.

3 Launch Adobe PageMaker 6 and open the *07Final.pm6* file in *07Project* to see how the completed newsletter will look.

SETTING UP THE FILE

1 Choose New from the File menu to open the Document Setup dialog box.

2 Set the Page Size to Custom, the Dimensions to 9 by 16 inches, and the Orientation to Tall. Make sure that the Double-sided and Facing Pages options are enabled.

3 Set Number of Pages to 2, and set all four margins to 0.75 inch.

4 Click OK, and save your new document in *Projects* as *07Work.pm6*.

CREATING A LEADING GRID

The following steps create an invisible grid that is usually referred to as a *leading grid*. The grid affects much more than leading, however. When this grid is in place, objects—text blocks and graphics—align in a way that makes it easy to achieve an underlying sense of order on the page. A page with a complex layout can easily begin to feel chaotic and disorganized. Enabling this grid makes it easier to maintain an integrated and harmonious appearance.

The first step is to set the tick marks on the vertical ruler to equal the vertical spacing (leading) that you are going to use for body text.

1 Double-click the pointer in the Toolbox to open the Preferences dialog box. Set Measurements In to Picas, set the Vertical Ruler to Custom, and type **14** in the Points box. Click OK.

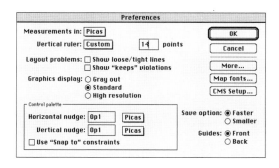

You set the vertical ruler to 14 points because the body text leading for this project is 14 points.

2 Zoom in on the left side of the page so that you can easily see the tick marks on the ruler.

The numbers on the ruler now show the number of 14-point lines rather than picas. Each text line is shown by a slightly larger tick mark and is divided into thirds by smaller tick marks. If the Leading Method for a paragraph is set to Proportional, the baseline of each text line rests on the second small tick mark for each line. If the Leading Method is Baseline, the baseline rests on the large tick mark.

Note: To set the Leading Method, click the Spacing button in the Paragraph Specifications dialog box.

3 Choose Guides and Rulers from the Layout menu. In the submenu, turn on Snap to Rulers.

You've now set the ruler tick marks equal to your basic body leading and told PageMaker to snap objects to those tick marks (Snap to Rulers).

4 Choose Guides and Rulers from the Layout menu again, and make sure that Show Rulers, Show Guides, and Snap to Guides are all enabled.

The steps you have just completed will help object move easily into place, and help ensure that objects are aligned.

SETTING UP THE MASTER PAGES

The majority of pages in this newsletter have three columns, so you begin by specifying a three column layout on the master pages. While you're on the master pages, you also create the title header that appears at the top of the inside pages.

Setting the columns

When you set columns on a master page, they appear on all publication pages that use that master page.

1 Click the master page icon at the bottom of the document window to display the left and right Document Master pages.

PageMaker shows you both master pages because you chose Facing Pages in the Document Setup dialog box.

2 Choose Column Guides from the Layout menu and specify three columns with 1 pica 6 points (1p6) of Space Between. Click OK.

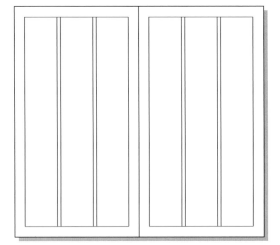

Because Set Left and Right Pages Separately is unchecked, your settings apply to both right and left document pages.

Creating the running head

1 With the zoom tool, drag a selection marquee near the top of the left master page and across the full width of the page. Make it only a couple of inches high.

2 Drag a guide from the top ruler down to approximately 3p1. Select the text tool, and drag a text column across the entire width of the page above the columns. Type in the words **Adventure—Travel** putting an em dash, with no spaces, between the two words.

Note: To type an em dash, hold down the Shift and Option keys and type a hyphen (Macintosh) or hold down the Control and Shift keys and type = (Windows).

3 Use the pointer tool to size and position the text block so that it extends the full width of the page. Position the bottom of the windowshade on the guide at 3p1.

The bottom of the windowshade snaps easily to the guide because you have Snap to Guides turned on.

4 Use the text tool to select the text. Display the character view of the Control palette, and make the text 10 point MyriadMM 830 Black 300 Cond. Click the All Caps button to make the text uppercase. Change to the paragraph view, and apply a left indent of 18 picas and a right indent of 18 picas.

Next, you use the Force Justify Alignment button in the Control palette to add letterspacing.

5 With the text still selected, click the Force Justify Alignment button in the Control palette.

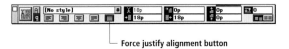

— Force justify alignment button

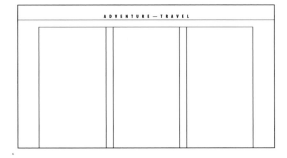

PageMaker adds equal amounts of space between each character to make the text fill the measure.

Note: If the text has word spaces, PageMaker justifies the line by adding all the necessary space to the word spaces. The workaround is to use nonbreaking spaces. When these are present, PageMaker does just the right thing to force justification: the word spaces are a little larger than the letterspaces, so the line is easy to read and looks nice.

TIP: THERE'S AN EASY WAY TO ACCESS MOST OF THE PAGEMAKER PLUG-INS: CHOOSE SCRIPTS FROM THE WINDOW MENU. OPEN THE SCRIPTS MENU, AND THEN OPEN PLUG-INS. YOU CAN NOW ACCESS ANY PLUG-IN BY DOUBLE-CLICKING ON IT.

So far so good: you've created a page header for the left-hand pages. Now you need to duplicate it on the right master page.

6 Select the header text block with the pointer tool, and copy it. Pan to the right master page, zoom in on the top, just as you did for the left master page, and paste. Then use the pointer tool to drag the text block so that it sits against the left side of the page (filling the page width) and so that the bottom of the windowshade is on the 3p1 guide.

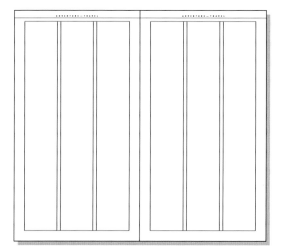

You've completed the master pages.

7 Save your document, and return to page 1 by clicking the page icon at the bottom of the Document window.

BEGINNING PAGE 1

You don't want the header to display on the first page.

1 Go to the Layout menu and disable Display Master Items.

The header that you created on the master page is no longer visible on page 1. It will still be visible on all pages that have Display Master Items enabled.

USING THE GUIDE MANAGER

Next, you use the Guide Manager to place a series of guides to help you position material on the page. The guides that you place by using the Guide Manager are exactly the same as the ones you drag from the rulers. Sometimes the Guide Manager is a more convenient way to place them, especially if you need a series of evenly spaced guides.

1 To display the Guide Manager, choose PageMaker Plug-ins from the Utilities menu and choose Guide Manager from the submenu.

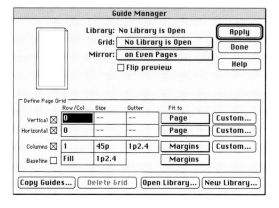

2 Deselect Vertical and Columns, and select Horizontal. To set your horizontal guides, click the Custom button that's on the same row as the word *Horizontal*. In the Customize Ruler Guides dialog box, click the New button.

3 The New Guide Position box is already highlighted, so type in the position for the first guide: **24p6**. Click New again and type in **49**. You don't need to type the **p** when nothing follows it, because you set your default measurements to picas in Preferences. Now click New and type in **53p3**. Finally, click New once more and type **59p6**.

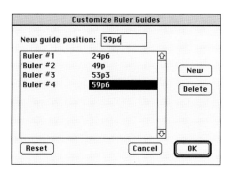

TIP: IF YOU'RE WORKING ON A WINDOWS SYSTEM, AND WANT TO CREATE A NEW LIBRARY, YOU MUST GIVE IT A NAME THAT ENDS IN ".PML".

4 Click OK in the Customize Ruler Guides dialog box, and then click Apply in the Guide Manager.

PageMaker displays the Apply Guides to Page dialog box.

5 Click Apply (Macintosh) or OK (Windows) to accept all the default settings.

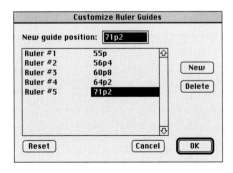

There are no existing guides that you want to replace, so you don't need to enable either of the Replace options. These guides are needed on page 1 only, so you don't need to choose a page range. Also, you don't want to apply the guides to a master page, so the default settings are exactly what you need.

6 Click Done. Go to page 2, and display the Guide Manager dialog box once more.

7 To place guides on page 2, repeat the process: Deselect Vertical and Columns, leaving Horizontal selected. Click the Horizontal Custom button. Click New for each guide you want to define, and define guides at 55, 56p4, 60p8, 64p2, and 71p2. Click OK, and then click Apply. In the Apply To box, be sure it says 2, and click Apply (Macintosh) or OK (Windows).

Note: You didn't have to change to page 2 to set the page 2 guides. You can specify whatever pages you want in the Apply To box.

8 Click Done to dismiss the Guide Manager dialog box.

9 Now is a good time to save your work. Remember to save often. In this Advanced book, we remind you only once in a while.

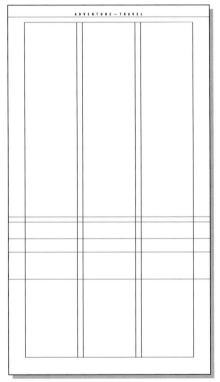

Page 2

The guides that you just created can be moved or deleted exactly like the ones that you drag from the rulers. They are, in fact, exactly the same.

PLACING ART ON PAGE 1

For this project, we have provided all of the art that you need, including the drop caps. Some—but not all—of the elements have been saved in a library. Several of the elements in the library were created in PageMaker itself and do not exist as separate files. The largest graphics are not included in the library, in order to preserve disk space.

1 Return to page 1, and choose Library from the Window menu to display the Open Library dialog box. Navigate to *07Project*, and double-click *07Lib.pml*. You should see several thumbnails, each with a title underneath. If you don't see both images and titles, click the Palette menu and choose Display Both.

The masthead items at the top of page 1 were created in PageMaker and saved in the library as AT Logo-Heading.

2 Drag AT Logo-Heading onto the top of the page. Release the mouse button to place the image, and then drag it with the pointer tool. When you drag it, a rectangle becomes visible. Place the left side of the rectangle against the left margin and the bottom of the rectangle on the guide at 24p6.

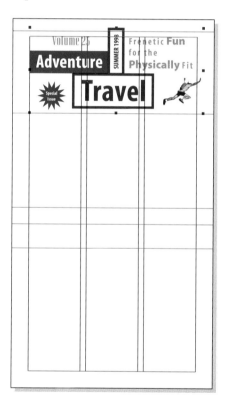

If black border doesn't appear as you drag the graphic, try dragging a little faster at the beginning. Once you've got the black border, you can slow down.

The next element is the large duotone photograph that goes on the top half of page 1.

3 Drag LeapDuo from the library, just as you did with the heading graphic, and position it so that the left side is against the left margin and the bottom rests on the guide that's at 49 picas.

PLACING THE TEXT

The *07Travel.doc* file contains the text of several articles for the current issue, including the bungee-jumping story. PageMaker's semiautomatic flow is the perfect way to place this story because if you used the fully automatic flow option (Layout, Autoflow), the text would fill all three columns. You don't want that, because the right column is reserved for another story. Manual flow would work, but you'd have to reload the cursor after each column.

1 Begin by displaying the page at Actual Size if it isn't already, and pan so that the two left columns below the large photograph are visible.

2 Display the Place Document dialog box, navigate to *07Project*, and double-click *07Travel.doc* (or single-click, and click OK).

PageMaker imports the text and gives you the automatic text-flow icon or the manual text-flow icon, depending on whether Autoflow is enabled in the Layout menu. Autoflow is disabled by default, so you probably have the manual text-flow icon.

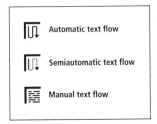

3 Hold down Shift to change to the semiautomatic text-flow icon.

4 Continue to hold down Shift and click inside the left column, starting a couple of inches below the photograph. You'll position the text more precisely later.

The text fills the column and stops. Your cursor is still a filled icon, ready to place more text.

5 Holding down Shift, click inside the second column at the same position to fill the second column.

There's more to the story, but you'll place that later.

6 Click on the pointer tool in the Toolbox to unload the cursor.

Note: When you click with a loaded text icon to place text, the text flows in and fills the width of the column if the icon is inside the column when you click. If the icon touches the column margin at all, PageMaker thinks you're outside the column and spreads the text the full width of the page margins. If that happens, roll the column completely up, and reload the text icon. Then place it again, being careful to have the pointer completely inside the column.

FORMATTING THE BUNGEE ARTICLE

You already know how to format paragraphs and how to create and apply paragraph styles, so for this project, you are just going to import the paragraph styles that you need from another publication. Later, you'll make a few changes to these styles, so you copy the styles from *07Styles.pm6*, rather than from *07Final.pm6*.

Importing styles

1 Choose Define Styles from the Type menu, and click Copy in the Define Styles dialog box.

2 In the Copy Styles scroll list, navigate to *07Project* if you're not there already, and double-click *07Styles.pm6*.

3 When you're asked if you want to copy the styles over the current styles, click OK. Click OK again to dismiss the Define Styles dialog box.

Your document now contains all the paragraph styles that you need to format the text in this newsletter.

Adding heads, graphics, and styles

The next step is to apply paragraph styles to all the paragraphs of the bungee-jumping story. You first apply the Body text style to all of the text. After that, all you have to do is apply headline styles where needed.

1 Choose the text tool, and click an insertion point anywhere in the article you just placed. Now Select All, and apply the Body text style.

Note: You can use the Styles palette or the Control palette to do this, or you can choose from the Styles list in the Type menu. It doesn't matter which technique you use.

The Body text paragraph style is now applied to the entire file that you just imported, not just the portion that's visible.

2 Select the first two paragraphs in the bungee article ("Bungee Jumping in Mexico" to "way to go"). Cut the two paragraphs, and then use the text tool to drag a text block across the top of the two columns under the photograph. Paste the two paragraphs into it.

3 Use the pointer tool or the arrow keys to position each of the two body text columns so that the first baseline rests on the 59p6 guide. Then click the newly pasted headline text block, and make sure that the text block fills the two-column width completely.

4 With the text tool, click in the first head, the one that says "Bungee Jumping in Mexico," and apply the Header 1 paragraph style.

Tracking and kerning

Compare the results with *07Final.pm6*, and notice that in the final version the headline fits in one line and there is not so much space between the letters. Typographers would say that the headline in *07Final.pm6* has a *firmer texture*. The perception of texture in type is a subtle, almost subliminal thing, but for that very reason, people respond strongly to it, even if they're not aware of doing so. Your goal as you work with type is to create a texture that's even and feels pleasant to look at—neither crowded nor loose. There are two ways to control typographic texture: tracking and kerning.

Tracking adjusts the space between letters evenly, adding or removing the same amount between each pair of letters. As type gets larger, letters need to be closer together to give a nice texture. Type that is less than 14 point almost never needs tightening, whereas most type over 30 point does need tracking. The exact amount required varies widely with the typeface.

The second technique for controlling texture in type is called *kerning*. Kerning adjusts the space between individual pairs of letters. As type gets larger, unevenness in letter spacing becomes more apparent. The letters **TA**, for example, look as though they have extra space between them compared with other letters. They need to be kerned (moved together).

PageMaker's Expert Kerning feature produces excellent type effortlessly by different kern values to each individual pair of characters. It combines these kern values with the information you supply about what degree of correction (Design Class) you need. The Design Class is the document type. It addresses the fact that text type should not be quite as tightly spaced as headline (display) type. Very large type (poster), on the other hand, can be spaced very tightly indeed and still look good and be easy to read.

The kind of adjustment between letters that you get from Expert Kerning is much more sophisticated than the effect you get by assigning a track or by manual kerning. Use Expert Kerning only on larger sizes of type, typically 36 points or over. In the next step, you use PageMaker's Expert Kern-ing feature to reduce space selectively between characters.

1 Select the whole "Bungee Jumping" headline with the text tool, (Macintosh only) and choose Expert Kerning from the Type menu. Set the the Kern Strength to .80 and the Design Class to Display. Click OK.

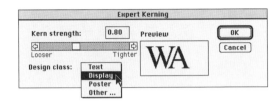

Watch as PageMaker's Expert Kerning reduces the space between each pair of letters. The headline should now fit on one line and match the one in *07Final.pm6*.

(Windows) In the Character view of the Control palette, choose Tight from the Track Menu.

2 Go to the second header ("For a honeymoon…"), and apply the Header 2 paragraph style.

3 Drag the "Bungee Jumping" headline so that the first baseline rests on the 53p3 guide. Make sure that the left side of the block is flush with the left margin and that it fills the two-column width exactly.

Adding a drop cap

The decorative drop cap for the bungee-jumping article has been provided for you in the library. It was created in PageMaker and is a combination of the letter L, a rectangle, and a text wrap.

1 Delete the **L** from the phrase *Let me say* at the beginning of the body text for the article.

2 Drag LCap out of the library, and release it onto the pasteboard. Use the mouse to place it flush left with the left margin, and position it so that the top of the box aligns with the top of the letters in the first line of body type.

Because the piece already has a wrap applied to it, the surrounding text positions itself nicely around the drop cap.

3 Select the first paragraph of body text with the text tool, and then display the paragraph view of the Control palette. Change the first line indent from 1 pica to zero.

Fixing a widow

The last line of the first paragraph ends with a very short line—a widow. That doesn't look good, but there's an easy way to fix it.

1 Display the character view of the Control palette.

2 Use the text tool to select the whole first paragraph (but not the drop cap graphic), and then click the small left-pointing Kerning button in the Control palette once or twice until the single word moves up one line.

Left kerning button ┐

3 Make sure that the bottom of the text block in each of the two columns is even with the bottom page margin.

Placing the circle graphic

Now it's time to place the circular graphic that goes between the two columns of the bungee-jumping article. It's called Circle Photo in the Library palette. This graphic has a wrap already applied to it. It's also a circular mask grouped with an underlying square object.

1 Drag Circle Photo from the library. Release the graphic onto the pasteboard or a white area of the page. After releasing the graphic, click it with the pointer tool to select it.

2 In the Control palette, click the upper left corner of the proxy, and then set the X value to 13p6 and Y to 69p11 .

Note: After dragging an object in from a library, you must click on it to select it prior to applying any attributes from the Control palette. The object looks selected when you first drop it on the page, but it isn't really.

3 This is a good time to save your work.

You may want to check *07Final.pm6* again to see if your work matches it.

ADDING THE CONTINUATION LINE

The bungee-jumping article continues on a later page, so you need to add a jump line where it ends on page 1 to tell the reader where the article continues. To do this, you must first place the rest of the article. The file containing this article is large because it contains other articles as well, so you are going to flow the remainder of the *07Travel.doc* file into the document so you can see what you're working with.

1 With the pointer tool, select the text block in the second column, and load the cursor by clicking the bottom windowshade handle.

2 Go to the second page, and hold down the Command key (Macintosh) or Control key (Windows) to toggle from manual flow to autoflow. Click in the top of the left column to place the text.

PageMaker flows all the unplaced text into the publication.

3 Return to the first page, and select the text block in the second column by clicking on it with the pointer tool.

4 Choose PageMaker Plug-ins from the Utilities menu, and choose Add Cont'd Line from the submenu. In the dialog box that appears, enable Bottom of Textblock and click OK.

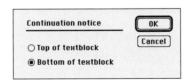

By choosing Bottom of Textblock, you tell PageMaker that you want the jump line to say "Continued on page …." If you choose Top of Textblock, PageMaker adds a line at the top that says "Continued from page…." PageMaker knows where you placed the next textblock of the article, and it inserts a line of text that contains the correct page number. It also creates a paragraph style called Cont. On , which has the default formatting for the jump line. You can edit this style exactly as you would edit any other paragraph style.

5 To change the look of the continuation line (or *jump line*), Command-click (Macintosh) or Control-click (Windows) the Cont. On style in the Styles palette to display the Edit Style dialog box.

6 Click the Type button, and set the font to 9-point AGaramond Semibold Italic and the leading to 14 points. Click OK, and then click the Para button. To remove the ruling lines from the style definition, click the Rules button and then deselect both Rules choices. Option-click (Macintosh) or Shift-click (Windows) OK to exit the nested dialog boxes.

The final step is to move the jump line up a bit. It's in a separate text block, so all you have to do is drag it.

7 Use the pointer tool to select the text block containing the jump line. Position it so that the bottom of the windowshade is on the bottom margin. You can do this by dragging it or by using the arrow keys on the keyboard to nudge it. Another option is to move it up by clicking the nudge buttons next to the Y value box in the Control palette.

Nudge button

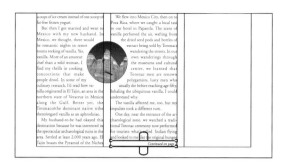

Note: An interim file is provided with the steps completed up to this point. If you want to complete the rest of this project without having to do the earlier steps, go to 07Project, *open* 07Inter1.pt6, *and save it in* Projects.

ADDING THE EDITOR'S NOTE

The Editor's Note sidebar rests on top of a screened-back blue rectangle that forms one of the major design elements on the front page. The rectangle serves as a point of focus and visually unifies the top and bottom of the page.

Creating the blue background

1 Take another look at *07Final.pm6,* before you begin this section, to remind yourself of what you're accomplishing here.

2 Return to *07Work.pm6,* and select the rectangle tool from the Toolbox. Drag a tall narrow rectangle on the pasteboard to the right of page 1. Don't worry about the size and position. You take care of that in the next steps.

3 Select the rectangle, and then be sure the upper left reference point of the proxy in the Control palette is selected. Set the width to 19p6 and the height to 77p6.

4 Display the Colors palette, click the Both (line and fill) button, and choose 20% from the Tint pop-up menu. Now click PANTONE Blue 072 CVU.

The whole rectangle is now a very pale (screened-back) blue.

Note: This blue occurs twice in the Colors palette but has a PS icon next to one occurrence. The latter one was brought into the document when you dragged the first of the two EPS graphics in from the library (LeapDuo). The other one is the non-PostScript version that came in with the first of the non-EPS graphics (AT Logo-Heading).

5 Zoom out and pan so that you can see the lower right corner of the page. Drag the rectangle so that its lower right corner nestles in the lower right corner of page 1.

6 With the rectangle selected, choose Send to Back from the Arrange menu so that the blue background is behind the photograph and the title art is at the top of the page.

7 Choose Lock Position from the Arrange menu. This locks the rectangle so that it will not accidentally be moved as you work on the page.

8 Save *07Work.pm6.*

Placing and formatting the text

In the next steps, you place and format the text for the Editor's Note. Take a look at the Editor's Note in *07Final.pm6* to see where you're headed. Notice that the title is white type against a dark blue box.

1 Display the Place Document dialog box, and double-click *07Editor.doc*. With the loaded icon, click in the right column about one-quarter inch below the big photograph.

2 Select the whole sidebar article with the text tool, and apply the Sidebar Text paragraph style.

In the next steps, you apply a paragraph style to the header, create a dark blue rectangle, place it behind the header, and group the rectangle and text block together.

3 Zoom in on the top of the Editor's Note article. Apply the SideHead paragraph style to the title ("Editor's Note") of the sidebar.

Don't worry if the text seems to disappear. The style you applied has Reverse as part of its definition. The text will be visible once more after you place the blue rectangle behind it.

4 Select the rectangle tool again, and draw a column-wide box over the "Editor's Note" title. Select the rectangle with the pointer tool, and use the Control palette to set the width to 14 picas (the width of the column) and the height to 2p4.

5 With the rectangle still selected, click the Both button on the Colors palette and apply PANTONE Blue 072 CVU. Choose Send Backward (*not* Send to Back) from the Arrange menu. If necessary, repeat this until the dark blue rectangle is behind the text.

6 Use the arrow keys on the keyboard or the vertical nudge buttons on the Control palette to nudge the blue rectangle so that it is centered vertically behind "Editor's Note."

Using the nudge technique works especially well for delicate positioning such as this.

7 At this point, the dark blue rectangle and the text block should both be flush left in the right-most column and have widths exactly equal to the column. The rectangle should still be selected, so Shift-click on the text column to add it to the selection, and choose Group from the Arrange menu.

Now the blue rectangle is "glued" to the column and can't be accidentally jostled out of position.

8 Click an insertion point in the first text paragraph of the Editor's Note. Display the Paragraph view of the Control palette, and change the first line indent from 1 pica to zero.

9 (Windows only) Use the text tool to highlight the last paragraph of the Editor's Note and get rid of the extra line by clicking the left Kerning button in the Control palette twice.

10 With the pointer tool, drag the assembled text-and-box object up so that the baseline of the line that begins "crave adrenaline rushes" is on the 59p6 guide.

The baselines of the Editor's Note article are now aligned with those in the bungee-jumping article because you used the same guide to place both, and the leading is the same.

FINISHING THE BUNGEE ARTICLE

Next, you go to page 2 and position the remainder of the bungee-jumping article.

1 Go to the top of page 2 and zoom in on the top of the page. Make sure that the top of each of the two text blocks aligns exactly with the top margin.

2 Pan down and, if necessary, zoom out so that you can see the bottom half of the two columns.

Earlier in this project, you used the Guide Manager to place guides on page 2. Now you use these guides to position the bottom of each text block.

3 With the pointer tool, grab the bottom handle of the left text block, and roll the column up until the bottom is on the 60p8 guide (the third one from the bottom). Roll the bottom of the middle column up to the guide that's at 55p.

4 Click the windowshade handle at the bottom of the text block in the second column to load the text icon, and flow the remaining text into the third column. Align the top of the text block with the top margin.

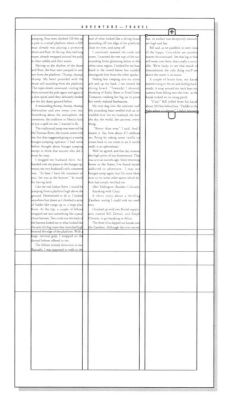

FORMATTING THE KAYAKING ARTICLE

Next, you apply formatting to the "Kayaking with Crocs" article, which is in the third column in *07Final.pm6*.

1 Zoom in on the middle of the middle column, and (Macintosh only) apply the Header 1 style to the "Kayaking with Crocs" line. Then highlight it with the text tool, and apply Expert Kerning just as you did for the headline of the bungee-jumping article: Choose Expert Kerning from the Type menu. Set the Kern Strength to .80, and make sure the Design Class is set to Display. Click OK.

Now you use the Column Break command to move the headline to the top of the third column.

2 Click anywhere in the "Kayaking with Crocs" headline, and display the Paragraph Specifications dialog box. Under Options, enable Column Break Before, and click OK.

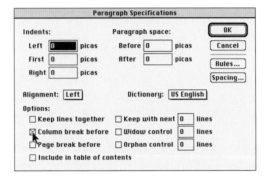

The head promptly pops to the top of the next column (i.e., it has a column break before it).

3 Select the next paragraph ("A short story…") and apply the Header 2 style.

4 Drag the Kayaking Photo out of the library, place it on the pasteboard, and then drag it to the top of the third column so that the solid rectangle that you see as it moves is placed against the top of the right column.

The photo already has a wrap applied to it, so it pushes the text down out of the way. Since Snap to Guides is enabled, the picture snaps smoothly into the column when you move it close to the column guides.

POSITIONING THE PULL QUOTE

1 Drag Pull Quote from the library, release it onto the pasteboard, and then click it to select it.

2 Be sure the top left reference point of the Control palette proxy is selected, and then set the X value to −41p2 and the Y value to 23p0.

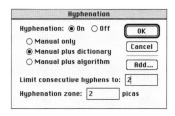

3 (Windows only) With the text tool, highlight the line to the right of the pull quote that begins *welcome* and click the left Kerning button in the Control palette twice.

CONTROLLING HYPHENATION

If you look over the body text that you've placed so far, you'll notice that there's a lot of hyphenation. On the second page, there's one place in the left column where three lines in a row are hyphenated (Macintosh only). You decide that you don't want more than two lines in a row to hyphenate. Since you want this to be true for all body text, you are going to change the definition of the two body text styles: Body text and Sidebar Text.

1 To display the Edit Style dialog box, Command-click (Macintosh) or Control-click (Windows) the Body text style in the Styles palette or choose Define Styles from the Type menu, highlight Body text, and click the Edit button.

2 Click the Hyph button to display the Hyphenation dialog box. Type a **2** in the box following Limit Consecutive Hyphens To. Click OK, and exit both dialog boxes.

3 Repeat the process for the Sidebar text style.

There's one more hyphenation problem. Look at the subhead of the kayaking article ("A short tale…"). One of the words is hyphenated. As a rule, headlines should not be hyphenated, so you're going to change the definition of the Header 2 paragraph style to turn off hyphenation. This time you display the Edit Style dialog box from the Control palette rather than from the Styles palette. It doesn't matter which you use.

4 Display the Edit Style dialog box again. Click the Hyph button, and then click the Off option next to Hyphenation. Click OK twice to exit the Edit Style dialog boxes.

Now there will be no hyphenation in any paragraph that has the Header 2 paragraph style applied to it.

LAYING OUT THE TIBETAN TREKS SIDEBAR

To finish page 2, you place the prepared title graphic for the Tibetan Treks sidebar and then place a graphic at the bottom of the page. You then modify the graphic in several ways: you enlarge it, color it blue, and alter it with PageMaker's Image Controls. Last, you change the layout to two columns, place the sidebar text, and add the drop cap.

Placing the sidebar title

1 Take another look at *07Final.pm6* to see what this part of the page looks like.

2 Drag Side Head out of the library and position it so that the left side is against the left margin and the top border of the photograph aligns with the guide at 56p4.

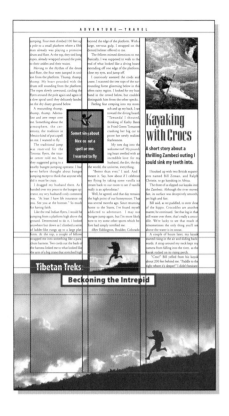

Placing the background graphic

1 Drag Tibetan Treks out of the library, and place it so that the lower left corner is in the lower left corner of the page.

2 Select the sidebar title graphic that you dragged from the library just previously, and apply Bring to Front so that it is in front of the enlarged background photograph.

3 Select the large Tibetan Treks photo, and apply PANTONE Blue 072 CVU from the Colors palette.

Applying special effects

Now you use PageMaker's Image Controls to screen back the photo and create some special effects.

Macintosh:

1 With the photo selected, choose Image from the Element menu and choose Image Control from the submenu. Experiment with clicking different buttons above the graph and with clicking the Lightness and Contrast controls.

The buttons produce an immediate effect, but for the other controls, you have to click Apply. There's one more technique available here if you're working on a Macintosh. With the pointer, drag across the width of the graph. Notice that the bars of the graph conform to the invisible line that you trace with your pointer. Click Apply to see the effect.

2 When you're done exploring, use the pointer to draw a line across the graph. The line should begin at the middle of the left side and go to the upper right corner of the graph. Click Apply, and then click OK.

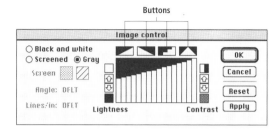

Windows:

1 With the photo selected, choose Image from the Element menu and choose Image Control from the submenu.

2 Set the Lightness to 90% and the Contrast to 24%. Click OK.

Placing the text in two columns

Now you've prepared the background graphic for the Tibetan Treks article. The next step is to place the text. This article is laid out in two columns rather than three, so you need to change the column guides.

1 Choose Column Guides from the Layout menu. This time, enter 2 for the number of columns. Keep 1p6 as the Space Between Columns, and click OK.

Notice that changing the number of columns does not affect text that is already placed on the page.

2 Display the Place Document dialog box and select *07Tibet.doc.* located on *07Project*, as a new story. Once your icon is loaded with the text, use Partial Autoflow again by holding down Shift as you click in the top of each column below the Tibetan Treks head ("Beckoning the Intrepid").

3 Use the text tool to select all of the newly placed text, and apply the Sidebar text paragraph style.

4 Drag (or nudge with the arrow keys) each of the two columns so that the first baseline sits on the 71p2 guide.

5 Use the pointer tool to roll the bottom handle of the left text block down so that it's even with the bottom margin of the page.

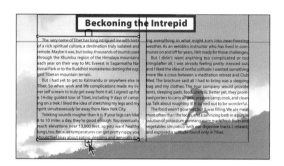

6 With the text tool, click an insertion point in the first paragraph of the text you just placed. In the paragraph view of the Control palette, change the first line indent from 1 pica to zero.

7 Drag the TCap graphic from the library. Position it visually by placing its left side against the left margin and the bottom even with the fourth baseline of the Tibetan Treks text.

8 Delete the first letter of the text—the T—since it is now duplicated by the drop cap.

9 Use the text tool to select all of the Tibet article except the first paragraph. In the Character view of the Control palette, change the track from No Track to Tight.

10 Save *07Work.pm6.*

USING THE STORY EDITOR

PageMaker's Story Editor is a text-only view that makes it fast and easy to edit text because there are no graphics to redraw, no confusing formatting, and stories are all together in one place, not spread out over various pages.

Some tasks can be performed only in Story Editor view. The most notable examples are find, change, and spellcheck.

By setting some preferences, you can control what you see in the Story Editor and how it looks.

1 Double-click the pointer tool in the Toolbox to display the Preferences dialog box; click the More button.

Note: Displaying the Preferences dialog box by double-clicking the pointer tool is exactly the same as choosing Preferences from the File menu.

2 In the Story Editor section of the More Preferences dialog box, choose the Font and Size that you'd like to use in the Story Editor. For this project, choose 12-point Helvetica.

These settings determine how text is displayed in the Story Editor. If you are sharing the file with other people, be sure to pick a font that is available to all of you.

3 Be sure Display Style Names is on. This lists the style name of each paragraph in a column to the left of the text.

When you're working in Story Editor, this is useful to help you keep track of what each paragraph is in the layout.

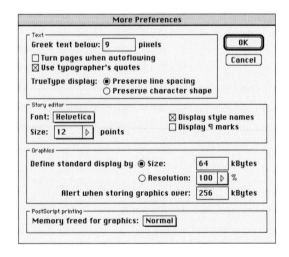

4 Click OK twice to exit the Preferences dialog boxes.

FIND AND CHANGE

If you look at the text you imported for the various articles, you see that there is an unusual character—ó—in places where there should be em dashes. Things like this happen sometimes when text is moved between applications and between platforms. PageMaker's Find and Change feature makes the character easy to fix. To use find and change, you must work in Story Editor view.

1 To display the Story Editor, click an insertion point on page 1 in the text of the bungee-jumping article.

Don't click next to the drop cap ("L"), because the drop cap is a separate story.

2 Choose Edit Story from the Edit menu.

This displays the story in Story Editor. Another way to accomplish the same thing is to triple-click on the story with the pointer tool.

3 Look at the last sentence in the second paragraph. There are two instances of the **ó** character in the sentence ("óthe dominant native tribe thereó"). Select one and copy it.

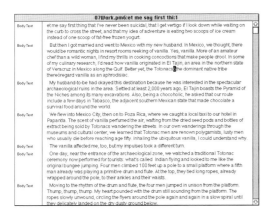

4 Choose Change from the Utilities menu to display the Change dialog box. Paste the copied character into the Find What box.

Note: You could also type the character directly into the Find What box. On a Macintosh, type Option-e o (hold down Option as you type e and then let go of Option and type o). In Windows, hold down Alt and type 0243 on the numeric keypad.

5 Type an em dash in the Change To box. The keystrokes for an em dash are Option-Shift-hyphen for the Macintosh. In Windows, you must use the special dialog box sequence: ^_.

6 The case (uppercase or lowercase) doesn't matter, and the character you're looking for is not a whole word, because it always turns up attached to other words, so leave the check boxes empty for Match Case and Whole Word. Enable All Stories in the Search Story option list.

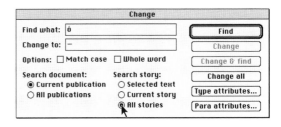

You could now click Change All to change each instance of that character to an em dash. A word of warning, though: Change All should be used with great caution. It's easy to change things you never meant to change. For instance, if that character is present as a legitimate character in a word, it's going to be changed anyway if you use Change All. It's far safer to check each occurrence before changing it.

7 Click Find. Look at the found character. (It's highlighted.) It's one you want to change, so click the Change & Find button.

PageMaker makes the change and automatically searches for the next occurrence of the character. This technique gives you control over the replacement process. It's a little slower, but there are no nasty surprises at the end of it.

8 For this project, change each occurrence of the character to an em dash. There should be seven in all.

Note: To skip over an occurrence without changing it, click Find Next.

9 Click the upper left corner (Macintosh) or upper right corner (Windows) of the Change dialog box to close it.

10 Save your work. (Hopefully, you've been saving at regular intervals.)

CHECKING THE SPELLING

Spell checking is another task that you can perform only in Story Editor view. You should still be in Story Editor, but because PageMaker creates a separate window for each story, you are in the window for the "Tibetan Treks" story.

1 To return to the beginning of the publication, choose the name of the publication that you're working in—*07Work.pm6*—from the Window menu. The submenu lists each open Story Editor window, using the first few words in each to identify it. Choose the one that begins "et me say" and then place your insertion point at the beginning of the story.

2 Display the Spelling dialog box by choosing Spelling from the Utilities menu.

Before you begin, look over the options. As a rule, you want PageMaker to suggest possible spellings to you, so verify that Alternate Spellings is enabled.

Usually, you want to know when the same word occurs twice in a row, since this is a common error. That's the Show Duplicates option. In this text, though, the writer uses phrases like *thump, thump, thump*, so don't enable Show Duplicates.

3 You want to check all the stories, so enable Search Story: All Stories. Click Start.

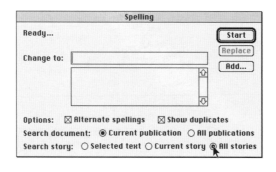

PageMaker looks for both misspelled words and unexpected capitalization, such as a sentence beginning with a lowercase letter.

4 The first word that the spell checker questions is *et*. You removed the **L** from the word *Let* because you added a graphical drop cap, so the word is actually okay. You don't want to add it to the dictionary because it's not going to occur often, so click Ignore.

PageMaker continues the spell check without changing the word or adding it to the dictionary. This project contains a lot of personal and place names that should be ignored. Others, like *hippo*, are odd or rare and don't need to be added to the dictionary. Click Ignore for all of the following words:

Tajin	Cruz
Totonacs	chocoholic
Tabasco	Poza
Rica	Papantla
Totonac	Tawanda
Kathy	Bev
Eddington	Crocs
Zambesi	Zeman
Ralph	Christie
hippo	Croc
betcha	Jon
Benson	Yangtze
who've	say…happy
Britta	Munstead
Khumbu	Everest
Sagarmatha	14-day
Med	simpatico

5 The next questioned word is *amatuer*. This word is wrong, but the correct spelling appears in the list of possible replacements. Click "amateur" in the replacement list to make it appear in the Change To box, and then click Replace.

PageMaker replaces the word and continues the spell check.

6 Ignore the next word, *Tajin*. The word after that is *Veracruz*. You want to use a different form of the name, so replace the word in the Change To box with *Vera Cruz* and click Replace. The change appears in the text. You don't want to add it to the dictionary, so click Ignore to continue spell checking.

Note: Sometimes when you type in a change and click Replace, PageMaker continues the search without waiting for you to click Ignore or Add. That means that PageMaker found the substitution in its dictionary.

7 Ignore the next few words that are questioned. They're all on your "ignore" list. When you get to *ubquitous*, choose the correct spelling, *ubiquitous*, from the list, and click Replace.

8 The next questioned word is *bungee*. This word occurs frequently in this project, so you want to add it to the dictionary. Click Add. Enable As All Lowercase, click OK, and then click Continue.

To specify capitalization for a word, enable Exactly as Typed if the word must always have the capital letters that you've typed in the Word box. If the word should be lowercase except at the beginning of a sentence, choose As All Lowercase. PageMaker is smart enough to know when to capitalize it.

9 The next word is *dented*. The word is okay, so click the Add button to add the word to the dictionary. PageMaker displays the Add to User Dictionary dialog box, which shows how it would hyphenate the word. You don't want it to hyphenate before the *ed*, so remove the two tildes from the word. Be sure that As All Lowercase is enabled, and click OK. Click Continue.

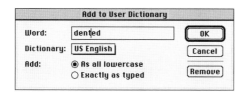

You use the tildes to tell PageMaker how preferable a hyphenation point is. Place a single tilde at each point in the word that is most desirable. Put two tildes at each point that would be acceptable but not ideal, and put three tildes at each point that should be used only if absolutely necessary. If you don't want the word to be hyphenated at all, remove all tildes from it.

10 The next few words are on your ignore list. When you get to *kayaking*, click Add and change the hyphenation to *kayak~ing*. Click OK and then click Continue. Ignore the next two words and then change *expatriats* to *expatriates* by choosing the correction from the list and clicking Replace. Ignore the next few words.

11 When the spell checker questions *whitewater*, click the Add button and change the hyphenation to *white~water*. Be sure As All Lowercase is enabled and click OK. Click Continue. Ignore *Yangtze* and then replace *reluctatly* with *reluctantly* from the list. Ignore the remainder of the words that the spell checker questions.

13 When the message "Spell check complete" appears in the dialog box, click the upper left corner (Macintosh) or upper right corner (Windows) to close it.

Exiting from Story Editor

1 There is one Story Editor window open for each of the three stories in the project. To close all of these windows at once, hold down Option (Macintosh) or Shift (Windows) and choose Close All Stories from the Story menu.

2 You have completed this project. If you have a printer available, you may want to print out your file.

3 Close all open files, and exit PageMaker.

CHAPTER

3

SAILING & RACING THE WIND TODAY

Sailboat design has changed only slightly from ancient times to the 1800s. If a sailor from the 19th century could travel back in time to an ancient Roman ship, for example, he would recognize enough of the rigging and gear to pitch in and pass as part of the crew.

With the number of people sailing for pleasure burgeoning, boat designers changed their focus from building on tradition to developing better designs,

methods, and materials. Even so, the early pleasure boats remained heavy because the primary construction material still was teak and other wood. Only in the last 50 years have modern materials produced lighter boats that require less maintenance. That means more time spent sailing, which has increased the sport's appeal to both leisure sailors and racers.

Today, sailboats are fast and sleek, built primarily of fiberglass, polyethylene, aluminum alloy, polyurethane, and other durable, yet lightweight materials. Contradictory though it seems, a few sailboats are made of concrete. Most recreational sailboats are sloops or cutters. Although some experts use the terms interchangeably, a sloop technically has one mast and one headsail, whereas a cutter has one mast but two or more headsails.

AN OPTIONAL "PULPIT"
ACTS AS A GUARDRAIL FOR
ADDED SAFETY AT THE
BOW OF THE SAILBOAT

19

8

This project is a book, complete with an index and table of contents that you create. Chapters One and Two of the book are provided for you. You assemble Chapter Three

SAILING PUBLICATION

using the template that is provided. This serves as a review of many of the skills you have acquired elsewhere in these projects. Then you spell-check the text, create a Book List, and insert index markers into Chapter Three using a variety of techniques. Finally, you generate an index and table of contents and learn how to format each one.

This project is a multichapter book about sailing. You are provided with two chapters that have already been completed. You use a template as a starting point to create a third chapter. Then you add index markers, create an index, create a table

SAILING PUBLICATION

of contents and integrate all these elements together into a book.

In this project you learn how to:

- Create a book list
- Insert index markers
- Create and format an index
- Create a table of contents

This project should take you about 2 hours to complete.

BEFORE YOU BEGIN

1 Return all settings to their defaults by deleting the *Adobe PageMaker 6.x Prefs* file from the *Preferences* folder (Macintosh) or by removing \pm6\rsrc\usenglish\pm6.cnf from the drive containing PageMaker (Windows).

2 Make sure that AGaramond, Corvinus Skyline, and the Myriad Multiple Master fonts are installed on your system.

3 Launch the Adobe PageMaker 6 application and open the *08Final.pm6* file in *08Project* to see how Chapter 3 will look when you have completed the steps in this project. You may want to look at *08Chap1.pm6* and *08Chap2.pm6* as well, to get an overall feeling for the book. Later, you will look at the example files for the table of contents and index.

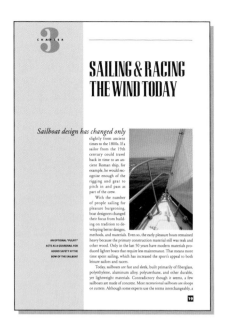

STARTING CHAPTER 3

You begin by opening the template file and saving it as the new Chapter 3 document.

1 Open *08Sail.pt6*, and save it in *Projects* as *08Work.pm6*.

Notice that when you open *08Sail.pt6*, your new document is untitled. This is because *08Sail.pt6* was created by choosing the Save As: Template option in the Save As dialog box. PageMaker opens only untitled copies of templates. This ensures that the template itself can't be overwritten.

2 Go to the Layout menu, and make sure that Autoflow is enabled.

Next, you turn off the display of guides to make it easier to see where the text goes. Then you place the text file that contains the text for Chapter 3 of the book.

3 Choose Guides and Rulers from the Layout menu, and make sure that Show Guides is deselected.

4 Display the Place Document dialog box, navigate to *08Project*, and choose *08Chap3.doc*. Be sure that Retain Formats is enabled, and click OK.

5 Place the top left corner of the loaded text right under the left end of the thin black line that goes across the top right part of the chapter opening page. Click to flow the text file into the document.

Style names were applied to the text when it was created in a word processor. Because the style names used in the word processor match those defined in the PageMaker template, enabling Retain Format applies the PageMaker style definitions to the tagged text. The text will therefore appear fully formatted with the PageMaker styles when it is placed.

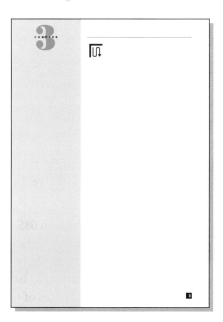

Notice that PageMaker creates as many additional pages as necessary to accommodate the placed text.

6 Enable the display of guides once more. The keyboard shortcut for toggling guides on and off is Command-J (Macintosh) or Control-J (Windows).

Because this is the third chapter in the book, you need to set the opening page to the correct number.

7 Open *08Chap2.pm6*, and look at the last page; the page number is 18. Close *08Chap2.pm6*, and return to the first page of *08Work.pm6*.

8 Choose Document Setup from the File menu, and enter **19** in the Start Page # box. Click OK.

Note: Later on, you'll be creating a book and using the book list to number the pages automatically between chapters. For now, it would be confusing to have Chapter 3 begin with page 1, so we enter the correct page number manually.

9 On page 19, position the text block so that the first baseline in the title rests on the guide that's at 1.953. Be sure that it remains positioned exactly between the vertical margins.

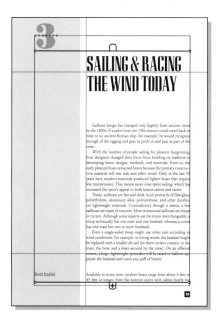

APPLYING THE CORRECT MASTER PAGES

This document has a special master page for the chapter opening ,in addition to the pair of Document Master pages that are appropriate for the rest of each chapter. When PageMaker added pages for the imported text, it used the master that was applied to the right-hand opening page for all the right-hand pages. In the next steps, you first look through the chapter to observe the problem, and then you apply the correct master pages to all the interior pages of the chapter.

TIP: TO DISPLAY THE NEXT PAGE OF A PUBLICATION, PRESS COMMAND-TAB (MACINTOSH) OR F12 (WINDOWS). TO DISPLAY THE PREVIOUS PAGE, PRESS COMMAND-SHIFT-TAB (MACINTOSH) OR F11 (WINDOWS).

1 To see a slideshow presentation of the pages, hold down the Shift key and choose Go to Page from the Layout menu. PageMaker moves through the document, displaying each pair of pages for a couple of seconds. To stop the scrolling, click anywhere with the mouse or press any key.

2 To apply the proper master pages, begin by choosing Master Pages from the Windows menu to display the Master Pages palette.

3 Click the triangle at the top right of the palette, and choose Apply from the Palette menu.

4 In the Apply Master dialog box, choose Document Master from the Master Page pop-up list. Type in **20-27** for the page range, and leave the Set Right and Left Pages Separately option deselected. Click Apply.

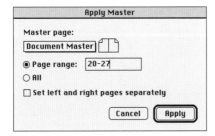

This applies the correct master pages (Document Master) to all the chapter pages except the opening page. Notice that Document Master is actually a pair of master pages, one for the right pages and one for the left pages. You usually want to apply the pair together, but you have the option of applying master pages separately to right and left pages.

5 To examine this option, choose Apply from the Master Pages palette menu again. Enable Set Right and Left Pages Separately and notice that you now have separate master page lists for right and left master pages. Click Cancel to dismiss the dialog box without making any changes.

6 Save *08Work.pm6*. Remember to save regularly throughout the project.

ADDING FORMATTING AND GRAPHICS TO THE TEXT

You need to make a few changes to the text formatting. Then you'll place a series of graphics, and add captions to some of the graphics before beginning work on the index and table of contents.

1 On page 19, use the text tool to click an insertion point in the introductory paragraph of body text. Then apply the Intro Paragraph style.

You can apply any paragraph style by clicking the name in the Styles palette, by choosing it in the Paragraph view of the Control palette, or by choosing it from the Style submenu of the Type menu. The result is the same, whichever technique you use.

2 Select the pointer tool, and display the Place Document dialog box. Choose *08ArtA.tif*, and be sure that As Independent Graphic is enabled. Choose No when asked if you want to copy it into the document, and then click anywhere on the page with the loaded icon to place the graphic.

3 To position the graphic after it's on the page, click it with the pointer tool to select it, and then click the top left corner of the proxy in the Control palette. Type in **4.98** for the X value and **4.019** for Y, and apply the settings.

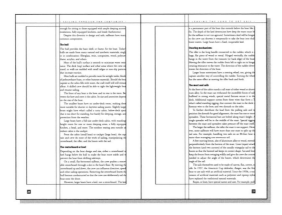

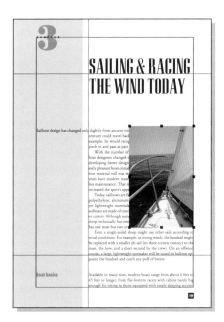

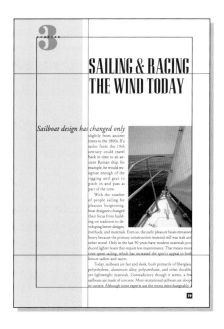

4 To make the text flow around the graphic, you need to apply a wrap to it. Select the graphic and choose Text Wrap from the Element menu. In the top row of icons, click the middle one. This highlights the right icon in the bottom row, which is what you want. Set the Bottom Standoff to 0 inches, and leave the rest set to the default standoff of 0.167. Click OK to apply the settings.

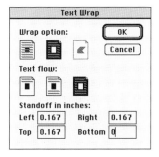

Now you apply character formatting to the beginning of the opening paragraph to create the designer lead-in.

5 Zoom in on the first paragrph, and use the text tool to select the first five words of the introductory paragraph, the one that wraps around the graphic. In the Control palette, click the italic button, set the point size to 23, and apply the settings.

You now need to import the text for the caption that appears in the space to the left on page 19. To see the effect of enabling Convert Quotes in the Place Document dialog box, you import the text twice, once without the Convert Quotes option enabled and once with it on. In typography and desktop publishing, you always want to use the typographer's curly quotation marks rather than the straight ones that a typewriter gives you. For placing the final caption, you use a technique called *drag-placing* that lets you control the area occupied by the placed text.

6 Display the Place Document dialog box, and choose *08Capt1.doc*. Deselect the Convert Quotes option, but leave Retain Format enabled. Click OK, and then click in the space to the left of the text column to flow the text onto the page. Zoom in on the caption so that you can see the shape of the quotation marks clearly, and observe that they are straight, like inch marks (which in fact they are).

7 Now delete the caption text block, and re-import it, but this time enable Convert Quotes. With the loaded text icon, drag diagonally to create a rectangular space for the text. Begin at the left margin, and as you drag, watch the hairline that appears in the top ruler. (There's one in the left ruler too.) Drag until the text block is just over 1⅜ inches wide, and make it roughly 2 inches high. When the text appears on the page, select it, and if necessary, use the pointer tool to reshape the text block so that the line breaks are the same as the ones in the illustration below. Then drag the text block with the pointer tool so that the lower right corner of the text is in the corner formed by the vertical guide at 2.75 and the horizontal guide at 9.781.

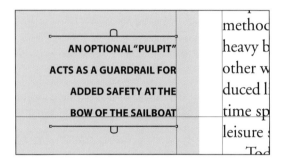

8 Finally, use the pointer tool to adjust the bottom of the main text block on the chapter opening page so it's even with the bottom page margin.

9 Save *08Work.pm6*, and then take a look at *08Final.pm6* to make sure that your page matches it.

10 Place *08ArtB.tif* on page 22 as an independent graphic. Choose not to copy it into the document when the query appears. Click anywhere on the page to place it, and position it by selecting the top left point of the Control palette proxy; set X to −5.5 and Y to 0.75.

Note: When Facing Pages is enabled in Document Setup, X values on left-hand pages are always negative.

11 Apply a text wrap to the graphic by choosing Text Wrap from the Element menu. In the Text Wrap dialog box, click the middle icon in the top row. Set the left standoff to 2.25, the bottom standoff to zero, and leave the others set to the default of 0.167. Click OK.

Next, you place the caption text that goes with this graphic.

12 Drag a horizontal guide to 6 inches.

13 Drag-place *08Capt2.doc*, making the width slightly less than 1.5 inches. Look at *08Final.pm6* to see what the line breaks should be, and adjust the width of the text block if necessary. Drag the text block so that the lower right corner of the text is at the intersection of the horizontal guide at 6 inches and the vertical guide at −5.75.

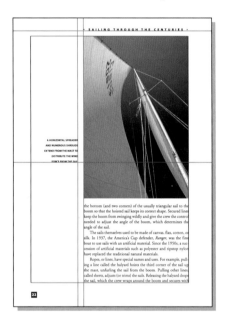

To complete the laying out of Chapter 3, you place a graphic and caption on page 24 and a graphic on page 26.

14 Turn to page 24, and place *08ArtC.tif*. As with all large graphics in this project, don't choose to copy it into the publication. Position it on the page by clicking the top left corner of the Control palette proxy and setting X to −7.75 and Y to 0.75. Choose Text Wrap from the Elements menu, and choose the center Wrap Option again. Set the Left and Bottom standoffs to zero, and leave the others at the defaults. Click OK.

15 Still on page 24, drag-place *08Captn3.doc*, making the area just over 1.5 inches wide when you drag. Drag the bottom handle of the windowshade down to be sure all the text is displayed, and compare it to the caption in *08Final.pm6* to make sure the lines are breaking correctly. Then drag the text block with the pointer tool so that the right side is against the vertical guide that's at −5.75 inches and the first baseline is even with the first baseline of the text under the graphic.

16 To place the remaining graphic, go to page 26 and display the Place Document dialog. Choose *08ArtD.tif*, and click on page 26 with the loaded icon to flow it onto the page. Position the graphic by selecting the upper left reference point of the Control palette proxy and setting X to −7.75 and Y to 6.702.

17 To apply the text wrap to *08ArtD.tif*, choose Text Wrap from the Element menu again, and click the center Text Wrap option. Set the top standoff to 0, and leave the other standoffs set to the 0.167 default. Click OK. If necessary, select

the main text block and roll it up so that the bottom of the text block is just above the image, and the last line of text begins with *founders of the New*.

When you originally placed the text, it ended on page 26, so that's where the last text block is. Since you've added several graphics, there's no longer room for all of the text and some of it is no longer placed. In the following steps, you place the remaining text.

18 Go to page 26. Use the pointer tool to select the text block and notice that the handle at the bottom of the windowshade is red, indicating unplaced text.

19 Click the red handle at the bottom of the text block windowshade to load the text icon, and then click near the top of page 27, between the margins.

Because you enabled Autoflow earlier in this project, PageMaker add extra pages as needed. In fact, it adds two pages, when only one additional page is needed, because you have the Facing Pages option enabled in Document Setup.

20 Return to page 27 and make sure that the top of the text block is resting on the top margin.

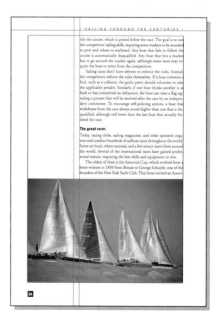

21 Save *03Work.pm6*.

You have now placed the text and graphic elements of this chapter and are ready to place index markers and to generate a table of contents and index.

Note: An interim file is provided with the steps completed up to this point. If you want to complete the rest of this project without having to do the earlier steps, go to 08Project, *open* 08Inter1.pt6, *and save it in* Projects.

CREATING A BOOK LIST

The next part is the heart of this project: to assemble all the chapters into a book so that page numbers will be automatically updated and so that you can generate an index and table of contents. In PageMaker, you create a book by opening any one of the files (or *publications*) that will be in the book and generating a book list. You add each chapter to the book list, and if you want the index and table of contents to be in separate publications, you add those files to the book list as well.

The index and table of contents don't *have* to be in separate publications. You can generate the information and place it in one of the existing publications. For this book project, however, the graphic designer has designed and created a template file for the table of contents and another for the index. When you create the book list, you'll include those two (currently empty) publications.

You can create the book list in any one of the publications that will be in the book. However, the book list needs to be present in a publication in which you are generating a table of contents or index, so once the book list is created, you'll copy it to the rest of the publications in the book.

To create a complete book list that includes the index and table of contents, begin by using the templates to create the empty files for these two publications.

1 Open *08TocTpl.pt6*. Since it's a template, you get an untitled document. Save this in *Projects* as *08Toc.pm6*. Next, open *08IdxTpl.pt6*, and save it in *Projects* as *08Index.pm6*.

2 You can create the initial book list in any one of the publications that will be part of the book. Since you've been working in *08Work.pm6*, go to that file.

3 Choose Book from the Utilities menu.

PageMaker displays the Book Publication List dialog box. In the next steps, you add the publications that are to be parts of the book and then arrange them in the right order.

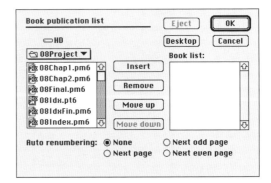

4 If there are any entries in the book list on the right, highlight each one in turn, and click Remove. In the scroll list to the left, navigate to *Projects* and double-click *08Toc.pm6* to add it to the book list on the right. (You could also click it once and then click Insert). Add *08Work.pm6* and *08Index.pm6* to the book list.

5 In the left scroll list, navigate to *08Project*, and add *08Chap1.pm6* and *08Chap2.pm6* to the book list.

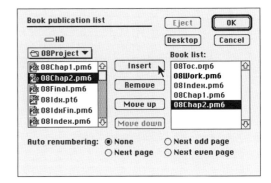

The order that the publications appear in the book list is important, because this is the order in which PageMaker numbers the pages. The publications should appear in the list with the table of contents first, the three chapters in order, and the index last.

6 In the book list, highlight *08Chap1.pm6*. Click the Move Up button twice so that *08Chap1.pm6* follows *08Toc.pm6*. Highlight *08Chap2.pm6*, and click the Move Up button twice so that *08Chap2.pm6* follows *08Chap1.pm6*. The order in the book list should now be as follows: *08Toc.pm6*, *08Chap1.pm6*, *08Chap2.pm6*, *08Work.pm6*, *08Index.pm6*.

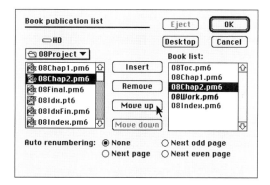

Before you close the Book Publication List dialog box, you need to tell PageMaker that the publications should be numbered consecutively and that each new chapter should begin on a right-hand (odd-numbered) page. PageMaker will then add a blank page, if necessary, to the end of a chapter so that the next chapter begins on a right-hand page. If you choose None as the Auto Renumbering option, PageMaker just uses whatever numbering you specified as the Starting Page # in the Document Setup dialog box for each publication.

7 Choose Next Odd Page, and then click OK. PageMaker asks you if you want to renumber the publication now. Choose No. Don't set the Auto Renumbering option yet. That comes later.

There's no need to renumber the publication until you've generated the table of contents, because the table of contents will add pages, and therefore will change the page numbers.

You'll need a copy of the book list in the table of contents and index files in order to generate their contents, so the easiest thing to do is to copy the book list to all the files in the book.

8 In *08Work.pm6*, where you created the original book list, hold down the Command key (Macintosh) or the Control key (Windows) and choose Book from the Utilities menu.

That's all there is to it. PageMaker places a copy of the book list in each publication that's in the book list.

8 Save *08Work.pm6*.

ADDING INDEX MARKERS

Creating an index has four stages: put index entries into each publication in the book, look the entries over and edit them if necessary, generate the index, and place the index in the publication where you want it to be.

Wait until you have finished editing your publication before you add the index markers. If you edit after you have added the markers, you run the risk of moving or deleting a marker as you edit, or of making an index entry inappropriate.

The mechanics of creating the index are relatively simple. Planning what index entries to use is a real art, however. All we can teach you here is the technique of inserting the entries and generating the index.

To add index entries, you should work in the story editor so that you can see the index markers. The following steps take you through several different techniques for adding index entries to a publication.

1 Place an insertion point in any paragraph of *08Work.pm6*, and choose Edit Story from the Edit menu. Another way to invoke the story editor is to triple-click on the story with the pointer tool.

2 Choose Display ¶ from the Story menu so that you can see the symbols that mark index entries. The marker symbol is a black rectangle with a white diamond inside.

The simplest and most basic way to insert an index entry is to highlight the text that should appear in the index, then display the Index Entry box, and add the entry. You begin by using Find to locate the phrase *International Yacht Racing Union* and then add it to the index.

3 Display the Find dialog box by choosing Find from the Utilities menu or pressing Command-F (Macintosh) or Control-F (Windows). To find the first phrase that you want to add to the index, type **International** in the Find What box, and click Find.

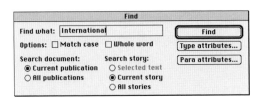

4 When PageMaker finds the word *International,* highlight the rest of the phrase *International Yacht Racing Union.* To display the Index Entry dialog box, choose Index Entry from the Utilities menu or better still, use the keyboard shortcut: Command-; (Macintosh) or Control-; (Windows). The highlighted text appears in the first-level Topic box. Be sure that Page Reference is selected, rather than Cross-Reference, and click OK.

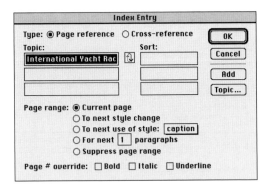

Notice that a marker symbol shows up to the left of your entry selection. This marker contains the indexing information that you entered in the Index Entry dialog box.

Choosing the Page Reference option in the Index Entry dialog box instructs PageMaker to give the page number on which the index marker appears. Later in this project, you use the Cross-Reference option to create entries like "See…" and "See also…"

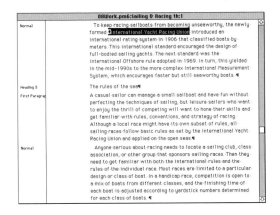

The technique in the previous steps indexes a phrase as it appears in the text. In some cases, however, the words in the text aren't in the right form or in the right order for the index entry, so you need to take additional steps to create the entry you want.

You create the next entry by typing text directly in the Index Entry dialog box, rather than by highlighting text.

5 Go back three paragraphs to the one that begins "By the 1720s." Place your insertion point anywhere in the paragraph, and display the Index Entry dialog box without highlighting any text first. All the topic boxes are blank. Type **racing boat to boat** in the top topic box.

If you clicked OK now, you'd create a first-level topic entry with that text. But you decide that it should be a second-level topic entry instead.

6 Click the Promote/Demote button to move the entry down one level, and then type **yacht racing** in the first-level topic box. Click OK.

```
                          ┌─ Promote/Demote button
┌──────────────────────────────────────────────┐
│              Index Entry                        │
│ Type: ◉ Page reference  ○ Cross-reference  ┌──────┐ │
│ Topic:                      Sort:          │  OK  │ │
│ ┌─────────────────┐ ┌↕┐  ┌──────────────┐  └──────┘ │
│ │ yacht racing    │ └─┘  │              │  ┌──────┐ │
│ └─────────────────┘      └──────────────┘  │Cancel│ │
│ ┌─────────────────┐      ┌──────────────┐  └──────┘ │
│ │ racing boat to boat│    │              │  ┌──────┐ │
│ └─────────────────┘      └──────────────┘  │ Add  │ │
│ ┌─────────────────┐      ┌──────────────┐  └──────┘ │
│ │                 │      │              │  ┌──────┐ │
│ └─────────────────┘      └──────────────┘  │Topic…│ │
│                                             └──────┘ │
│ Page range: ◉ Current page                          │
│             ○ To next style change                  │
│             ○ To next use of style: ┌───────┐       │
│                                     │caption│       │
│             ○ For next ┌─┐ paragraphs└───────┘      │
│                        │1│                          │
│             ○ Suppress page range                   │
│ Page # override: ☐ Bold ☐ Italic ☐ Underline        │
└──────────────────────────────────────────────┘
```

You've created a main (first-level) index entry that says "yacht racing" and a second-level sub-entry that says "racing boat to boat." To understand what first-level and second-level entries are, look at *08IdxFin.pm6*. Find the "yacht racing" entry. "Yacht racing" is a first-level topic, and "racing boat to boat" and the other two indented entries under it are the second-level topics. PageMaker lets you create three levels of topic entries.

7 Return to the story editor view of *08Work.pm6*. For basic first-level entries that don't need any editing, there's a good keyboard shortcut. In the paragraph just before the one you're in ("Yacht racing began"), highlight the words *Charles II*. Press Command-Shift-; (Macintosh) or Control-Shift-; (Windows).

That's all you have to do. PageMaker creates the index entry.

8 Enable All Stories in the Find dialog box, and use Find to locate the word *artificial*. Display the Index Entry dialog box. The word *artificial* is already displayed in the top topic box, so add the word *materials* to the entry and click OK.

In the next step, you index a topic that is discussed in two sequential paragraphs. You indicate this in the Index Entry dialog box so that if a page break occurs between the two paragraphs, PageMaker will list both pages in the index.

9 Use the Find dialog box to find the phrase *Thames Tonnage rule*. Notice that there are two paragraphs in a row that discuss this topic. Display the Index Entry dialog box. The highlighted material appears in the top topic box, but it should be a second-level entry, so click the Promote/Demote button to move it to the middle (second-level) topic box. Then type **Rating systems** into the first-level box. Click the button next to For the Next __ Paragraphs, and type a 2 in the box. Click OK.

```
┌──────────────────────────────────────────────┐
│              Index Entry                        │
│ Type: ◉ Page reference  ○ Cross-reference  ┌──────┐ │
│ Topic:                      Sort:          │  OK  │ │
│ ┌─────────────────┐ ┌↕┐  ┌──────────────┐  └──────┘ │
│ │ Rating systems  │ └─┘  │              │  ┌──────┐ │
│ └─────────────────┘      └──────────────┘  │Cancel│ │
│ ┌─────────────────┐      ┌──────────────┐  └──────┘ │
│ │ Thames Tonnage rule│   │              │  ┌──────┐ │
│ └─────────────────┘      └──────────────┘  │ Add  │ │
│ ┌─────────────────┐      ┌──────────────┐  └──────┘ │
│ │                 │      │              │  ┌──────┐ │
│ └─────────────────┘      └──────────────┘  │Topic…│ │
│                                             └──────┘ │
│ Page range: ○ Current page                          │
│             ○ To next style change                  │
│             ○ To next use of style: ┌───────┐       │
│                                     │caption│       │
│             ◉ For next ┌─┐ paragraphs└───────┘      │
│                        │2│                          │
│             ○ Suppress page range                   │
│ Page # override: ☐ Bold ☐ Italic ☐ Underline        │
└──────────────────────────────────────────────┘
```

Now, if the two paragraphs were to be separated by a page break, both page numbers would appear in the index.

For the next indexing technique, you learn how to use Find and Change to find a phrase and "change" it to an index entry. I use quotation marks because the word doesn't really get changed; the index entry is added. You want to find all occurrences of the word *clubs* and create an index entry for each one. You can use the Change dialog box to do this quickly and easily.

10 In story editor, use the text tool to click in the title at the beginning of the story. If the Find dialog box is still displayed, dismiss it. Then choose Change from the Utilities menu, and enable All Stories. Type the word **clubs** in the Find What box. Type the characters ^; into the Change To box. Click Find.

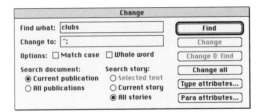

For each occurrence that you want to index, you click the Change and Find button. If the occurrence of the found word is not one that you want to index, you click Find Next to skip it without creating an index entry.

11 The first occurrence is in the paragraph that begins "By the 1720s." It's about the first racing clubs, so click the Change and Find button to add an index marker and find the next occurrence of the word. The second occurrence is also appropriate, so click Change and Find again.

12 In preparation for the next procedure, copy the next occurrence of the word *clubs*.

13 The third occurrence is in a paragraph that doesn't really say anything substantial about racing clubs, so click Find Next to find the next occurrence of the word without adding an index marker to the current occurrence. There are no more instances of the word *clubs* in the remaining text, so PageMaker posts the Search Complete dialog box. Click OK to dismiss it.

Next you want to find occurrences of the word *club* (rather than *clubs*) and index the occurrences as *clubs* where appropriate. The technique that you used in the last step—putting "^;" in the Change To box—won't work here, because you want the index entry (*clubs*) to be slightly differ-

ent from the word you're searching for. In the next steps, you use two different techniques: You paste the entry from the Clipboard, and you use the topic list.

14 Click in the beginning of the story again. Dismiss the Change dialog box, and display the Find dialog box. Enable Whole Word and All Stories. Type **club** in the Find What box, and click Find. The first occurrence is one you want to index, so display the Index Entry dialog box. (The quickest way is the keyboard shortcut.) You copied the word *clubs* to the clipboard in a previous step, so now click in the top topic box, and use Paste to paste in the word *clubs*. Click OK to insert the index marker.

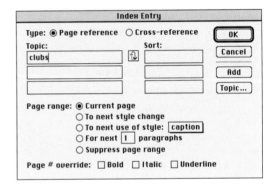

15 To find the next occurrence of *club*, click Find Next in the Find dialog box or use the keyboard shortcut: Command-G (Macintosh) or Control-G (Windows). The next occurrence of *club* is not one for which you want to create an index marker, so Find again, using the dialog box or keyboard.

16 The third occurrence needs to be indexed. Display the Index Entry dialog box and click the Topic button. Choose the letter *C* from the pop-up menu next to the words *Topic Section* to display entries beginning with the letter *C*. Highlight *clubs*, and click OK twice to exit the nested dialog boxes.

17 Find *club* again. Index it as *clubs* by using either technique: the topics list or pasting from the Clipboard. Find again. Index the occurrence. After this fifth occurrence, you get the Search Complete dialog box. Click OK to dismiss the window.

For the next entry, you take advantage of PageMaker's easy way to index names.

18 Put your insertion point at the beginning of the story and use the Find dialog box to find the name *Dixon Kemp*.

You want to index this as *Kemp, Dixon*, but you don't have to reverse the name manually. PageMaker does it for you.

19 Press Command-Shift-Z (Macintosh) or Control-Shift-Z (Windows).

PageMaker adds the index marker.

20 To see how the index entry will look, highlight the marker that PageMaker just added to the left of *Dixon Kemp* and choose Index Entry from the Utilities menu. The dialog box shows the index entry for the highlighted marker. Notice that the index entry reads "Kemp, Dixon" even though the text that you originally highlighted read "Dixon Kemp." Click OK.

For the next and last index entry, you find a name and then edit it in the Index Entry dialog box.

21 Click an insertion point in the first paragraph of the story. Use Find to locate the name *Sir William Perry* and use the keyboard shortcut given earlier to create an index marker (Command-Shift-; for Macintosh or Control-Shift-; for Windows).

You've created an index entry that will read "Sir William Perry," but you want to change it so that it reads "Perry, Sir William."

22 Highlight the index marker that you just created, and display the Index Entries dialog box, either by using the keyboard shortcut or by choosing Index Entry from the Utilities menu.

The dialog box shows the current entry.

23 Edit the entry in the top Topic box to read "Perry, Sir William" and click OK.

You have edited an existing index entry.

Index cross-references

There's another type of index entry called a *cross-reference*. It refers to another index entry instead of a page number. In the next steps, you create a cross-reference index entry that says "Organizations, *see* Clubs." It doesn't matter where your insertion point is when you create an entry of this type, since the page number isn't listed and PageMaker doesn't create an index marker for the entry.

1 Display the Index Entry dialog box and type **Organizations** in the first-level box.

2 Click the Cross-Reference radio button.

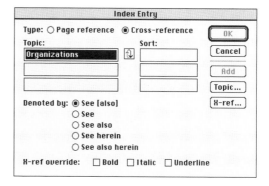

The lower part of the dialog box displays a new set of options.

3 Click the radio button next to *See*. To make the word *See* appear in italics, click the box next to Italic in the X-Ref Override section of the dialog box. Click the X-Ref button.

PageMaker displays a new dialog box where you can specify the topic to which you want to refer. Since you always want to refer to an existing index topic, PageMaker makes it easy for you by displaying all existing topics in the list at the bottom of the dialog box. All entries beginning with the chosen letter of the alphabet are displayed.

To browse through existing topics, you can either click the Next Section button to see the entries for the next letter of the alphabet or click on the letter next to Topic Section and go directly to the letter you want from the pop-up menu. Use the two techniques to browse through existing index entries for this project.

4 When you are finished browsing, choose the letter *C* from the Topic Section pop-up list in order to see a list of entries in the current chapter that begin with the letter *C*.

Note: To see all the index entries in all the publications in the book list, click the Import button.

5 Click *clubs* in the list of *C* entries, and then click OK. Click OK again in the main Index Entries dialog box.

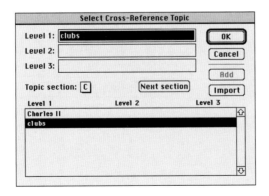

You have now created an index entry that says "Organizations, *See* clubs."

6 Now is a good time to save *08Work.pm6.*

Previewing the index

You can edit any entry by highlighting its marker symbol and then displaying the Index Entry dialog box. The information for the highlighted marker will be displayed. You can then make whatever changes you wish. PageMaker offers you an even more convenient way to edit entries, however. You can create a preview of the index by using the Show Index feature and then edit any entry from within that listing.

1 Still in the story editor, choose Show Index from the Utilities menu.

PageMaker goes through all the publications that are in the book list for the publication you're in. In this case, you copied the complete book list to every publication in the book in an earlier step, so PageMaker finds the index entries for the whole book. When the search is complete, it displays the Show Index dialog box. The Index Section is set to *A*.

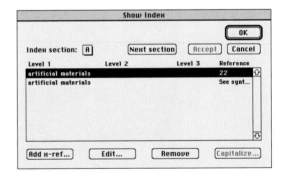

2 To see entries beginning with other letters, either click the letter next to Index Section and choose a letter from the pop-up menu or step through the alphabet by clicking the Next Section button. Click OK.

3 Now choose Show Index again, but this time hold down the Command key (Macintosh) or Control key (Windows). Holding down the Command key causes PageMaker to display the entries for only the current publication.

4 Choose *O* from the Index Section pop-up menu.

Organizations is highlighted, since it's the only entry beginning with *O*.

5 Click the Edit button. In the Edit Index Entry dialog box, change the capital *O* in Organization to a lowercase *o*. Click OK to return to the Show Index dialog box. Click Accept, and then click OK to exit. Hold down Option (Macintosh) or Shift (Windows) and choose Close Story from the Story menu to close all open story editor windows.

GENERATING AN INDEX

1 Open *08IdxFin.pm6* in *08Project* to see how the finished index will look.

2 In *Projects*, open *08Index.pm6*, the file that you created from the index template. Choose Book from the Utilities menu to confirm that this file contains an up-to-date book list, and then click Cancel to dismiss the dialog box.

Note: You can create an index for a booked publication only from a file that contains a book list. This file has a book list because earlier in this project you created a book list in 08Work.pm6 and then copied it to all the other files on the list, including this one.

3 Choose Create Index from the Utilities menu. In the Create Index dialog box, be sure that Include Book Publications is enabled.

If this is not checked, PageMaker indexes only the current publication, not the whole book.

4 The Title box contains the text that will appear as the title of the index. For this project, you can accept the default of "Index."

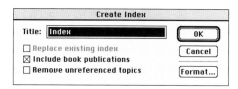

If you have used a topic list, Remove Unreferenced Topics ensures that you won't get any index entries that aren't actually used.

In the next step, you change the space that occurs between the entry and the first page number. The default is two spaces, but you change it to a non-breaking en space. This prevents entries in which the number is on a line by itself.

Note: To see what the other codes mean, look in Appendix A of the Adobe PageMaker User's Guide, "S*pecial Characters.*"

5 Click the Format button. The Following Topic box is highlighted by default, so type a caret followed by a greater-than symbol (^>). This is the dialog box code for an en space. Click OK to exit the Index Format dialog box, and then click OK again to generate the index.

3 Highlight Heading 2, and repeat the process—click Edit, click Para, enable Include in Table of Contents, click OK twice. Do the same thing for Heading 3, and then click OK to accept all the style changes. Save the chapter.

You have just specified that the text of all three heading levels in Chapter 3 should automatically be included in the table of contents. In the real world, you'd have to do the same thing for each of the other chapters, or better still, you would copy the Chapter 3 styles into the other chapters. In this project, however, the work has already been done for you in the other two chapters.

4 In *Projects*, open *08Toc.pm6*, the empty file that you created earlier from the table of contents template. Take a quick look at the list of styles, and notice that they are the same ones that appear in your chapter publications.

Later on, you'll see that PageMaker creates some new paragraph styles for the generated table of contents text.

Next, you want to specify that each publication (chapters, TOC, and index) should begin on a right-hand page.

5 In *08Toc.pm6*, choose Book from the Utilities menu, and enable Next Odd Page in the Auto Renumbering section. Click it again if it's already selected. Click OK. Choose Yes when asked if you want to renumber the pages now.

PageMaker goes through all the publications in the book, updating the page numbering and adding blank pages where necessary to ensure that each publication begins on a right-hand (odd-number) page. Now it's time to generate the actual table of contents.

6 Choose Create TOC from the Utilities menu.

PageMaker displays the Create Table of Contents dialog box. The text in the Title box is the text that will appear as the title of the table of contents.

7 For this project, accept the default title of "Contents."

8 Be sure that Include Book Publications is enabled.

You would deselect this only if you wanted to create a table of contents or paragraph list for just the current publication—not a common situation.

9 For Format, accept the default of Page Number After Entry.

10 For Between Entry and Page number, the ^t designated a tab between the entry and page number. You can use regular spaces instead, if you like, or you could use ^m to put in an em space. For now, accept the tab.

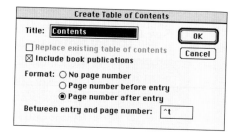

Note: Look in the Adobe PageMaker User's Manual *under* "Special characters: typing, finding, and changing" *for instructions on how to enter other special characters in dialog boxes.*

11 Click OK.

PageMaker posts a window that informs you of its progress as it goes through the publications looking for designated paragraphs. When it has completed the task, it presents you with an icon loaded with the newly generated text.

12 Click the loaded text icon in *08Toc.pm6* near the top of the text column to place the generated text.

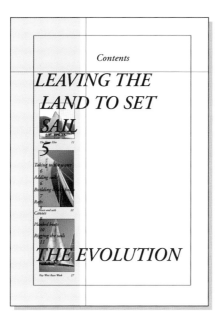

13 Save *08Toc.pm6*.

Your table of contents text is in place, but the appearance isn't right. PageMaker created a new paragraph tag for each requested paragraph style, but it used the formatting of the source paragraphs as a default style definition. You now need to edit the TOC paragraph styles.

FORMATTING THE TABLE OF CONTENTS

1 Go to the first page of *08Toc.pm6*, and look in the Styles palette. Notice that PageMaker has added several new styles to the list. Each one begins with the letters *TOC*.

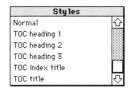

You begin by editing the paragraph style for the title.

2 Choose Define Styles from the Type menu. Highlight TOC Title, and click Edit. Click the Type button, and choose Corvinus Skyline as the font. Enter **56** in the Size box, and set Case to All Caps. Deselect Bold, and set the Track to Normal. Click OK. Next, click the Para button in the Edit Style dialog box. Set the Alignment to Left, Left Indent to 2.25, the First Indent to 0, and the Space After to 1 inch. Click OK twice to return to the main Define Styles dialog box so you can choose the next style to work on.

In the next steps, you define the other four styles that begin with *TOC*.

3 Select TOC Heading 1 from the Style list. The Type settings for this style are 12-point MyriadMM 830 Black 300 Cond. The Case is already set to All Caps, because PageMaker picked up the attribute from the Heading 1 style definition in the chapters. The Para settings are Left Indent 2.25, First Indent 0, and Paragraph Space Before 0.25. After clicking OK to make the Para settings, click the Tabs button to set a tab. Click the icon for right aligned, and then choose the dotted line from the Leader pop-up menu. Next, type **6.7** in the Position box, and choose Add Tab from the Position pop-up menu. Click OK to exit the Indents/Tabs dialog box and OK again to return to the Define Styles dialog box so that you can edit the next style.

4 TOC Heading 2 should have Type settings of 13-point AGaramond Regular. The Para settings are Left Indent 2.25 and First Indent 0. Then click the Tabs button and set a right aligned, dot-leadered tab at 6.7. Don't forget to choose Add Tab from the Position pop-up menu after typing in the position.

5 For TOC Heading 3, the Type settings should be 13-point AGaramond Regular and the Para Settings should be Left Indent 2.5, First Indent 0. Again, set a right-aligned, dot-leadered tab at 6.7.

6 Exit from the nested Define Styles dialog boxes.

7 Hold down the Shift key to constrain the movement to a single direction, and drag the text block so that the baseline of the title ("Contents") rests on the guide at 2 inches.

Making paragraph styles match

You're almost done. The word *Index* is still not formatted correctly. It should look the same as the lines that have the TOC Heading 1 style aapplied to them. In the next steps, you make the style for that line—TOC Index title—the same as the TOC Heading 1 style. This is necessary because you are going to be generating the index one more time. The number of pages in the table of contents changes as you apply formatting, and the new table of contents will reflect the changed numbers. If you change the definition of the TOC Index title style, the index title will be correctly formatted when the new table of contents is generated and placed.

1 Drag the bottom handle of the text block down a little below the bottom margin so that you can see the large word *Index*. Click in the line with the text tool and look in the Styles palette to see that the line has the TOC Index title paragraph style applied to it. Notice the capitalization and spacing of the style name.

2 Click an insertion point in one of the lines that has the TOC Heading 1 style applied to it. Command-click (Macintosh) or Control-click (Windows) on the [No style] entry in the Styles palette to display the Edit Style dialog box.

3 Type **TOC Index title** in the Name box, being careful to duplicate the capitalization and word spacing of the style name. Click OK.

You have now redefined the TOC Index title style to be exactly like the TOC Heading 1 style. When you regenerate the table of contents, everything will be formatted correctly.

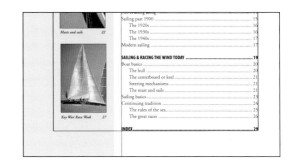

The entry for the index should now be sitting exactly on the bottom margin of page 1 of the table of contents.

Removing the extra pages

Now that the TOC paragraph styles are formatted, there are several empty pages. You need to delete these empty pages and then regenerate the table of contents in order to get the correct page numbers.

1 With *08Toc.pm6* active, choose Remove Pages from the Layout menu.

2 Specify pages 2 to 3, and click OK.

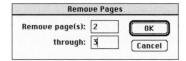

Regenerating the table of contents

1 Choose Create TOC from the Utilities menu.

2 Enable Replace Existing Table of Contents, and click OK.

PageMaker generates a new table of contents and replaces the old text with the new table of contents text. The new table of contents takes up only one page. The page numbers in the rest of the book have changed to reflect the shortened table of contents.

Formatting the dot leaders and page numbers

The next problem is that the dot leaders of the bold entries are too heavy. They take their formatting from that of the character immediately preceding them, so you need to format the space that precedes each one. In fact, you can't format the dot leaders directly. To see this for yourself, select a TOC Heading 1 leader without selecting the space that precedes it, and apply 13-point AGaramond (not bold) to it. The leader is still big and bold because it's taking its formatting from the preceding character.

1 Go to the first entry that has the TOC Heading 1 style applied to it ("Leaving the land…"). Select the space immediately before the dot leader, the leader itself, and the number following the leader. Apply 13-point AGaramond from the Control palette.

2 The next TOC Heading 1 paragraph ("The evolution of sailing…") doesn't have a space before the dot leader, so type a space after the word *sailing*. Then select the space, leader, and page number and apply 13-point AGaramond as before.

2 In the same way, apply 13-point AGaramond to the remaining TOC Heading 1 line and to the index title line.

Your table of contents should now match the sample file *08TocFin.pm6*. You've completed the table of contents, and in fact, you've completed the book.

TIME OUT FOR A MOVIE

If your system is capable of running Adobe Teach movies, play the movie named *Prepress Tips* to hear prepress professionals talk about how to prepare PageMaker files for successful printing. For information on how to view Adobe Teach movies, see "Watching Adobe Teach Movies" at the beginning of this book.

PRINTING THE BOOK

You can print a booked publication from any one of the publications within the book. You should first check the book list contained in the publication to be sure it's up-to-date.

1 Click anywhere in *08Toc.pm6* to make it the active publication. Choose Book from the Utility menu, and look over the list to be sure it contains *08Toc.pm6, 08Chap1.pm6, 08Chap2.pm6, 08Work.pm6,* and *08Index.pm6,* in that order. Be sure that Autonumbering is set to Next Odd Page. Click OK (or Cancel, since you didn't change any settings).

TIP: TO SAVE PRINT
SETTINGS FOR USE
LATER IN A SESSION,
MAKE THE SETTINGS,
AND THEN HOLD DOWN
SHIFT AND CLICK
DONE. TO SAVE THESE
SETTINGS PERMAN-
ENTLY, CHOOSE PRINTER
STYLES > DEFINE FROM
THE FILE MENU.

2 To display the Print Document dialog box, choose Print from the File menu or use the keyboard shortcut: Command-P (Macintosh) or Control-P (Windows). Make sure that a PPD appropriate for your printer is selected, if you have a PostScript printer. Otherwise, select the appropriate printer.

3 Enable Print All Publications in Book.

This choice is available to you because the publication that you're in has a book list in it. If the current publication doesn't contain a book list, this choice is grayed out. The other choices in the Print Document dialog box are the same as for a nonbook document.

4 Select Print Blank Pages to print any blank pages that PageMaker may have added to make each publication begin on a right-hand page.

5 If you are going to print at this point, click Print. If not, choose Cancel.

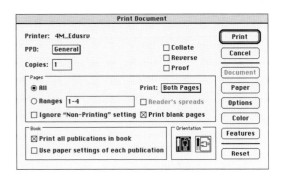

5 Close all open files, and quit PageMaker.

INDEX

Colophon

DOCUMENTATION

Authors: Jann Tolman, Patrice Anderson

Project Designers: Andrew Faulkner, Sharon Anderson

Art Director: Sharon Anderson

Illustrator: Jeffrey Schaaf

Design Assistant: Jamie Gross

Book Production: Jeffrey Schaaf

Book Production Management: Rebecca Gross

Publication Management: Kisa Harris

Photography: Billy Black (Project 8: Key West and Eggemoggin races), Dugald Bremner (Project 4: page 2, page 3 upper right), Project 7: bungee jumper, kayaker, trekker), Kisa Harris (Project 3: mountain/TOC, parachuter; Project 4: train), Scott Peterson (Project 1; Project 3: product shots), Beth Wald (Project 4: page 3 upper left, page 5 upper left and right), Graham Walsh (Project 2), Joanie Yokom (Project 8: mast, sail)

Cover Design: Sharon Anderson

CD Cover Design: Patti Fuji

Adobe Teach Movies: Glen Janssens, Paul Lundahl, Jamie Gross, Andrew Faulkner

Adobe Press: Patrick Ames

Special thanks to: Patrice Anderson, Kay Diamond, Necia Doughty, John Doughty, Jamie Gross, Carita Klevickis, Abbo Peterson, Jim Rzegocki, Patti Sokol, Kathleen Spears, San Francisco Public Library Public History Room, San Francisco Martime Museum

ALPHA TEST TEACH PARTICIPANTS

Patrice Anderson, *Adobe Instructional Design Manager*

Sharon Anderson, *Sharon Anderson Design*

Dean Bernheim, *Adobe Product Support*

Andrew Faulkner, *Andrew Faulkner Design*

Kisa Harris, *Adobe Educational Services*

Linda Kowalski, *Continental Printing*

John Roll, *Consultant*

Jim Rzegocki, *Adobe Training Specialist*

Patti Sokol, *Patti Sokol Consulting*

Carol Takoni, *Waller Media*

Jann Tolman, *Consultant*

Min Wang, *Adobe Creative Services*

BETA TEST TEACH PARTICIPANTS

Sharon Anderson, *Sharon Anderson Design*

Carol Butts, *Adobe Customer Service*

Andrew Faulkner, *Andrew Faulkner Design*

Jennifer Flathman, *Adobe Customer Service*

Jamie Gross, *Andrew Faulkner Design*

Kisa Harris, *Adobe Educational Services*

Linda Kowalski, *Continental Printing*

Tan Matosian, *Adobe Instruction Design Manager*

Patti Sokol, *Patti Sokol Consulting*

Angie Vincenti, *United Way of Santa Cruz County*

PRODUCTION NOTES

This book was created electronically using Adobe PageMaker 6 on a Power Macintosh 8100. Art was produced using Adobe PageMaker, Adobe Illustrator, Adobe Photoshop, and SnapJot. Plates for the book were created using CTP direct-to-plate technology. The Minion and Frutiger families of typefaces are used throughout this book.

Adobe Systems ...vides a range of ...tional materials ...r its application ...ftware through ...Adobe Learning ...rces programs.

Adobe Learning Resources

These resources include:

The Classroom in a Box™ educational product line for class-rooms and student labs; Adobe Acrobat™ training on CD-ROMs for end-user customers; and, customized classes for corpora-tions. For more information: email adobe.train@adobe.com.

In addition, the Adobe Instructor Certification Program is open qualified instructors. For information on becoming an Adobe Certified Instructor, contact rpedigo@adobe.com or fax 206-470-7127 or see our home page on the World Wide Web.

End users needing a referral to a Adobe Certified Instructor please contact: rpedigo@adobe.com	Visit the Adobe home page on the World Wide Web for current Learning Resources: http:\\www.adobe.com

Your input is invaluable!

Send an email to adobe.train@adobe.com. Let us know what you think of this, or other, Classroom in a Books. Mention the book's title and number your responses to the questions below (or just write us):

1 What do you like best about the book?

2 What would you suggest to improve the book?

3 What topics should be added to the book?

4 Where did you get the book? (e.g., training class, bookstore, mail order publisher)

5 Would you like to see the book localized? If so, in which language?

If you don't have email access, write a letter to:
Adobe Learning Resources Group, Adobe Systems Incorporated
P.O. Box 7900, Mountain View, CA 94039-7900

What's on the Classroom in a Book
Advanced Adobe PageMaker 6 CD?

The contents of this CD include:

1 all the **graphics** and **illustrations** you will place into each of the eight projects contained in this book

2 all the **sample text** you will flow into the documents you are creating

3 a complete **font set** chosen by professional designers for practicing Adobe PageMaker's powerful typographic tools

4 six specially created Adobe Teach **multimedia** training examples highlighting Adobe PageMaker's unique capabilities

5 **Adobe Acrobat Reader software** to view the Adobe Teach components, and access information on the Adobe Instructor Certification program

The Classroom in a Book staff recommends you use a double-speed, or faster, CD-ROM reader for accessing the files on the CD. The manuals that came with your computer and your CD-ROM player will detail set-up instructions.